Caligula

Caligula

An Unexpected General

Lee Fratantuono

(with photographic illustration by Katie McGarr)

Pen & Sword
MILITARY

First published in Great Britain in 2018 by
Pen & Sword Military
An imprint of
Pen & Sword Books Ltd
47 Church Street
Barnsley
South Yorkshire
S70 2AS

ISBN 978 1 52671 120 5

A CIP catalogue record for this book is
available from the British Library.

Printed and bound in England
by TJ International Ltd, Padstow, Cornwall.

Pen & Sword Books Limited incorporates the imprints of Atlas, Archaeology,
Aviation, Discovery, Family History, Fiction, History, Maritime, Military, Military
Classics, Politics, Select, Transport, True Crime, Air World, Frontline Publishing,
Leo Cooper, Remember When, Seaforth Publishing, The Praetorian Press,
Wharncliffe Local History, Wharncliffe Transport, Wharncliffe True Crime and
White Owl.

For a complete list of Pen & Sword titles please contact
PEN & SWORD BOOKS LIMITED
47 Church Street, Barnsley, South Yorkshire, S70 2AS, England
E-mail: enquiries@pen-and-sword.co.uk
Website: www.pen-and-sword.co.uk

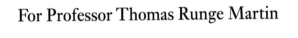

For Professor Thomas Runge Martin

Contents

Preface and Acknowledgments

Another book on the emperor Caligula invites (indeed demands) explanation and justification. For many years, the 'standard' English biography/history of Caligula and his reign was the work of J.P.V.D. Balsdon, *The Emperor Gaius (Caligula)*. This 1934 Oxford monograph revealed something of its intention even from the imperial nomenclature of its title: it would be a serious study of an emperor who was far more complex, and far less crazed, than the ancient treatments of Rome's notorious emperor from the pens of Suetonius and others would suggest. This was to be a book about the emperor Gaius, not the madman Caligula whose monstrous deeds fill the pages of Suetonius' life and have grimly mesmerized so many across time and space. Coincidentally, Balsdon's work appeared in the same year as the historical novel of Robert Graves, *I, Claudius* – a work that is better known today thanks to British television than to the original (and captivating) novel and its sequel, *Claudius the God*. There is no question that the general perception of Caligula owes more to Graves than to Balsdon.

Balsdon was supplanted in some ways by Anthony Barrett's *Caligula: The Corruption of Power*, which appeared from Yale University Press in 1989. Barrett's magisterial treatment of Caligula would reappear in a significantly revised second edition of 2015 from Routledge, with the new title, *Caligula: The Abuse of Power* (Barrett explains in the preface to the second edition that he is more inclined now to believe that Caligula was essentially unfit for office from the start, and that he abused power rather than suffered corruption because of it). The second edition of Barrett was in part motivated by the many books on Caligula that appeared after the first, prominent among them being three English commentaries on Suetonius' life of the emperor (by David Wardle, Hugh Lindsay and Donna Hurley). All three are invaluable aids for the study of Caligula and his reign.[1]

The three major Suetonian commentaries on the *Caligula* offer detailed notes on the Latin text of Suetonius – an author who has been served splendidly in recent years by the appearance of a new Oxford text of Robert Kaster, complete with companion volume on textual problems in the *Lives of the Caesars*.[2]

Barrett's work is certainly in the general school of Balsdon, though with a more balanced approach to the *princeps*. Readers who come to Barrett from Balsdon will not find so many ready excuses of Caligula's behaviour, or so much effort expended in defending the emperor against a hostile historiographical tradition. But the general approach is similar, and the conclusions not vastly dissimilar – though Caligula will likely never find another apologist as devoted as Balsdon.

Some voices have been raised in defence of the ancient tradition of Caligula as insane monster. Here the work of Arther Ferrill holds sway. His 1991 Thames and Hudson study, *Caligula: Emperor of Rome*, has a neutral title for a book that dismisses the arguments of those who would try to sanitize the Caligulan reign. For Ferrill, while this or that detail of the historical record may be suspect, on the whole the ancient narrative is sound, and Caligula was insane. Ferrill's book has been criticized by some for being a less than critical assessment of the Caligulan principate, a volume that ultimately takes almost everything said by a Seneca or a Tacitus at face value or as gospel truth. These criticisms are not entirely fair, though in the end Ferrill stands on one extreme and Balsdon on the other, with Barrett somewhere betwixt the two, though far closer to his Oxonian predecessor Balsdon than to Ferrill. Ferrill is in some ways a valuable counterbalance to his more sympathetic predecessors. At the very least, he serves as a reminder that we are possessed of too little evidence about the Caligulan principate to be sure of even the most general lines of interpretation of his reign. Tacitus has been viewed with suspicion by some for not being so removed from the anger and partisanship that he refers to in his own work (*sine ira et studio*, etc.) – but we sorely miss the Tacitean treatment of the Caligula years. Indeed, we may wonder if it is noteworthy that his principate is missing from the manuscript tradition of the *Annales*. The simple fact is that as for many luminaries of Roman history, we are missing considerable information about Caligula's life. All Caligula monographs are probably too long – the temptation to speculate is so great. That said, his reign has undeniable intrinsic interest, and apart even from the perhaps inevitable indulgence in the lurid that his life invites, his reign is of unquestioned significance in the development and progress of the Julio-Claudian principate.

Barrett's book has enjoyed translations into foreign languages, and Aloys Winterling's 2003 German monograph on Caligula (*Caligula: Eine Biographie*) has been translated into English (2011). Winterling is very much in the 'school' of Balsdon; like others of the same 'school', he finds the story of Caligula's sororial incest to be suspicious, and he engages in the same rationalization and careful defence that Balsdon practices. Pierre Renucci's 2011 French language monograph *Caligula*, for Éditions Tempus Perrin, sees a link between the defects in character attributed to Caligula, and the very milieu and structure of Julio-Claudian Rome. Renucci's work is very much in the mold of Barrett, seeking not so much to rehabilitate Caligula as to offer a more nuanced appraisal of his life and deeds. Renucci's study of Caligula follows admirably on his work on *Auguste, le révolutionnaire* (2003) and *Tibère, l'empereur malgré lui* (2005), all to be highly recommended to francophone students of the Julio-Claudians (Renucci also has a 2012 Claudius in his series). In Arther Ferrill's *Bryn Mawr Classical Review* of Barrett, he notes that exceedingly little new evidence was unearthed in the half century between Balsdon and Barrett: fair enough. The same is true for the nearly three decades since the first edition of Barrett.

The present study is not a scholarly treatment of Caligula in the manner of Balsdon or Barrett. It aims at providing the general reader with an overview of the sources for the life of Caligula, the surviving accounts of ancient writers that reference his reign. It provides a running commentary or *explication de texte* for those sources, and offers some guidance along the way to points of dispute and further inquiry by providing bibliographical references. It attempts to show that Caligula's foreign and military policy was, on the whole, relatively sound, and to elucidate how many of the Caligulan initiatives that for various reasons (not least the emperor's assassination in late January 41) were never seen through to completion but were finished by his successors – something of a belated tribute, at least after a fashion, to the soundness of some of his policies. It hopes, however, to be of interest to more scholarly audiences, if only because Caligula seems to be one of those subjects of unending fascination – a fact that may speak to baser elements in the human psyche. My students are often amazed to ponder that there is not so very much time at all between an Augustus and a Caligula; for them, the fears that may have been very real for a poet like Virgil in the wake of the advent of the Augustan regime came to full fruition in the principate of Gaius. Whatever pretences dominated in the Tiberian Age – at least when Sejanus was not exercising his reign of terror – were completely abandoned under the young Gaius. And the principate would indeed never fully recover. That said, one cannot, I think, escape the sense that the surviving historical record is heavier on the editorializing side than the historical-critical – though the 'real' Caligula may have been no help at all in preventing that outcome.

The book before you is not, however, another attempt to rehabilitate Caligula; this has been done, and done well, by those inclined to conclude that the historical tradition is vitiated by a hopelessly prejudiced outlook on the emperor Gaius. As a representative work in that curious genre known as 'popular' studies of ancient historical topics, it does not presume to add particularly original thoughts to the vast literature on Caligula. In the absence of new evidence, there is not likely to be much room for innovation in the study of his principate, only of the judicious application of philological, archaeological and historical methodologies to reappraise and re-evaluate what we have. Future discoveries may of course provide for promising new avenues of inquiry.

On the whole, this work subscribes to the Barrett theses on Caligula; those views, we might note, are not much altered between his 1989 first edition and the 2015 second. Much work was done on Caligula in the intervening quarter century, but it is significant that Barrett's essential views were not altered with the passage of time. Greater emphasis will be found in these pages, however, on the image of Caligula as Julian scion, and on Caligula's attitude toward the Trojan, Venusian ancestry of his Julian *gens*.

That said, this book does examine all aspects of Caligula's life, though with varying degrees of attention. It considers closely the historiographical tradition on the emperor, including the notorious and infamous anecdotes told of him since his own days. Some brief mention is given to the *Nachleben* or afterlife of Caligula; here, Camus' play is a gem. Much of the afterlife is unseemly and frankly unworthy of consideration, and is best left to the investigation of the prurient.

The title of this volume is *Caligula: An Unexpected General*. That title references several points of appraisal of Caligula's life as a conductor of Roman foreign policy and of at least prospective military operations in Germany, Gaul and Britain. While Caligula was literally born *in castris*, and was the veritable mascot of his father Germanicus' troops, he had no military experience in his youth, and on the day he assumed power in the wake of Tiberius' death, he could hardly rest on the laurels of having achieved anything militarily (cf. Augustus and Tiberius before him). Caligula was thus an 'unexpected general' in terms of the military background he brought to the principate; we are told that the names Caligula and Gaius alike grated on him, and certainly the former reminded him of his essentially mock military experience.

The title also reflects the possibility that Caligula was actually quite competent in his military initiatives and planned execution of military and foreign policy manoeuvres, his lack of experience notwithstanding. There is good reason to think that even if Caligula had less than stellar results in his domestic affairs with the Senate in particular, on the whole he was possessed of a good sense of what needed to be done in the arena of foreign affairs (with the singular exception of his relations with the Jews). The 'unexpected general' set the course in some regards for the foreign policy of Claudius and beyond.

It is as ever a welcome task to express gratitude to those who have aided in the production and composition of this book. Phil Sidnell, my editor at Pen & Sword, remains a patient and learned guide through the process of turning proposal into product. Caitlin Gillespie was kind enough to lecture at Ohio Wesleyan on Roman Britain and the Boudica revolt under Nero (the subject of her forthcoming Oxford study, *Boudica: Warrior Woman of Roman Britain*); I have benefited much from her work in my research. Alden Smith and Michael Putnam remain much appreciated sources of encouragement and support in the classics community.

Blaise Nagy (now Professor Emeritus of Classics at the College of the Holy Cross) is always generous with his willingness to read and offer wise counsel on my writing. To him I continue to owe a debt of gratitude.

The students of my biannual seminar on the Roman Empire were a particularly delightful group on which to test certain sections of the present work. In particular, I have benefitted from the suggestions and advice of Sarah Foster and Elizabeth Kish. The Roman imperial history students regularly delight in Suetonius, Tacitus and even Dio Cassius; they found the British Broadcasting Company production of Robert Graves' *I, Claudius* as wonderful a treat to view as I did when first I saw the late, exceptionally gifted John Hurt perform his classic role as Gaius Caligula. Working with the undergraduate Roman Empire students is a daily exercise in appreciating how stories and legends take hold in the mind, and in appreciation of how the enduring influence of the classics continues to offer priceless lessons for contemporary life.

Once again, one of my volumes is significantly enhanced in quality and aesthetic grace by the work of my freelance photographer, Katie McGarr, of Trek Afar Photography. Katie travelled extensively through areas associated with the reign of Caligula to capture images for this book. She is tireless, devoted to her craft and gifted with a fine mind and a keen eye for historical and archaeological travel photography. Her talent and expertise make every project a pleasure to see through to the finish, and she has my enduring gratitude for her art and labours. This book is in several regards as much hers as mine, not least in terms of the amount of dedication and effort that she displayed in shooting and editing.

Lastly, I am pleased to dedicate this study to an inspirational scholar and mentor. Thomas R. Martin was a professor of mine at the College of the Holy Cross in Worcester, Massachusetts, from the very first semester in which he commenced teaching there in the autumn of 1992 as the Jeremiah W. O'Connor Chair in Classics; under his tutelage I read from Plato's *Crito*, Sophocles' *Antigone* and then Herodotus. It is a humbling privilege to offer this small token of thanks to Tom for all that he taught me in classwork at Holy Cross, and for the example of his scholarship on ancient history and numismatics, not least his splendid history of ancient Rome for Yale University Press. *Ad multos annos, magister optime.*

Lee Fratantuono
12 October 2017
Delaware, Ohio, USA

Chapter One

The Life of Caligula by Suetonius, Part I (Caligula the *Princeps*)

W e would be much the poorer in our study of the emperor Caligula if we did not have access to the biography written by Gaius Suetonius Tranquillus ('Suetonius').[1] Born in c. AD 70, Suetonius is perhaps most famous today as the author of a set of a dozen imperial biographies known as the *De Vita Caesarum* or (as it is commonly known in English) 'Lives of the Caesars'. The lives of the twelve Caesars were likely composed early in the second century AD; all of them survive intact, except for the opening chapters of the first (on Gaius Julius Caesar).[2] If one wanted to name the principal primary source that survives from antiquity for the life and reign of Caligula, one might reasonably be tempted to cite Suetonius' life – though, as we shall see, the biography must be used with even more of the caution and circumspection that ancient biography and historiography always demand.[3] At the very least, Suetonius provides the only surviving complete narrative of the emperor's life.[4] It is a challenging source, not least for the lack of ready chronology and convenient timeline, and the relative lack of information about source material and source criticism. But together with surviving material from the monumental Roman history of Dio Cassius, it constitutes the major extant evidence for the short reign of the unforgettable Gaius.[5] Indeed, of the Julio-Claudian emperors it is Caligula who has fared the worst in terms of ancient testaments to his life and reign.

We shall proceed first through the first twenty-one chapters of Suetonius' life, chapters in which the biographer purports to describe Caligula the *princeps* as opposed to Caligula the *monstrum*.[6] These chapters offer something of a survey of the accomplishments of Caligula as emperor that may be considered positive or at least neutral in import; there are shades of the monster to come, but on the whole these are calm and even happy remembrances of a brief period after the death of Tiberius. The early section of Suetonius' life is as much impressionistic as anything else; it gives both highly specific details of the emperor's biography, and general commentary and reflection on both his character and the times. It provides a résumé of accomplishments that on the whole might be considered not undistinguished, given the short tenure of Caligula's reign.

The first six chapters of Suetonius' life of Caligula, however, are devoted not to its subject, but to commentary on and praise of the future emperor's father, the celebrated hero Germanicus. Born Nero Claudius Drusus Germanicus in 15 or 16 BC, he was known as Julius Caesar Germanicus after his adoption by his uncle Tiberius in AD 4.[7] Germanicus was the son of Tiberius' brother Drusus the Elder, who had died in the summer of 9 BC.[8]

One might succumb easily enough to the impression that Suetonius deliberately opens his life of Caligula with an extended praise of Germanicus principally to heighten the contrast between the father and the son. The laudatory treatment of Caligula's storied father sets the stage for the biographer's treatment of the child who would be most famous (or infamous) – the emperor Caligula. Germanicus was married to Agrippina, the daughter of the emperor Augustus' dear friend Marcus Vipsanius Agrippa and his wife Julia (the daughter of Augustus). The surviving children of the union were the daughters Agrippina (the Younger), Drusilla and Livilla, and the sons Nero, Drusus and Gaius.

Suetonius reminds his readers that when Augustus died and the legions refused to accept Tiberius as his successor, it was Germanicus who compelled them to maintain their allegiance, even after he was offered their support in assuming power himself.` The narrative is clear: any future persecution of the family of Germanicus by Tiberius constituted a supreme act of ingratitude and simple bad manners. Germanicus would be dead at 34 of suspected poisoning while in the East; Tiberius was suspected of involvement in the whole affair.

Suetonius notes that two of Agrippina's children died in infancy, while another – a son – died just as he was 'beginning to become a boy' (Latin *puerascens* – a very rare word). This son was the subject of a Cupid statue that Livia is said to have dedicated in the temple of the Capitoline Venus; Augustus, for his part, is said to have had a statue of the boy that he would kiss whenever he entered the room.[9] It is thought that this mysterious boy must have been born in AD 11, only to die sometime in the year of his brother Caligula's birth

– a haunting case, at any rate, of how one could imagine what might have been had this older brother of the future monster survived.

From Suetonius, we learn that Gaius was born on the thirty-first day of August, AD 12, the son of a consul. Suetonius is certain of the date; he notes that the surviving sources give conflicting testimony as to the birthplace – he settles on Antium, the modern Anzio in Latium.[10] Caligula's real name at birth was Gaius Julius Caesar Germanicus.[11]

Suetonius engages in careful historical source criticism for the question of Caligula's birthplace, noting that Gnaeus Lentulus Gaetulicus put it at Tibur, and Pliny the Younger among the Treviri in Germania (cf. modern Trier). He also cites the evidence of a letter of Augustus to Agrippina that speaks of Caligula being sent from Rome to Germany when he was not yet 2. Antium is the site that Suetonius settles on for the natal place of the future emperor, noting that once he was in the imperial purple, he even thought of transferring the capital to Antium, and that he always preferred the locale to any other for retreat and rejuvenation.[12]

Gaius was born a little less than two years, then, before the death of Augustus in AD 14. His eventual successor – his uncle Claudius, Germanicus' brother – was born in 10 BC. Rome's first four emperors were thus all alive between AD 12-14 – a remarkable circumstance. All were members of the so-called Julio-Claudian dynasty, which could fairly be called the first ruling family of the Roman Empire.

It is beyond the scope of this study of Caligula to examine the vast problem of the transition from a Roman Republic to an Empire – but suffice to say that a major problem of the Age of Augustus was the question of who would succeed the great saviour of Rome in his capacity as *princeps*, or 'first citizen'. By AD 12, it was clear that the successor would be Tiberius. Less certain was what would happen in the event of Tiberius' death (and we do well to remember that he was born in 43 BC and was thus already somewhat advanced in age by the standards of the times). Germanicus was an obvious enough candidate, especially given his immense popularity and skilled competence in military affairs. Augustus had had enormous difficulties in securing a reliable succession plan; his decision to compel Tiberius to adopt Germanicus was seen as a sign of great trust and confidence in the young man. If late Augustan, early Tiberian Rome had a celebrity, is was Germanicus. It is not difficult to imagine that Germanicus' popularity engendered a serious resentment and jealousy in Tiberius. Indeed, perhaps Germanicus was too popular for his own good.

For Gaius' noble father would die under mysterious circumstances in Syria in October of AD 19, when his son was but 7 years of age.[13] He died near Antioch, convinced to his dying breath that the emperor's friend, Gnaeus Calpurnius Piso, had poisoned him. Piso had certainly been appointed governor in Syria as a means of controlling Germanicus; two men of more opposite temperament likely could not be found. Piso would be prosecuted for *maiestas*, or treason, if not the death of Germanicus, though he committed suicide before the end of his trial, to the end declaring both his lack of culpability for the death and his loyalty to Tiberius.[14]

If anything, the early life of Gaius was inextricably associated with the soldiers his father commanded. To that childhood (indeed infancy) association with the common soldiery Gaius owed the nickname by which he is today best known: Caligula. The *caliga* was a half-boot that was worn by Roman soldiers; the name 'Caligula' is the diminutive of *caliga* and thus means 'Little Boot' or bootikin.[15] We may well assume that Agrippina dressed her infant in a miniature army outfit; the child was the virtual mascot and certain darling of his father's troops.[16] Indeed, we are told by Suetonius that after the death of Augustus, when the soldiers in Germany were contemplating mutinous revolt, it was the mere sight of baby Caligula which calmed them. The infant had been spirited off from camp to save him from any threat of harm from the rebellious soldiers; the mere thought that anyone would think that they could harm the little boy was enough to quell the disturbance and reduce them to contrition and repentance.[17]

The tradition developed that Caligula was virtually (if not actually) born 'in camp' with the army. The story about the rebellion of the soldiers and the flight of Agrippina and Caligula is told by the great Roman historian Tacitus in his *Annales*, or annals of imperial Rome.[18] Tacitus states plainly that Caligula was born *in castris*, or 'in camp'; this tradition was also recalled in verses of 'poetry' (not to say doggerel) that Suetonius preserves that refer to the fitting birth of the future emperor in the camp of the army.[19] Of the first three emperors of Rome, Caligula certainly had the most 'military' upbringing, given both the nature of the times and his father's career. He travelled with his family to Syria for his father's ill-fated appointment there;

by the time he was 7, he had seen more of the Roman world than either of his predecessors at the same age. It is not the purpose of the present work to offer a psychological study of the future emperor – but there can be little doubt that the dramatic circumstances occasioned by Germanicus' life made a formative impression on him.

After the death of his father, Suetonius records that the young Caligula lived first with his mother Agrippina and then, after her exile, with his great-grandmother Livia, the widow of Augustus.[20] Livia was destined to live until 28 September AD 29, a long fifteen years after the death of her great husband, and an annoying, uncomfortably protracted tenure into the reign of her son Tiberius. Suetonius notes that Caligula gave the funeral oration for Livia; he was then but 17 years old, and not yet of age. This is a decade that in some sense could be called a lost one in the short life of Gaius; we know precious little about what happened to him between the autumns of AD 19-29, formative years of his life to be sure. After Livia's death, he was assigned to the care of his grandmother Antonia Minor, the younger daughter of Mark Antony; he remained with her until he was summoned by the emperor to his more or less permanent retreat at Capreae, likely sometime after late AD 30.[21] Antonia would play a significant role in ensuring the safety of the young Caligula in dangerous times (especially given the rise of Tiberius' disreputable associate Sejanus). Less certain is whether she lived to regret any efforts expended on his behalf.

For the first ten chapters of Suetonius' life of Caligula, though, there is no hint of the reputation of the 'monster' for which the emperor would later be notorious. This changes in the eleventh chapter, when the biographer indicates that even then (that is, at a young age) there were signs of depravity. Caligula is charged with being an eager witness to torture and execution. He is accused of gluttony and adultery (the latter while disguised in a wig and a long robe).[22] He was fond of the theatrical world of dancing and singing – activities that were held in suspicion by upper-class Romans, and in which Suetonius says that Tiberius permitted Caligula to indulge, in the hope that they would mollify his savage, cruel nature.[23] It would appear likely, however, that Tiberius had no real hope that Caligula could be rehabilitated; Suetonius credits the old emperor with the quip that he was nurturing a viper for the Roman people, and a Phaëthon for the world.

Phäethon in classical mythology was the son of the Sun, a solar child whose doom was guaranteed when he visited his father to demand some token of his paternity. Given the chance to have any wish he craved, he desired to drive the chariot of the sun for but one day – a wish that spelled fiery ruin for the world, and, eventually, Phäethon's own death when Jupiter ended the disastrous ride with a timely thunderbolt.[24]

In Tiberius' sentiments, we may see something of a desire to improve his own reputation by a *deterior* comparison with what would follow him. If Tiberius worried about being hated and about his posthumous reputation, then at least he could rest secure in the knowledge that his successor would be far worse, and that his own memory would seem positive in light of what followed him. Ingenious, cynical – and perhaps eminently Tiberian.

The reality, however, is more complicated. Tiberius had a son of his own, Drusus the Younger, who had been born in 13 BC as the offspring of Tiberius and his first wife, Vipsania Agrippina.[25] Names are notoriously confusing in early imperial Roman family trees and political adoptions; the man known best to history as Drusus the Younger was born Nero Claudius Drusus, and became Drusus Julius Caesar in AD 4 after Tiberius was adopted into Augustus' Julian family.

Drusus died, however, on 14 September AD 23, under the mysterious circumstances that seem all too common in ancient historical narratives of the period.[26] Germanicus' sister Livilla would seem to have poisoned him, in connivance with her lover Lucius Aelius Sejanus, the powerful prefect of the Praetorian Guard, who for a while was virtual ruler in Rome while Tiberius remained in seclusion at Capreae.[27] Drusus did have a son of his own – the ill-fated Tiberius Gemellus. But in the autumn of 23, there were still two older brothers of Caligula – Germanicus' sons Nero and Drusus. Nero would eventually be banished to Pontia, where he would die in AD 31. Drusus was arrested and sent to prison in Rome in AD 30; he was infamously starved in prison, reduced to the pathetic state of eating his own mattress stuffing. Death came in AD 33. In the complicated circumstances of the later years of Tiberius' reign, Sejanus himself fell in the autumn of 31 – but by then, apparently, Tiberius had decided that Drusus would have too sore a memory of Tiberius were the emperor to release him.[28] Sejanus was killed on 18 October 31; Livilla was handed over to her mother Antonia and starved to death the same autumn.[29]

By the time he was 19, circumstances had conveniently reduced the imperial family quite appreciably in number – Gaius, little Caligula, had survived. How did it manage to happen?

One theory certainly is that in Caligula, Tiberius saw a kindred spirit, a fellow lover and practitioner of perversion and depraved acts (sexual and otherwise), a sharer in sordid deeds who would also provide Tiberius with a better reputation simply by virtue of his own horrible nature. In accord with this thesis, perhaps Tiberius realized that Caligula was so bad and so ostentatious in his wickedness that his very survival as emperor would depend on some softening of the rougher edges, some toning down of the excesses.

Another theory – not mutually exclusive with the first – is that time and chance simply worked in favour of Caligula. According to this theory, Sejanus would have seen to the destruction of Caligula – but the intervention of Antonia came just in time to save what remained of the House of Germanicus. Caligula certainly benefitted from the powerful women who shielded him from harm. Livia was no doubt a formidable source of protection, and then Antonia (especially) in turn.[30] Caligula had the advantage of having been the third surviving son of Germanicus, not the first or second.[31] His outspoken mother Agrippina caused enough problems for a long time for herself and those surrounding her; there were plenty of people to eliminate in the family, and Caligula was far enough along in the queue to benefit from a degree of sheer luck.[32]

By the age of 19 – in AD 32 – Caligula's fortunes were looking ever more promising. Ultimately, Tiberius would leave his estate to Caligula jointly with his grandson Tiberius Gemellus; there seems to have been no serious consideration of any place for 'Uncle' Claudius, the brother of Germanicus. There had already been precedent for the transition from one *princeps* to another (i.e. in 14); one might expect that things would go relatively smoothly whenever Tiberius died.[33]

Suetonius proceeds to the question of Caligula's first marriage, which was to Junia Claudilla, the daughter of Marcus Junius Silanus.[34] The exact year of the marriage is in dispute; at any rate, it would not be a long union. Caligula was soon enough made augur, a prestigious appointment in the apparatus of Roman religion – the *augures* were official diviners and announcer of unfavourable omens. Suetonius associates the appointment as a replacement for Caligula's brother Drusus; before he was invested with the insignia of office, however, he was apparently promoted to that of *pontifex*. This far more important priesthood had significant oversight over the festivals, sacrifices and other liturgical celebrations and commemorations of the state religion. The prestigious appointment is associated with Caligula's character (especially his *pietas*, a concept that is impossible to translate well into English but that encompasses the difficult relationship between both mortals and the divine, as well as between fathers and sons and familial interactions – 'loyalty' is perhaps a better rendering than 'piety'). Suetonius also observes that after the downfall of Sejanus, Caligula was increasingly encouraged to expect the succession from Tiberius, so that such promotions as the pontifical were to be seen as natural enough props to the career of the suddenly quite important young man.

Junia Claudilla died in childbirth at an uncertain date. Caligula is said then to have seduced Ennia, the wife of Quintus Naevius Sutorius Macro, the prefect of the Praetorian Guard after the death of Sejanus.[35] If Suetonius can be trusted, Caligula promised to marry Ennia should he become emperor; the apparent rationale for the affair was so that Caligula could ingratiate himself with the prefect. This strategy on the part of Caligula may seem strange and counterintuitive; we shall return soon enough to the question of the future emperor's involvement with the wife of Macro and the place of the affair in the machinations of the succession.

Macro was instrumental in the end of Sejanus, and was a major player in the chicanery that likely attended the death of Tiberius. The story goes that Caligula poisoned his adoptive father, and when the imperial ring was taken a little too fast from the hand of the dying Tiberius, a convenient pillow guaranteed that asphyxiation would make a new emperor.[36] Friendship with Macro would provide a praetorian safeguard to the young Caligula's new reign. He certainly had no intention of sharing his newfound power with the even younger Tiberius Gemellus.

Suetonius' verdict on the question of parricide is that it is likely enough that Caligula killed Tiberius, since there are sources that record that later in life, the emperor noted that he had thought of killing the old man – indeed, that he had entered Tiberius' bedroom with a dagger, only to lose his nerve out of pity for the pathetic elderly emperor. This was a source of pride and boasting for Caligula; he was an exemplar of *pietas* not only in his willingness to seek to avenge the death of his mother and his brothers, but also in his devotion to his 'new' father Tiberius – he would not kill his emperor. Tiberius is said to have known of the would-be assassination, but to have done nothing to ask after the matter.

It is interesting to note that Suetonius places the rumours and stories about the role of Caligula in the death of Tiberius among the actions of the *princeps* and not the *monstrum*. Certainly there was little if any mourning for Tiberius. Did Caligula poison Tiberius? Did he strangle the old man, or use a pillow to smother him? Did he order that Tiberius' ring be taken from him while he still breathed, only to suffocate him when the ornery emperor appeared unwilling to cooperate in surrendering it? Did he order the crucifixion of a slave who made the fatal mistake of crying out at the assassination? We cannot be sure – but apparently Caligula enjoyed bragging of how he could have slain Tiberius, but did not.

Pietas catapulted Caligula to the office of *pontifex*, and *pietas* was the emperor's boast in the matter of his reviled predecessor. Tiberius was hated – but Caligula would not raise his hand to slay his adoptive father. *Pietas* was a defining quality of the Julian *gens*, the characteristic trait of the Trojan hero Aeneas. It is not surprising that Caligula would seek to cloak himself in this signal virtue of his storied family. The implication is that the Claudian family – the Tiberian side of the imperial dynasty – was rather lacking in this quality.[37] *Pietas* was also associated with Germanicus; Suetonius records that whenever Caligula's father came upon the graves of famous men, he would stop and make sacrifices to their shades out of reverence and respect for the dead.[38] He was the first to try to collect and assemble the bones and remains of those who had perished in the Varus disaster of AD 9.[39]

Tiberius died on 16 March, AD 37 at the age of 78.[40] His death came near Misenum, in the vicinity of Naples in Campania. His predecessor Augustus had been deified, but there would be no such *post mortem* apotheosis for Tiberius.

Chapter 13 of Suetonius' life notes what we might consider the zenith, the apex of Caligula's reign – its first day. After the long years of the morose and increasingly dour Tiberius, Caligula was seen as a young breath of fresh air, the scion of Germanicus and harbinger of a Golden Age. His very survival as one of the few members of Germanicus' family left alive was another element of the joy and rejoicing that accompanied his journey from Misenum to Rome.

At 24½ years of age, Gaius was emperor – and the Romans were delighted that this young man had assumed the purple. They lavished affectionate names on the new emperor – indeed, the subject of nomenclature is a recurring theme in the Suetonian life, not least in the celebrated nickname of Gaius. He was called a constellation or star – Latin *sidus* – but also a 'chick' (Latin *pullum*) and a baby (*pupum*), terms of endearment that may have offended Caligula. Could the populace really hope that the man who had obtained the empire (*Sic imperium adeptus*, Suetonius says)[41] would endure such names for long?[42]

Perhaps not surprisingly, the will of Tiberius was disregarded by both the Senate and the *turba*, or mob. There would be no joint rule of Caligula and Tiberius Gemellus.[43] Over a period of three months, from mid-March to June, more than 160,000 animals were sacrificed in the general mood of celebration and feasting. The cynic could note that soon enough there would be human offerings whose deaths would come as the price of having Caligula in power.

But for the present at least, *pietas* continued to be the order of the day. Caligula is said to have travelled to the islands of Pandateria and Pontia, to recover the ashes of his mother Agrippina and his older brother Nero, so that they might be honourably buried in the Mausoleum of Augustus in Rome.[44] Ever the showman, Caligula made a point of departing for the islands in stormy weather, so as to highlight all the more effectively his devotion. The month of September, Caligula determined, would be named Germanicus after his father.[45] Yearly funeral sacrifices were to be made in honour of his mother Agrippina. His uncle Claudius would be named consul, colleague with his nephew in the office. His grandmother Antonia was to be given the same honours that Livia had once enjoyed.[46] Tiberius Gemellus was adopted and given the title *princeps iuventutis*, or 'Prince of Youth'. The names of his sisters were to be included in all oaths alongside his own.[47] There was a clear implication in the honour shown to Gemellus that he was the intended successor – though no doubt Caligula expected to reign for a far longer time than the four years he was destined to wear the purple. The appointment of Gemellus was perhaps no more than a sop to the Tiberian faction that may have questioned the whole transition from a Claudian ascendancy to a Julian. In any case, the young man was not destined to live long. Claudius was in some sense a convenient enough substitute for Germanicus. It appears that he truly was not taken seriously in the corridors of power (at least not by Tiberius or Caligula), and that as a surviving brother of Germanicus he could safely be honoured with such tokens of *pietas* and affection as the shared consulship with his nephew – he was no threat and no danger to the young Gaius. Not surprisingly, the title of 'Prince of Youth' would later be assumed by the emperors themselves; it could always be hazardous to appoint a successor too soon, after all. We might note that Augustus had bestowed the same title on Gaius and Lucius Caesar, the children of Agrippa and Julia; both would die prematurely, as would Gemellus.

Suetonius notes that when Caligula crossed over to the islands near Campania, vows were made for his safe return, and there was general anxiety about his security, such that no one dared to miss the chance to speak of their care for the young new *princeps*.[48] He fell ill, and there were crowds around the imperial palace all night, with some even vowing to fight as gladiators for his healthy recovery. Lives were vowed in exchange for that of Caligula. Artabanus, the King of Parthia, came of his own free will to meet with the Roman consular legate Lucius Vitellius; he crossed the Euphrates and paid homage to the Roman eagles and standards, and to the statues of the Caesars. We shall return to this question of the mysterious illness of Caligula, a calamity that remains uncertain with respect both to epidemiology and duration, especially in terms of the question of whether or not the illness marks the transition in Caligula's rule from that of *princeps* to *monstrum*. Augustus had been sickly for much of his life, and there may have been some recollection of the fragile health of the beloved, divinized first *princeps*.

Loyalty and devotion to family were hallmarks of the emperor's early reign. But *pietas* was not necessarily associated with Caligula in the days when he was with Tiberius at Capreae.[49] It is said that the young man was approached with complaints about the treatment of his mother and his family, and that he never acceded to their wishes to join in complaints about Tiberius' behaviour. He never cooperated with anyone in questioning Tiberius' actions. Even his own mistreatment was ignored; eventually it was said of him that no one had ever been a better servant or a worse master.[50] Later of course – once he was safely ensconced in power – Caligula could claim that he had contemplated killing the old man. But certainly in the years before AD 37, no one could count on Caligula for help in defending the honour of the *domus Germanici*. To be fair, no one could readily expect that Caligula could do much in the circumstances – he was in an undeniably difficult, even perilous position. He survived, though arguably no thanks to credit of his virtue or courage. The language of the quip against Caligula was rooted in the metaphor of slavery; Caligula was a *dominus*, to be sure – but he was also a *servus*. Implicit in this comment is the idea that the *princeps* should not be a *dominus*, since the word inevitably evoked the image of slavery. One of the more interesting aspects of the study of Caligula is the question of the political transformation of Rome during this third imperial rule, and the changing hues and tones of the principate in the transitions from Augustus to Tiberius and now to Caligula. Indeed, we shall come to see that for some scholars, the brilliant achievement of Caligula was his determination that Rome needed to be a monarchy in the style of the great Eastern powers – a sentiment that was anathema for those possessed of love and respect for the republican traditions of the city.

But again, the early days of Caligula were marked by generosity and good fortune. Those who had been exiled under Tiberius were all recalled, and any outstanding charges were rescinded and annulled. Documents related to the cases of his mother and brothers were burned;[51] alleged evidence of a threat against him was ignored. Freedom and liberty were to be restored, as it were, in the wake of the dark days of the incessant treason trials and climate of apprehension in the city.

Tiberius was given a splendid funeral and a eulogy by Caligula that was marked by tears and a generally lachrymose performance. Nobody could argue that Caligula was unfaithful to his predecessor, to whom he owed his adoption and advancement to imperial power. These were indeed the days of the Golden Age, it would seem; the past was being rehabilitated and reconciled to the present, and a true descendant of Augustus was setting right the perceived mistakes of the past – but with no condemnation of Tiberius. If there were any real oddity to the transition to Caligula, it was in the relegation of Tiberius Gemellus from the role of co-heir to that of adopted son. But no one seemed to care very much about Drusus' son.[52] Caligula had now buried Livia and Tiberius, and had spoken the customary words of honour and eulogy. At the height of his popularity, Caligula had somehow managed to survive unspeakably complicated and challenging circumstances in the imperial circle.

Those who are familiar with the legendary sexual perversions of Caligula may be surprised to find that Suetonius notes that another early edict of the new emperor was the banishment from Rome of the so-called *spintriae*.[53]

These perverts were particularly associated with Tiberius' sexual playground retreat at Capreae – Caligula was respectful toward Tiberius, but he saw to the excision of the cancer of perversion from the city.[54] Indeed, Suetonius notes that Caligula was ready to kill the *spintriae*; he could barely be restrained from his desire to drown them in the sea.[55] Here, too, we may see the clear hint of the monster, of the sadist with his perverse delight in the sufferings of others.

The writings of Titus Labienus, Cremutius Cordus and Cassius Severus had all been banned under the days of Tiberius, but Caligula ordered that they be recovered, circulated and read.[56] The *rationes*, or 'accounts', of the empire were also published; they had been released in the days of Augustus, but discontinued under Tiberius. Roman equestrians guilty of especially scandalous acts were punished, yet those culpable for minor faults were excused. Moderation was the order of the day, and the climate of fear and apprehension that had been fostered in the days of Sejanus and Tiberius alike was to be dispelled. In one sense, Caligula could not win. If he acted nobly, he could be accused of dissimulation and a mere attempt to curry the favour of the populace.

Tiberius' will had granted legacies and bequests, as had that of Livia; the latter testament had been suppressed by order of Tiberius, but now Caligula honoured the prescriptions of both (ignoring, of course, the key detail about the place of Tiberius Gemellus in the *post mortem Tiberii* arrangements). According to the last chapter of Suetonius' life of Tiberius (76), the will stipulated that Gaius and Gemellus should be equal inheritors, and each sole inheritor in case of the death of the other.[57] As for Livia, Suetonius refers to her as 'Julia Augusta' in his mention of the will – the title she had been granted after her husband Augustus' death.[58] Caligula was doing all he could to emphasize his Augustan connections. Why Tiberius had avoided honouring the will cannot be known with complete certainty; he clearly resented his long-lived mother.[59]

Some details preserved in Suetonius offer memorable anecdotes of these seemingly blissful days. A freedwoman was given 800,000 sesterces, because she had refused to implicate her guilty patron, even under the torture that was customary when slaves were interrogated (an example of a reward – however outrageously generous – for a display of *pietas*). Those who had suffered losses from fire were awarded recompense.

Caligula was duly recognized for all these munificent and merciful acts. He was awarded a golden shield, which was to be carried by the colleges of priests every year on an appointed day, with senatorial participation in the procession. Boys and girls of the nobility sang of his greatness in choral ode. The day on which he commenced his reign was called the Parilia, the name of the festival of 21 April that marked the very birthday of Rome.[60] According to the surviving *Acta Fratrum Arvalium*, or 'Acts of the Arval Brethren', that date was 18 March – the day the Senate in Rome declared Caligula *Imperator*.[61]

Caligula assumed the consulship with Claudius on 1 July; the office was held for two months. A second consulship followed, which commenced on 1 January AD 39 and lasted for a month. The third was held until the Ides of January (i.e. 13 January) in 40. The fourth and final tenure in office was held until 7 January 41 – in other words, Caligula's consulships grew ever shorter. The third, Suetonius notes, commenced at Lugdunum (modern Lyons), and without a colleague – not because of Caligulan arrogance or contempt for precedent, but because he was unaware that his partner in office had died before the Kalends of January (i.e. 1 January).

The emperor was notably generous. The common people were given a gift of 300 sesterces a piece, and two lavish banquets were offered to the Senate and the equestrians, at the second of which, the men were given gifts of togas, and their wives and children red and scarlet scarves. The holiday known as the Saturnalia (a precursor of the Christian Christmas) was extended by a day, which he named 'Iuvenalis' (a day of youth).[62] Interestingly, Suetonius had also noted that the Saturnalia was more or less suspended in AD 19 when Germanicus died; public mourning was so intense in the wake of his death that the great winter holiday was ignored in favour of displays of grief.[63]

Gladiatorial shows were also held, and boxers were featured from both Africa and Campania. The emperor presided – but he also let other officials oversee the games, so as to give them honour and a chance at popular favour. Caligula was a great patron of the theatre, and plays were held in many locales, even at night. Games were held in the Circus, including beast hunts with panthers or cheetahs.[64] The so-called 'Troy game', or *lusus Troiae*, was also held, a traditional equestrian display in which two teams of young noblemen enacted the battle for Troy, the city that was at the heart of the Roman foundation legends of Aeneas and his son Ascanius or Iulus – the progenitor of the Julian clan, or *gens*.[65] Chariot racing, including contests where all the participants were of senatorial rank, was also popular in Caligula's Rome.

All of this might be seen as classic imperial practice to curry the favor of the populace, and it would be difficult to indict or impugn Caligula for any of his actions with respect to largesse and the games. Any criticism of Caligula attendant on his indulgence in games and, for that matter, literary and theatrical pretensions may raise the question of whether the attacks were anachronistically levelled against his posthumous memory in light of the excesses of Nero, who was even more infamous for such decadence. The interest in the Troy game certainly bespoke a certain pride in the part of the young emperor for his celebrated family lineage, for the descent of the Julian line from Venus and Aeneas through Iulus and, of course, Julius Caesar. Indulgence in some of these initiatives might be reasonable, especially in light of the emperor's youthful exuberance.

Stranger, though, is the story that Caligula constructed a bridge of boats across the Bay of Naples and rode across it and back on two successive days, the first time on a horse with military decorations, the second in a two-horse chariot with a Parthian boy hostage by name of Dareus, with the Praetorian Guard and Gallic chariots to accompany him in mock triumph.

Suetonius more or less defends Caligula from charges that he was merely seeking to imitate the great Persian monarch Xerxes, who had famously bridged the Hellespont between Asia and Europe, or that he was attempting to threaten Germany and Britain with military invasion.[66] He notes that when he was a boy, his grandfather recalled that the Tiberian astrologer Thrasyllus had declared to the emperor that Caligula had no more chance to be emperor than to ride over the Gulf of Baiae with horses. Caligula was now emperor – and he would prove Thrasyllus wrong at any expense.[67] It is possible that we may also identify here a real frustration with a lack of achievement in *res militares*; Caligula had no record of service, and there may even have been some more or less good-natured wagging about how the emperor was a play soldier – a reflection, in other words, of the whole *caligula* story from his infancy that seemed permanently to infantilize him. Again, at the risk of indulging in psychological analysis, the young *princeps* may have had a profound need to compensate for his very real lack of experience for his office.

A festival was also held at Syracuse in Sicily, along with games at Lugdunum in Gaul, where there was also a contest in Greek and Latin oratory. The losers, Suetonius notes, were obliged to write in praise of the victors, with the least successful compelled to erase what they had written either with sponge or tongue, unless they chose to be beaten with rods or cast into a river. The details about the punishments and cruel behaviour may easily be taken as further evidence of Caligula's character, which had not yet reached the level of monstrosity that was still to come. For the losing contestants to have to lick their words was a deep humiliation, while being beaten or thrown into a nearby river was a physical punishment quite inappropriate to the occasion (to say the least). One has the impression that Caligula presented this all as a source of amusement and mockery; again, the warning signs were there of what was likely to transpire as the emperor grew more comfortable in his power.

We may note in contrast that Suetonius praises Germanicus for his literary interests and achievements; he was an orator as well as an author of Greek comedies.[68] One might be tempted to think that the son inherited some of the literary interests of the father, though to worse ends.

The temple of Augustus and the theatre of Pompey were finished, while an aqueduct in the region near Tibur and an amphitheatre were started.[69] Temples and city walls in Syracuse were repaired. Plans were also commenced to rebuild the palace of Polycrates at Samos, finish a temple of Apollo at Miletus, develop a city high in the Alps and dig a canal through the Isthmus of Corinth in Greece.[70] Building projects were a hallmark of the Age of Augustus, but Tiberius was not particularly known for his development of the city of Rome (or of any other). Caligula was thus harking back to the days of his glorious ancestor. His Rome would be a source of architectural splendour and achievement, and foreign locales – especially in Greece – would also be favoured with renewal and renovation.[71]

The project in the Alps, we might note, is mysterious; there is no clear sense of what Caligula had in mind. He travelled through the Alps, as we shall see soon enough, when he journeyed to the German border at the Rhine – but what he planned for somewhere in the mountain range is unknown. It is possible that he wanted to establish some place that could be associated with the great deeds of his father in Germany.

Hactenus quasi de principe, reliqua ut de monstro narranda sunt;[72] thus far, Suetonius notes, we have discussed the *princeps* – the rest concerns the monster.[73] Suetonius thus memorably separates the two sections of his life – the first comprises but twenty-one chapters, while the second extends to sixty.

One third of the biography is devoted to the emperor, and a portion of that is actually a quasi-eulogy of his father Germanicus. The bulk of the biography is the stuff of notoriety and sordid report, and is the account of Caligula that is best known to the popular imagination. It is an enduring picture of savagery and disgusting crime.

We may take stock at this juncture of the Suetonian picture of Caligula as *princeps*. The biographer is notoriously bad about chronology and dating (indeed, to the point of frustration), but it is clear enough from both Suetonius and (as we shall see) other sources that there was a 'good' and a 'bad' period to Caligula's principate.[74] Interestingly, Suetonius associates Caligula's father Germanicus with the same division in the imperial tenure of Tiberius.[75] He notes that after the death of Germanicus, there was no restraint on Tiberius; the *saevitia*, or savagery, of Tiberius had been held in check by Germanicus, given that the emperor had respect and fear (*reverentia* and *metus*) for the young man. In other words, he feared that excessive cruelty and unrestrained autocratic tendencies might result in popular uprising and the rise of his implicit young rival. If anyone in Rome believed that Germanicus' death had permitted Tiberius to indulge in his worst passions, then the accession of Caligula would easily enough be taken as the harbinger of a positive future.

But for those who subscribed to the idea that one's character was fixed in the stars as it was from birth, whatever good Caligula did was simply the result of pretence and an ability to fool people for at least a short while. The mask eventually came off; for those who were observant enough, the signs were always there that the monster lurked beneath the surface. *Dissimulatio* was the key to understanding the young Caligula, at least according to this logic. He had tricked enough people into thinking that he was a reasonable, even principled ruler.

The perhaps excessive interest in the games and the theatre could easily enough be taken as evidence of a decadent if not degenerate spirit; the episode of the bridge of boats was certainly readily suspect. But Caligula was significantly younger than his two predecessors at the time of his accession, and unlike them, he had no military record to offer as testimony to his potential or actual greatness. Youthful indulgence would readily have been offered as an excuse and justification for some of his more questionable early actions.

The Praetorian Guard was the source of his military power, and whatever lingering loyalty was present in the army toward the family of Germanicus. Grandiose projects such as the desire to cut through the Isthmus of Corinth could easily be taken as evidence of a hubristic nature.[76] We are certainly left with the picture of a young emperor who was eager to prove himself and his worth to the world. The son of Germanicus and descendant of Augustus had an immense task thrust upon him in the wake of Tiberius' death.[77] It was to Caligula's great advantage that Tiberius was so unpopular. If Tiberius recognized in Caligula someone who would be more hated than he was, then at least at the commencement of his reign Caligula could enjoy the benefits that were attendant on succeeding the reviled old *princeps*. Twenty-three long years had been spent under the reign of Tiberius. Caligula, at 24, would have seemed a breath of fresh air – his life had almost exactly coincided with the number of years Tiberius had ruled. The reign of Caligula the monster would show in part that little Gaius had mastered the lessons of perversion and wickedness that had marked the worst excesses of Tiberius' Rome.

We turn now to the unforgettable Suetonian account of Caligula the *monstrum*. It is the more colourful and memorable section of the life, and the work that has certainly had the most enduring impact on the modern perception of Caligula. It will ultimately be our task to determine how fair and reasonable Suetonius' treatment of the *princeps* is, and to try to glean from his sordid stories some sense of the political and especially military realities of the short reign of Gaius.

Chapter Two

The Life of Caligula by Suetonius, Part II (Caligula the *Monstrum*)

S uetonius commences his investigation of Caligula the 'monster' with another consideration of the question of names. Caligula was called *pius* – the adjective or appellation that characterized him as loyal and devoted to the memory of his parents, and highlighted his respect for the gods. He was *castrorum filius* – literally, 'a son of the camp' – and *pater exercituum*, or 'father of the armies'. He was also *optimus maximus Caesar* – 'best and greatest Caesar'.

All of these titles, Suetonius notes, were 'assumed' – *cognominibus adsumptis*. The impression one forms is that the emperor wanted to change his image, from Bootikin to something rather more dignified and noble. We may note the use of both *filius* and *pater*: perhaps the young Caligula could not decide between favouring the affectionate image of a son or embracing the Augustan model of a father.[1]

And yet, Suetonius notes, one night at a dinner party, when kings who had come to fulfill the duty of embassy and displays of respect for the *princeps* were debating the question of who was most noble in lineage, Caligula interrupted the discussion with a quote from Homer that there should be one lord and one king.[2] He came near, the biographer notes, to assuming the diadem and converting the *species principatus* into the *regni formam* – the image or semblance of a principate into the form of a monarchy.

Caligula, simply put, wanted to be King of Rome. Roman history recalled the reign of the early kings, and the expulsion of the last – Tarquinius Superbus, or Tarquin the Proud – by Brutus in 509 BC. The Roman Republic had been established in the same year, with the accession of the first consuls and the dawn of a new Rome that despised the notion of monarchy. Republican sentiments certainly questioned various aspects of the new system that had more or less been refined over the long tenures of Augustus and Tiberius – but neither Augustus nor Tiberius ever aspired to an outright declaration of monarchical ambition.

Caligula was dissuaded from his intention by being reminded that he was above such regal conceits – he was higher than a king. The only rank higher than king was god, and so from that day on, Suetonius observes, Caligula began to assert his *divina maiestas*, or divine majesty.

In all of this there is a remembrance of the 'other' Gaius, Julius Caesar. He too had flirted with the idea of kingship, and was also honoured as a god.[3] Caesar had been circumspect about the whole question of his divinity, though not as much as his adopted son Augustus, while nobody ever thought about declaring Tiberius a god either in life or in death. Caligula would be the first emperor to be quite open and direct about his divinity.

What is interesting in all this is the significant detail that Caligula was advised or admonished (*admonitus*) that he had surpassed the principate and even monarchy. For Suetonius, the idea was not necessarily Caligula's own – though it was apparently one to which he readily assented. This is not to exonerate Caligula from his pretensions to godhood – but rather to note that perhaps some of his courtiers and advisors inherited more than they expected from their flattering advice.

And so statues of the immortals – not least the great chryselephantine statue of Zeus from Olympia – were brought from Greece so that the heads could be replaced with heads of Caligula. The statue was never actually brought to Rome – one of the artistic blessings of the emperor's short reign.[4] But Caligula did extend part of the imperial palace out to the Forum and made the temple of the brothers Castor and Pollux its vestibule.[5] He apparently often stood between the statues of the brothers and displayed himself for the adoration of those who drew near; he was called 'Iupiter Latiaris', or Jupiter Latiaris – the Jupiter of Latium or the Latin League.[6] Some scholars wonder if the address was meant not so much to flatter Caligula as to insult him (in other words, he was being derided as rather less impressive a Jupiter/Zeus than the one of Olympia).[7]

Caligula was not satisfied with sharing the temple of Castor and Pollux. He had his own shrine constructed, with priests and sacrificial victims. There was a golden statue of the emperor, which was dressed each day in the clothing worn by Caligula. The animal victims included flamingoes and peacocks (unquestionable markers of decadence and luxurious excess). At night, the divine emperor would invite the moon goddess Selene[8] to share his bed, while by day he would converse with the Capitoline Jupiter, now whispering into the ear of the god and now shouting, including a threat quoted from Homer that the god had better lift him up, or he would lift up the god.[9] The Iliadic verse is from Ajax to Odysseus during the wrestling match at the funeral games for Patroclus; the point of the fairly *recherché* reference seems to be that Jupiter should hasten to recognize Caligula as an equal, lest he be removed ignominiously. And indeed, Caligula soon enough reported that the god invited him to share his abode on the Capitol, so Caligula arranged for the palace to be joined thereto by a bridge, and plans were undertaken to build a new imperial home in the vicinity.

In all of this, perhaps the best that can be said of Caligula is that he apparently knew his *Iliad* very well indeed; he had certainly absorbed the lessons of his education in Homer's text.

Suetonius asserts that Caligula was deeply embarrassed by his descent from Agrippa on account of his low birth.[10] He conceived the idea that Augustus had committed incest with his daughter Julia, so that Agrippa could in some way be removed from the imperial family tree.[11] In some of this we may see a reflection of the tensions between the two sides of Caligula's family; he was descended from both Augustus via Julia's marriage to Agrippa, and from Mark Antony – the two opposing sides of the great climax of the civil wars at the naval Battle of Actium in 31 BC. Agrippa had been the admiral most responsible for the victory in that engagement; disrespect for Agrippa could have been a calculated way to honour Antony without slandering Augustus. That said, the story of incest between Augustus and Julia was a monumental slight against the very father of a Rome that had been reborn in the wake of so many years of internecine strife. At any rate, the inbreeding that had been a characteristic practice of the imperial family had resulted in a conflicted Caligula who could not decide which triumviral ancestor deserved to be honoured more conspicuously. And Agrippa's dearth of noble associations certainly did not accord with Caligula's pretensions to divinity.

In accord with his wish to excise the memory of Agrippa from his family background, Caligula is said to have banned the annual celebrations in honour of the victory of Actium and of the triumph of Agrippa at Sicily over the forces of Sextus Pompey. Caligula is said to have declared that these battles were deadly and calamitous to the Roman people – true enough, in the sense that

they were cases of civil war that resulted in the deaths of numerous Romans –
and so they should not be celebrated.

Caligula also attacked the memory of the late Livia, calling her – in one of the
more memorable quotes from the Suetonian life – a 'Ulysses in a *stola*' (*Ulixem
stolatum*). The *stola* was the usual dress of a Roman matron, while Ulysses was
the Latin name of the wily Greek hero Odysseus. Odysseus was an inveterate
survivor of challenge after challenge, both at Troy and after, and Caligula,
we must remember, had spent formative years with his great-grandmother.
He insulted her own lineage, arguing that she was the granddaughter on her
mother's side of a mere local magistrate at Fundi. Suetonius claims that, on
the contrary, his own research showed that Aufidius Lurco was a high-ranking
Roman official.

Here we find an interesting prosopographical problem.[12] The ancestor in
question was Alfidius, not Aufidius, so either Caligula deliberately lied about
the name, or Suetonius made an error in his research. In short, it is possible
that Caligula was right about Livia's ancestry – and no doubt easy to imagine
that both he and others were willing to say negative things about her in the
years following her death.

More notably, when Antonia asked to see her grandson Caligula, the
emperor would only meet her in the presence of the praetorian prefect Macro.
Antonia is finally said to have been driven to death (i.e. suicide) by such insults
and indignities – though some said that Caligula poisoned her.[13] Antonia died
on the Kalends of May in AD 37 – not so very long after the accession of
Gaius to the purple. Scholars have disputed the veracity of Suetonius' story
about Caligula's involvement in the death, noting that the emperor would have
had barely a month to dispose of his grandmother, and at the very time when
he was broadcasting his *pietas* and filial devotion.[14] In short, while we may
readily believe that Caligula insulted Livia, it strains credulity to imagine that
he poisoned Antonia. The cynical view would be that he wanted to avoid the
problem Tiberius had with Livia – an old woman of respected years who might
prove a check on his imperial whims.

Caligula is said to have shown Antonia no honour, and to have viewed her
burning funeral pyre from his dining room couch. Further, he had a tribune
sent in to see to the death of Tiberius Gemellus, thus removing one seemingly
significant threat to his monarchical ambitions.

The alleged denial of honours to Antonia would seem at variance with the report of Suetonius at 15.2 of his life, that Caligula bestowed on his grandmother whatever privileges Livia had enjoyed. As for Gemellus, Suetonius records the story that the young man's breath smelled of medicine, which Caligula assumed was an antidote that was being ingested to protect against poisoning. In reality, Gemellus had a terrible cough that would not improve; Caligula would seem to have been the doctor who solved the consumptive problem.[15] Even Balsdon – who often is careful to explicate Caligula's actions to show the hostility of some ancient traditions – observes (p.37) that 'The public peace was consulted when a possible rival of the Emperor was removed; but that does not excuse the act or its author.'[16]

Another victim of the emperor was his father-in-law, Marcus Junius Silanus, who like Gemellus was driven to take his own life. The story is told that when Caligula was departing on a sea voyage in stormy weather (i.e. the trip to retrieve the ashes of his relatives), Silanus did not follow him, planning, it would seem, to seize power should anything happen to Caligula on the dangerous voyage. Suetonius notes that Silanus was simply prone to seasickness and thus wanted to avoid the trip. Tacitus notes in his *Agricola* (4.1) that his father-in-law, Agricola's father, was Julius Graecinus, who was slain for refusing to prosecute one Marcus Silanus.[17]

Caligula's uncle Claudius was spared, if only to remain a *ludibrium*, or object of mockery. The survivor would live to see many more days, not to mention succession to his nephew's throne.

Suetonius also indicts Caligula for the regular practice of incest with his sisters – all of them.[18] The sisters in question were Agrippina (the mother of the future emperor Nero), Livilla and Drusilla.[19] Of the three, Drusilla was apparently the favorite. Antonia is said to have caught Caligula and Drusilla in a compromising position when they were still minors. Drusilla was later married to Lucius Cassius Longinus, but Caligula nevertheless treated her as his own lawful wife, and even made her his heir during his mysterious illness. [20] After Drusilla died (10 June AD 38), Caligula is said to have declared a period of public mourning and lament, during which it was a death penalty offence to laugh, bathe or dine in the presence of one's parents, wife or children. Caligula fled Rome in grief and travelled through Campania to Syracuse on Sicily, returning to the capital without cutting his hair or shaving his beard. His oaths thereafter were always taken *per numen Drusillae*, that is, through the *numen*, or 'divine power', of Drusilla – a goddess indeed.

Drusilla can claim the status among the Julio-Claudians of being the first woman to enjoy *post mortem* deification.[21] Suetonius details that the other sisters of Caligula were not held in such high esteem; their sexual favours were prostituted by the emperor to his favourites, and they were even implicated by Caligula not only as adulteresses, but also as knowledgeable of the conspiracies against him.

Frustratingly, Suetonius alludes but briefly to what must have been one of the more serious of the alleged early plots against him – that of Marcus Aemilius Lepidus. Caligula had actually compelled Drusilla to divorce her husband Cassius Longinus and to marry Lepidus. Considering that the emperor had named Drusilla his heir in the event that he did not recover from his serious illness, it was clear enough that Lepidus – Drusilla's legal husband if not regular bedmate – would succeed Caligula. Whatever happened, Lepidus did not survive his wife by long.

Letters were made public by Caligula in the handwriting of his sisters Agrippina and Livilla – letters obtained by deceit and base seduction (Latin *stuprum*). Three swords were dedicated to the god Mars Ultor – Mars the Avenger – in token of how the emperor's life had been saved from the machinations of Lepidus and the two surviving sisters.

Suetonius had already mentioned Caligula's brief marriage to Junia Claudilla;[22] now he proceeds to less honourable nuptial arrangements. Livia Orestilla was to be married to Gaius Calpurnius Piso. At their wedding, the emperor is said to given orders that the bride be taken not to Piso's house but to his own.[23] A few days later he divorced her, and two years later he exiled her, on a charge of suspicion that she had returned to Piso. Suetonius notes that other sources claim that at the wedding of the unfortunate couple, Caligula had sent a note to Piso instructing him not to have sexual relations with his (i.e. the emperor's) wife; Livia Orestilla was then carried off by Caligula, and the next day a declaration was announced that Caligula had obtained a wife in the same manner as Romulus (who had been responsible for the abduction of the Sabine women) and Augustus (who had obtained another Livia, of course, though apparently the reference is also to a charge that the first emperor had removed a woman from a dining table without notice of her husband).[24]

The second wife in the unseemly nuptial catalogue – Caligula's third overall – was Lollia Paulina.[25] In this case, Suetonius records that the emperor had heard that Paulina's grandmother had been exceptionally lovely. Caligula immediately called for the granddaughter, who at the time was married to the ex-consul Gaius Memmius Regulus.[26] She was also married and quickly divorced, with the command that she should never again engage in sexual relations.

The last wife was Caesonia, noteworthy for being neither beautiful nor young. She was already the mother of three daughters, and known for reckless spending and extravagant ways. And yet Caesonia seems to have been Nero's favourite, the only wife to whom he was faithful (leaving aside whatever did or did not happen with Drusilla). She was often taken with him when he appeared before the army, dressed in a military cloak with shield and helmet, while he exhibited her in a state of nakedness to his friends. He did not marry her until she gave birth to a daughter – whom he named Julia Drusilla, and whom he dedicated to the goddess Minerva from her infancy.[27] For Suetonius, the little girl quickly displayed ample evidence that she was the child of Caligula, given as she was to scratching the faces and eyes of her little playmates.

Other victims of Caligula are briefly enumerated: Ptolemy, the son of King Juba of Mauretania, the grandson of Mark Antony and son of Cleopatra Selene (the triumvir's daughter by Cleopatra), met an untimely death.[28] So did the praetorian prefect Macro, and his wife Ennia. Macro was no doubt seen by most of his contemporaries as another potential Sejanus; his enforced suicide would have come as no surprise and no source of grief to most.

Senators are also said to have been done away with, with the emperor continuing to summon them for some time after their deaths, only finally to announce that clearly they had taken their own lives. More fortunate members of the senatorial order were given humiliating tasks, such as running for several miles beside the imperial chariot or even serving at table in servile dress. Suetonius further claims that consuls were deposed for forgetting to celebrate Gaius' late August birthday. He had his quaestor viciously whipped on a charge of conspiracy.

Those who came by night to secure free Circus seats made the fatal mistake of causing a ruckus and noise. They were driven out with clubs, and in the process more than twenty equestrians were killed, along with many women and a crowd of others besides. Caligula started fights and riots when he scattered free tickets around at the theatre, all with the intention to encourage the commoners to take the seats reserved for the equestrians. At gladiatorial spectacles, Caligula would remove the awning and force people to endure the sun at the hottest part of the day – only to compel them to watch second-rate shows with aged, decrepit gladiators, as well as noblemen compelled to fight in mock battles – nobles who were noteworthy for some physical deformity or source of amusement.[29] And sometimes the emperor shut up the granaries, simply to create a famine.

Savagery was a characteristic of the emperor. From manufactured hunger, Suetonius moves on to charge that when the cattle to feed the beasts in a gladiatorial spectacle were too expensive, Caligula simply had the animals fed on live criminals.[30]

We have already seen how men had made lavish vows of their own lives in exchange for the health of the emperor when he had fallen ill; Caligula called in the promises.[31] One man who had promised to fight as a gladiator was now compelled to do so, and he was not released from the arena until he had been victorious in a sword fight, and after much pleading to be set free. Another man who hesitated to take his own life was handed over to his slaves, who forced him through the streets after he had been decked out like a sacrificial victim; he was finally hurled down from a height to his death.

Men of honourable rank (*honesti ordinis*) were punished with degrading service in the mines, or assigned to crews in charge of road work – or to be thrown to the beasts to be devoured. Some were shut up in cages and forced to stay on all fours like animals,[32] or otherwise were sawn in half. The victims of these excessive and cruel punishments were those who had criticized Caligula's shows, or who had failed to swear by his *Genius*.[33]

Parents were compelled to witness the executions of their children,[34] while a gladiatorial show manager was beaten with chains in his presence for several days, until finally he was slain after the emperor was disgusted by the smell of the man's putrefied brain.[35] A writer of Atellan farces was burned alive in the arena because of a *double entendre*.[36] An equestrian who protested his innocence as he was being thrown to wild beasts was removed from their enclosure, suffered the loss of his tongue, and was then cast back to his death.

Caligula had made it a point to show mercy and clemency to those who had been condemned under Tiberius. But when he learned from one returned exile that the man had spent his time in banishment praying for the death of Tiberius and the accession of Caligula, he had once ordered the general execution of all those whom he had exiled, suspecting that they were all praying for his death and the reign of another.

Caligula wished for the death of a senator; he arranged it that when the poor fellow arrived at the *curia*, he would be condemned as a *hostis publicus*, or 'public enemy', and slain by his senatorial colleagues with sharpened styluses. The victim was eventually savagely mangled and indeed torn to pieces, but Caligula was not satisfied until the body was dragged through the streets and all the man's limbs, member and bowels were heaped up before him.[37] Caligula had increased appreciably in savagery from the youth who delighted in the sight of executions and other corporal punishments.[38]

We have seen that Caligula apparently knew his Homer well. Speaking of the world of Greek letters, Suetonius records that Caligula used to say that there was no quality in his character that he praised and approved of more than his ἀδιατρεψία, which Suetonius glosses as *inverecundia*.[39] The Greek word does not occur elsewhere in extant texts; it would naturally mean something like 'steadfastness' – or, in a negative sense, simple stubbornness and an ornery nature.[40] One problem here is that the Latin *inverecundia* would properly mean 'shamelessness'. It is not a literal translation of the Greek, and may have been an error of some scribe who inserted it into the text. Scholars have attempted to argue that the point here – Suetonius knew his Greek after all – is that for Caligula, steadfastness meant steadfastness in inflicting harm on others and in engaging in unspeakable acts. If anything, the emperor was always consistent in this (despite the seeming arbitrariness of so many of his decisions). Nothing could dissuade the emperor – not fear of the gods, not the admonitions of counsellors and relatives, not any sense of trepidation or fear for the future or of retribution.[41]

Suetonius offers examples of this self-proclaimed characteristic trait of Caligula that hark back to other episodes to which he has alluded. Antonia apparently warned Caligula against excessive behaviour, but she was told that everything was permitted to him, and to act in any way he wished against anyone.[42] In the case of Tiberius Gemellus and his cough medication, Caligula is said to have exclaimed, '*Antidotum adversus Caesarem?*' – 'Is there medicine against Caesar?' When Agrippina and Livilla were banished, he noted that he had swords as well as islands at his disposal. An ex-praetor who had gone to Anticyra (in Phocis in Greece) for reasons of health and rejuvenation kept asking for extensions of his sick leave. Caligula finally noted that a man who was not cured by hellebore (a medicinal herb) needed to experience bloodletting – a play on the famous medical practice that endured until the late nineteenth century. After signing the death warrants of several Gauls and Greeks, the emperor noted that he was conquering 'Gallograecia'.[43]

Executions were drawn out and torturous. When someone was mistakenly done away with through a confusion of names, he noted that the victim was also deserving of death.[44] Caligula was fond of reciting a line from tragic verse: '*Oderint, dum metuant*' – 'let them hate me, so long as they fear me'.[45]

Documents that had allegedly been burned were produced, as Caligula attacked the Senate *en masse* as partisans of Sejanus and persecutors of his mother Agrippina and his brothers.[46] Caligula noted that the savagery of Tiberius was understandable, given the plethora of informers and agents of Sejanus who were active – an interesting twist on the earlier policy of distancing himself from the Tiberian reputation for *saevitia*, or cruelty.[47]

Caligula's oft-quoted verse about letting everyone hate him, so long as they feared him was borrowed from Roman republican tragedy, but his line '*utinam populus Romanus unam cervicem haberet!*' – 'if only the Roman people had but one neck' (i.e. so as all the more easily to hack off the heads of all) – was all his own.[48] The context was that the crowd was applauding a faction he opposed in the games; the triviality of the circumstances made the remark all the more memorable for its viciousness and contempt for humanity.

Somewhat more mysterious are the Suetonian anecdotes that the crowd one day demanded the thief Tetrinius (for punishment, or to be forced to participate in the games), and that Caligula replied that they were all Tetriniuses, and especially the story of a gladiatorial combat in which a member of the defeated side suddenly picked up his trident and killed the victors. The fight was between the so-called *retiarii*, or 'net-men' who wielded tridents, and the *secutores*, who fought with light arms. The circumstances of the fight that Suetonius describes are not entirely clear. Five net-men yielded to the *secutores* without a struggle, and when it was decreed that they should be killed, one of the *retiarii* took up his weapon again and killed the swordsmen. Caligula complained that this was a most foul murder, and criticized the crowd who had put up with seeing it.

The question of the exact point of the story hinges on the issue of whether or not the contest was supposed to be a serious one. There is certainly an ironic element in Caligula's complaint about 'the most cruel slaughter' (*crudelissimam caedem*). The episode remains 'obscure' (so says Wardle in his commentary); once again, everyone in Caligula's orbit – in this case both the gladiators and the crowd – was damned no matter what was done.

Caligula is also said to have complained that his reign was characterized by no disasters on the scale of the *Varusschlacht* of the Augustan Age (when the legions of Varus were slaughtered by Arminius' coalition of German tribes), or of the collapse of the amphitheatre at Fidenae.[49] The very prosperity and security of the Caligulan reign ensured that it would be consigned to oblivion. The emperor need not have worried on this point, needless to say.

Cruelty extended to meal time. Executions under torture were carried out during feasts, and a soldier skilled at decapitation was assigned to lop off the heads of prisoners as they drew near the emperor. The dedication of a bridge at Puteoli was marked by the drowning of spectators who had been tricked into boarding a boat to come to Caligula from the shore. Those who tried to climb back to safety were cudgelled with oars and boathooks. A slave accused of theft had his hands cut off and hung around his neck. A gladiator who thought he was fighting a mock battle with the emperor was killed with a very real dagger; Caligula then ran about with a palm of victory to celebrate the slaughter.[50] Dressed at the altar in the vesture of the *popa*, or official responsible for dazing sacrificial victims with a mallet blow, Caligula surprised the *cultrarius* whose task was to cut the animal's throat by smashing his own head. Caligula burst into laughter at a dinner in the presence of the consuls; when asked what was so amusing, he noted that at a single nod of his head he could have both their throats cut.

The emperor treated his wives and girlfriends similarly, kissing the neck with the reminder that he could have her beheaded whenever he wished. The tragic actor Apelles was mercilessly flogged when he hesitated too long as to the question of whether Caligula or Jupiter was greater – but Caligula made sure to praise Apelles' voice as he groaned in agony.[51] The devoted Caesonia was threatened with torture so that she could explain to Caligula's satisfaction why she loved him so ardently.

Statues of famous men were destroyed. The poems of Homer were considered for abolition. In this Caligula allegedly cited Plato, who in his *Republic* excluded narrative poetry and epic from the ideal state.[52] The poet Virgil was dismissed as a man of no talent and mediocre learning, while the historian Livy was considered verbose and careless.[53] Caligula is said almost to have banned the writings of both men, and to have removed their busts from libraries along with their works.[54] Lawyers were warned that he would see to it by the power of the gods that they never gave advice contrary to his wishes.

Suetonius had already alluded to Caligula's seeing to the death of his cousin Ptolemy; now he details the reasons for the murder.[55] The Mauretanian king had come to a gladiatorial display in Rome – and the crowd was overly fond of the monarch's purple cloak. Men with fine heads of hair were made to have the backs of their heads shaved. There were also other insults levelled at members of great families.

Aesius Proculus (the son of a chief centurion) was dragged from his seat at the games and made to participate as a contestant; he was called Colosseros or 'The Colossal Cupid' *ob egregiam corporis amplitudinem* for the 'outstanding size of his body'. Despite defeating two opponents in the arena, he was bound, dressed in rags, displayed to the women of the city and then slain.[56] If there was anything consistent in Caligula's actions, it is that he envied anyone and everyone whatever they had that he did not. For example, the fugitive slave who was the priest of Diana at Nemi (the slave who obtained his office by killing his predecessor) was assigned a stronger opponent after remaining in office for more years than suited Caligula.[57] A gladiator was praised so highly by the crowd for his victories that Caligula fled the amphitheatre in such haste that he tripped and fell on his toga, noting that the audience was readier to praise a mere slave for next to nothing then to honour their deified emperors or the god present among them.[58]

Sexual misdeeds were the hour of the day for Caligula.[59] Bisexual liaisons were numerous and perverse. There was the aforementioned incest with his sisters, and also the sending of bills of divorce in the name of absent husbands to those women with whom he was illicitly involved. The pantomime Mnester was one of his lovers; Mnester would later be infamous as a lover of Claudius' notorious wife Messalina – and he would perish in her downfall.[60] Lepidus – the ill-fated husband of Drusilla for a spell – was also among the catalogue of Caligula's partners in sexual misconduct.

Expensive pearls were drunk down that had been dissolved in vinegar.[61] Caligula was fond of saying that a man should either be frugal or be Caesar.[62] And so dishes of gold were the norm; large sums of money were scattered among the people. His main goal was to do whatever men said was impossible.[63] Expense was no consideration. Indeed, within only a year, all the money that Tiberius had amassed had been spent in profligate, wanton fashion.

As if a Xerxes or a Lucullus, Caligula tried to turn land into sea and sea into land by building projects on moles at sea, and by tunnelling through rock – and all with great haste, since death was the penalty for delay in construction. Once the money was exhausted, attempts were made to make more by illicit means, not excluding false accusations. Caligula was determined to have his name included in last wills and testaments to inherit wealth; once he secured such a bequest, he would accuse the testator of mocking him unless he died at once – and he sent poisoned treats and delicacies to hasten the inheritance.

Indeed, impatience was one of the hallmark qualities of the emperor. Caesonia once rose from a nap to be informed that while she slept, Caligula had condemned forty men on different charges simply by using one sentence of death.

Thirteen gladiators were once sold for the high sum of nine million sesterces, because Caligula warned the auctioneer not to ignore the 'bidding' of the praetor Aponius Saturninus, who had fallen asleep on a bench and kept nodding his head in slumber.[64]

While in Gaul, Caligula sold the possessions of his condemned sisters at enormous cost, and soon became all but addicted to the idea of finding whatever he could to pawn off at high profit. Outrageous taxes were imposed on the population, and a brothel was even opened in the imperial palace, with matrons and freeborn boys exposed for sale and perversion – the point being to raise money by any means possible.[65] Caligula was in addition an avid dice player, and more than willing to increase his winnings by lies and falsehood.[66]

After the birth of his daughter Drusilla, Caligula complained that money was even tighter now that he was a father.[67] He made clear to the people that he accepted cash for his daughter's upkeep and dowry, and that he would happily receive New Year's presents of coins.[68] He was so obsessed with money that it is said that he would pour forth huge masses of gold coins and walk barefoot over them, wallowing in the gold with his whole body, even out of lust for the very feel of the riches.[69]

Suetonius proceeds to the question of military affairs. Here at last the biographer turns to the military history of the short Caligulan reign, and he begins with a reminder that Caligula – unlike Augustus and Tiberius – had no military experience. There would be only one military adventure in Caligula's life, and it commenced (at least in Suetonius' estimation) with a desire to fill out the number of his precious German bodyguards, the Batavian contingent that was to prove quite loyal to him in the circumstances of his assassination (though to no avail).

The Batavians were allies of Rome in various military campaigns against other Germans. They had helped both Drusus the Elder and Germanicus, and would remain a feature of imperial bodyguards through the Age of Nero. The Batavians, who inhabited the ancient Netherlands, would take a prominent role in the complicated history of the so-called Long Year of AD 69.

One of the frustrating aspects of Suetonius' narrative is that he eschews a careful explication of the military and political situation. His narrative is subsumed under the heading of Caligula the *monstrum*, and it is a ludicrous impetus that sets in motion the whole 'campaign'. We shall be able to piece together some details of what exactly happened from careful comparison of Caligula with other extant sources – but for the moment, the emphasis remains on Caligula the tyrant and irrational libertine.

Caligula began his military adventure by raising and levying troops from all available quarters, so as to amass as impressive a force as possible. The march to Germany was made at times so hurriedly that the praetorian cohorts could scarcely maintain pace with the emperor; at other times in so leisurely a fashion that eight bearers carried Caligula on a litter, and the inhabitants of the town the army traversed were compelled to sweep the streets to eliminate dust, as well as to water them.[70]

Caligula reached his camp (of course Suetonius does not identify the site), displaying the harshness and severity of his discipline by dismissing all those officers who were dilatory in bringing auxiliaries.[71] Some older centurions were dismissed from their posts for reasons of age and physical infirmity, just days before they would have been dismissed anyway. Other soldiers were harangued for their avarice and greed; the pension for those who had served their time in the military was slashed by 50 per cent.

Suetonius is quite dismissive of Caligula's achievements after all of this drama and disciplinary rigour. He accepted the surrender of one Adminius, the son of Cynobellinus, the British king, who had been banished by his father. Adminius went over to Caligula with a small detachment of men. Cynobellinus, king of the Catuvellauni of south-eastern Britain, is perhaps most famous to anglophone audiences for Shakespeare's play *Cymbeline*.[72] Caligula is said to have responded to the surrender with the exultation of one who had conquered the whole of Britain. He sent messengers to announce in Rome that the island had been subjugated, with the news to be conveyed to the consuls in the temple of Mars Ultor, in the presence of the entire Senate.

Finding soon enough, however, that he had no ready arena for military campaigns, Suetonius' Caligula is said to have had some German prisoners taken across the Rhine and hidden, so that word could be brought to him after lunch that the enemy was about to launch a surprise attack.[73]

Caligula responded to the 'threat', of course, and returned with branches from trees that had been adorned like trophies, and new decorations were ordered for those 'brave' men who had accompanied him into battle – *coronae exploratoriae*, or garland crowns, in honour of expert 'scouts' (Latin *exploratores*). The crowns were decorated with images of the sun, the moon and the stars. For Suetonius, the point is that such an award made a farce of the tradition of military honours and insignia.

Hostages were also taken from a *litterarius ludus*, or primary school; on this occasion, Caligula departed a feast quickly and pursued the youths so that they could be brought back as 'evidence' of another triumph. Caligula is said to have quoted a line from Virgil's *Aeneid* when he returned to the banquet: *durarent secundisque se rebus servarent*.[74] Caligula may have criticized Virgil, but he was apparently not only able but willing to offer a timely and witty quote from the poet.

Caligula also sternly rebuked the Senate and people, noting that they were enjoying all manner of merriment in Rome while he was enduring the harshness of the German campaigns.

We now come to the single most memorable military 'exploit' for which Suetonius 'credits' Caligula: the notorious episode of the seashells. Caligula indicated that he was now going to finish the war, and he drew up his forces on the coast, at the shore of the ocean. Ballistas and other artillery were arranged. At that fateful moment, the emperor ordered his men to fill their helmets and the folds of their clothes with *conchas*, or seashells, which he called the spoils due to the Capitol and the Palatine in Rome. A lighthouse was built to commemorate the victory, as if it were the famous Pharos lighthouse at Alexandria. The soldiers were promised a donative of 100 *denarii* apiece, and were bade to depart happy in their newfound wealth.[75]

What exactly happened at the seashore on that climactic day of Caligula's campaigns has been studied with vigour by scholars of the reign of the enigmatic Gaius. Some have argued that the whole incident was based on a misunderstanding of a technical report of what Caligula actually ordered.[76] According to this theory, what Caligula really enjoined was that the soldiers should pick up *musculi* (cf. English 'mussel'), a technical term for a sort of shelter used in siege warfare. The main problem with this theory is that no evidence survives that Caligula used the word *musculus* (as opposed to *concha*).[77] David Woods argues that *conchae* were small boats, and that Caligula may have employed the noun in an innovative sense; the boats would have been captured British vessels that represented the conquest of the island. The linguistic novelty was misunderstood at an early date, thus occasioning yet another story of how insane Caligula really was.[78] Hurley and others take the reference to mean that pearls were collected – but from the wrong side of the English Channel, as it were, in a mock victory over the Britons (Caligula was actually on the modern Dutch shore).[79]

Suetonius observes that Caligula was careful to choose the most suitable candidates for his triumphal procession in Rome. Certain Gauls of outstanding height were chosen and ordered to grow their hair long and dye it red, and were made to learn something of the German language and take on new, barbarian names. Financial preparations were made for the triumph; the cost to Caligula was to be kept at an absolute minimum, and yet no expense was to be spared in pursuit of the goal of making this the grandest celebration Rome had ever seen – since, after all, the goods and resources of all humanity (excepting, one might think, the emperor) were at their disposal. The triremes in which Caligula had sailed out on the ocean where also to be carried overland to Rome.

Caligula's work in the north was, however, not yet quite finished. We are told that he also contrived to slaughter the legions that had mutinied after the death of Augustus in the summer of AD 14. These were the legions that had allegedly endangered his life in his infancy, the legions that his father Germanicus had confirmed in their loyalty to Tiberius and the new order. Caligula was apparently persuaded not to persist in this wish, but did insist on carrying out the ancient practice of decimation.[80] When he saw that the legionaries were ready to pick up arms and defend themselves against the prospect of even this more limited slaughter, he fled back to Rome and chose to vent his rage against the Senate. He complained bitterly that he had been cheated of triumphal honours by the Senate, though he had himself declared under penalty of death that no triumph should be prepared for him on his return.

Indeed, when senators met his entourage on the road to welcome him back to Rome, he is said to have announced that indeed he was returning, and with this in his hand – namely, his sword. Further, he was returning to the equestrians and to the people, but not to the Senate, for whom he was no longer a citizen or a *princeps* (so profoundly had they insulted him).[81] He pursued not a triumph but on ovation on 31 August – his birthday – in AD 40. Suetonius notes that within four months he was dead.[82]

For his biographer, Caligula's death came in time to prevent still greater atrocities than those he has already recorded. He is said to have intended to have slaughtered the leading senators and equestrians, and to have contemplated a retreat then to Antium (his birthplace) and then to Alexandria in Egypt.[83] Two *libelli*, or notebooks, were found among his papers *post mortem*; one was entitled *Gladius*, or 'Sword', and the other *Pugio*, or 'Dagger' – both contained lists of men marked down for slaughter.[84] Many poisons were also found in his possession. Claudius is said to have had them poured out into the sea, which created an environmental hazard and the death of many fish.[85]

Suetonius here interrupts his narrative, thus creating an effective cliffhanger before the account of the assassination. He proceeds to a physical description of the emperor: he was notably tall and extremely pale, and his body was too big for his very thin neck and legs. His forehead was broad and grim in its countenance, his hair thin, with the crown of his head almost entirely bald, though elsewhere his body was hirsute.[86] To look on the emperor from a height, or to mention a goat in his presence, was a capital offence. He was already unattractive facially, but practiced making savage and severe expressions to instill fear.

Suetonius records that Caligula's health was not good, either in body or in mind.[87] He suffered as a child from the 'falling sickness' (that is, the *comitialis morbus*, or epilepsy). While he was reasonably resilient as an adolescent, in his adulthood he was sometimes suddenly faint and incapacitated, unable to walk or even to hold up his head. He contemplated a retirement for the sake of clearing his head (*purgando cerebro*, literally 'for purging his brain'). It was believed that his last wife Caesonia had poisoned him with a love potion.[88] Insomnia was a perpetual problem; he never slept for more than three hours a night, and even that was fitful and plagued by nightmares, including one in which he dreamed that the image of the sea was speaking to him.[89] In consequence of his terrible time sleeping, Caligula would sometimes wander the long porticoes and cry out for the light, urging the coming of dawn.[90]

For Suetonius, Caligula's mental weakness (*valitudo mentis*) explained what the biographer identified as a major contradiction in the emperor's character: he was possessed of supreme confidence (*summa confidentia*), but also extraordinary anxiety and fear (*nimius metus*). He was terrified of thunder and lightning, though in general he despised the gods. In Sicily, though mocking all manner of miraculous events in different locales, he fled by night in panic from Messana because of an eruption of Etna. Once, when riding in a chariot on the far side of the Rhine, when he found himself in a narrow place and someone commented that circumstances would be quite difficult should the enemy suddenly appear, he immediately galloped off on a horse to safety – and this despite his repeated boasts and taunts about the inferior Germans. When he at last arrived at the bridges over the Rhine and saw that there was a great mass of servants and baggage, he insisted on being carried across from hand to hand over the heads of the slaves, so as to escape the possible hazard all the more swiftly.

News of an uprising in Germany filled him with such dread that he prepared to flee from Rome, with the thought that should the Germans cross the Alps and invade Italy, he could at least settle in some transmarine province. Caligula's apprehensions were apparently so well known that when he was finally assassinated, the killers argued to an angry soldiery that the emperor had killed himself after hearing bad news about some foreign peril.[91]

Caligula was no Roman in his dress and footwear; he was not even always a man or, for that matter, a mortal. He wore embroidered cloaks that were decorated with precious stones, and also favoured long-sleeved tunics (which were considered effeminate by the Romans) and bracelets (also associated with women). He indulged in silk – another mark of womanly dress – and the *cyclas*, a sort of robe that also gave evidence to his transvestite tendencies. He wore Greek slippers and the boots of the tragic actor. Sometimes he donned the *caliga* associated with the emperor's bodyguards and executioners, and sometimes simply women's shoes.

In all of this we may perhaps see an interest in the sort of clothing associated with the Trojans in, for example, Virgil's *Aeneid*.[92] This is the sort of outlandish costume that the heroine Camilla is fascinated by when she sees the Trojan priest of Cybele Chloreus in Book 11. Indeed, Suetonius records that sometimes Caligula even appeared in the dress of Venus, the patron goddess of the Julian *gens* and inveterate divine ally of Troy.[93] He also, to be fair, appeared with a golden beard and the thunderbolt of Jupiter or the trident of Neptune, and sometimes too with the caduceus of Mercury. He also favoured the costume of a triumphing general, and assumed the breastplate of Alexander the Great that he had removed from his sarcophagus. Pretensions of military glory and of divine right abound.

Caligula is said not to have been much given over to the study of literature, but he was more intrigued by oratory and eloquence.[94] He was apparently a gifted public speaker, especially when he was involved in making some charge against someone or railing against some imagined criminal or malefactor. He was an anxious and high-strung speaker, given much to dramatic flourish and flair. He accused Seneca of composing *commissiones meras*, simple school exercises[95] – and he deplored anything that was especially polished in style. The Seneca in question is either Seneca the Elder (54 BC – AD 39) or his nephew Seneca the Younger (4 BC – AD 65); the latter would be the tutor of Nero and one of the casualties of his pupil's reign. It is likely that the younger Seneca is referenced here. Once again we are given a glimpse into Caligula's judgments on the great writers of classical literature. For Suetonius' Caligula, Seneca's speeches constituted *harenam sine calce* – 'sand without lime'. We might imagine that the point of the metaphor from building was that Seneca's speeches lacked structure, that the building, as it were, was weak from the very foundation.

Caligula's speeches brought condemnation and salvation to many. He dispensed justice based on which of his speeches he thought was best (so that if he were to be particularly proud of something he wrote in accusation, he would use his estimation of his talent as the decisive factor in dealing with the defendant – not the question of guilt or innocence).

Caligula was also much given to the arts of the arena. He appeared as a Thracian gladiator, as a charioteer at the races, and also as a singer and a dancer.[96] The Thracian gladiator fought with a small shield and a short, curved sword. Thrace was a notoriously wild, warlike region in the south-east of Europe, corresponding to lands today held by Bulgaria, Greece and Turkey. When Caligula fought in the arena, he used real weapons – though his foes were not so lucky.[97]

Caligula's interest in the dramatic arts is said to be so ardent that he could not resist singing along with the tragic actor, or imitating gestures. He would be a frustrated artist, it seems, in that on the day of his assassination he was planning a *pervigilium*, or all-night festival, in which he was to make his stage premiere.[98] He once summoned three consulars near the close of the second vigil of the night to witness one of his nocturnal dances.

And yet, Suetonius records, despite all of his activities and achievements – Caligula could not swim.[99]

Those whom Caligula favoured, he favoured to the point of madness – among them the pantomime Mnester.[100] Caligula would kiss Mnester even in the theatre in public; if anyone interrupted Mnester's dancing with even the slightest noise, the emperor would see that they were flogged at once by his own hand.

One mysterious anecdote regards the fate of a certain Roman knight who created some sort of disturbance.[101] The knight was ordered by a centurion to proceed to the harbour at Ostia and to bear a message to King Ptolemy of Mauretania that ordered the king to do neither good nor ill to the sender. The point of the story seems to be that the knight was tortured by not knowing if he was carrying his death warrant.

Thracian gladiators were given the task of commanding Caligula's bodyguard. The armour of the gladiators known as *murmillones* was reduced.[102] A gladiator by the name of Columbus was victorious in a contest, but suffered only a light wound in the process; Caligula had poison added to the wound, which was thenceforth known as *columbinum*.[103]

In the chariot races, Caligula was a major devotee of the so-called Greens, regularly dining and spending the night in their quarters. The green driver Eutychus was once given the outrageous sum of two million sesterces as an imperial present. Soldiers were sent out the day before the games to ensure quiet in the neighbourhood, and to prevent the horse Incitatus from being distressed.[104] Incitatus was favoured with a marble stall, an ivory manger, purple blankets and a gemstone collar. A house was provided for the horse, complete with slaves and furniture. Guests were invited for events in the horse's name – and allegedly, Rome was destined to receive its first equine consul.[105]

All of this madness contributed, Suetonius makes clear enough, to the conspiracies that were formed to take the emperor's life. One or two were detected, the biographer notes, and others were delayed. But two men joined forces, as it were, and succeeded in their initiative and common cause.[106] Here Suetonius proceeds to the narrative of the assassination of Gaius Caligula.[107] The most powerful of the emperor's freedmen were aware of the plot, as were officers of the Praetorian Guard. Suetonius is careful to note that the Guard was not aware of an earlier conspiracy, though they knew that Caligula suspected and hated them. Sword in hand, he openly declared that he would kill them if they thought he deserved death –he continually accused them of disloyalty, and played one officer against another in a grim game of devotion.

It was finally decided to assassinate the emperor at the Palatine games, which commenced on 17 January.[108] The timing would be when the emperor departed at noon (for lunch and rest). The lead part in the conspiracy was taken by one Cassius Chaerea, a tribune of the Guard. Caligula is said to have taunted Cassius with every form of insult, especially sexual ones; the emperor would give him watchwords such as 'Priapus' and 'Venus', and make obscene hand gestures when he gave the tribune his hand to kiss.[109] The Venus password is reminiscent of the Julian *gens* and the principal place of the goddess in the mythology of the descent of the line from Aeneas and Iulus.

Prodigies (of course) attended the assassination.[110] The statue of Jupiter at Olympia laughed so loudly that the scaffolding erected around it collapsed and workers fled in terror.[111] A man named Cassius appeared, and reported that he had been ordered in a dream to sacrifice a bull to the god.

The Capitol at Capua was struck by lightning on the Ides of March, and also the room of the doorkeeper of the imperial palace in Rome.[112] The soothsayer

Sulla declared that death was at hand.[113] The Fortune goddesses at Antium warned that Caligula should beware a Cassius.[114] In consequence, Caligula ordered the death of Gaius Cassius Longinus, the proconsul of Asia, because he forgot that Chaerea's family name was Cassius.[115]

The day before his death, Caligula had a dream that he was standing by the side of the throne of Jupiter, and that the supreme god kicked him with his right toe and hurled him down to earth. While sacrificing, he was sprinkled with the blood of a flamingo – a change from the days when the emperor's cult included sacrifices of flamingoes.[116]

Mnester danced the tragedy that had been performed by Neoptolemus during the games at which the father of Alexander the Great, Philip of Macedon, had been killed in 336 BC The play in question was the *Cinyras*, the plot of which concerned the notorious story of how Myrrha fell in mad love with her father and connived to commit incest with him.[117] In a mime called *Laureolus*, in which the actor (playing a robber) falls and vomits blood, actors and understudies tried so hard to prove how good they were at acting that soon the stage was swimming in blood.[118] A night time spectacle was also bring prepared, in which underworld scenes were being shown with Egyptians and Ethiopians. This last stage reference is apparently to the *pervigilium*, or all-night event, mentioned earlier;[119] the Egyptians and Ethiopians were connected to the rites of the goddess Isis, but the exact point of the reference is uncertain.

Suetonius now describes the assassination. It was the ninth day before the Kalends of February, that is, 24 January – the year was AD 41.[120] It was about the seventh hour, i.e. 1.00 pm. Caligula was uncertain about lunch; he was suffering from an upset stomach because of excessive indulgence on the previous day. He was persuaded at last to depart for his meal by friends – likely enough men who had knowledge of the plot. He had to pass through a *crypta*, or covered passage; some noble boys from Asia were there, rehearsing parts for the stage. Caligula stopped to watch and encourage the youths. The leader of the troop complained that he was cold; otherwise Caligula is said to have wished to returned and watch the show.[121]

Suetonius records two versions of the actual killing. The first account is that while Caligula was talking to the boys, Cassius Chaerea came up from behind and stabbed him in the neck with the words, '*Hoc age*' (in English we might say, 'take that!').[122] The other tribune involved in the conspiracy – Cornelius Sabinus – then came up and stabbed the emperor in the chest.

The other version is that Cornelius Sabinus was able to dismiss the crowd by means of centurions who were complicit in the plot. Sabinus asked the emperor for the watchword, and on being told that it was 'Jupiter', Cassius Chaerea responded in Latin, '*Accipe ratum*' – 'So be it'.[123] As Caligula looked around, Cassius smashed his jaw with a blow.

It would seem that in either version, the emperor was lying on the ground, writhing in pain from the wounds and crying out that he was still alive.[124] He was then generally assailed by the conspirators, suffering thirty wounds, with everyone shouting, '*Repete*' – 'Strike him again'. He was stabbed in his private parts too – no doubt in reflection of his sexual perversions. His litter bearers tried to defend him with their poles, and soon the German bodyguard responded. Some of the assassins were killed, as were some innocent senators unfortunate enough to be caught up in the tumult.

Suetonius gives a summation of the life of the prince and monster. He lived for twenty-nine years, and ruled for three years, ten months and eight days. His body was secretly conveyed to the gardens of the Lamian family and hastily buried after an equally swift burning that did not succeed in completely consuming the body. When his sisters returned from exile, they evidently did not hold a grudge: he was dug up, properly cremated and then given a more fitting burial.[125] Ghosts haunted the caretakers of the garden before the exhumation and entombment, In the house where the assassination had taken place, there were hauntings and finally a mysterious destruction of the building by fire.

There were other casualties of that memorable January day. A centurion slew Caesonia, the devoted wife, and the daughter's brains were dashed out against a wall. Caesonia and Drusilla thus joined Caligula in a rare family slaughter.

Suetonius notes that the Age of Caligula was such that after the death, people did not at first believe that the emperor was really dead, assuming that he had faked the assassination in order to learn what people really thought about him.[126] The conspirators had made no decision about a successor, and the Senate was keen on restoring the Republic. The consuls went so far as to plan the first meeting of the senators in the Capitol and not in the *curia*, because the latter carried the name of 'Julian'. Some senators argued that the memory of the Caesars should be completely abolished, and the temples of all of them should be destroyed.[127] Some men observed that every Caesar named Gaius had died violently, ever since the time of the death of the Gaius Caesar who fell in the days of (Lucius Cornelius) Cinna. This last reference is to Gaius Julius Caesar Strabo, who died in 87 BC. As the commentators duly note, the statement about the doom of those named 'Gaius' is not strictly true – but the main reference is once again to Julius Caesar.

At the end of Suetonius' life, then, we are left with the memory not only of the notorious Caligula – but also of his accomplished ancestor, the storied inaugurator of the very line of the Caesars that Suetonius is investigating via his series of biographies. As we examine other extant sources for the life and reign of Caligula, we shall uncover and explore other parallels and points of intersection between the lives of the two Gaiuses ... an investigation that will offer some insight into the place of Troy in the Roman historical imagination.

Chapter Three

The Evidence of Dio Cassius for the Life and Reign of Caligula

Other than Suetonius' life, we are most indebted to the historical writings of Dio Cassius for information about the life of Gaius Caligula.[1] Dio lived from *c*. AD 150-235. Born in Bithynia in Asia Minor, his father was the Roman governor in Cilicia; he himself rose to high office and esteem in the empire (living even through the difficult days of another questionable emperor, the infamous Commodus), though today he is best remembered for what survives of his eighty-book history of Rome. Book 59 concerns the reign of Caligula. The end of the book is lost (so also the beginning of Book 60); for the missing material we are dependent on the work of the Byzantine scholars John Zonaras and John Xiphilinus. Zonaras was the author of a Greek history of immense scope (from creation through to AD 1118), in which the Roman history is largely drawn from Dio, while Xiphilinus prepared an epitome or abridgement of Dio (itself also incomplete), at the order of the Byzantine emperor Michael VII Doukas.[2]

Dio begins his account of Caligula's reign by addressing the question of Tiberius' will and the matter of the place of Tiberius Gemellus in any succession plan. The prefect Macro takes on a prominent role in the narrative: he is the liaison of Caligula to the Senate, and soon enough the consuls and Senate declare Tiberius' will to be null and void on account of the former emperor not being of sound mind at the time of its composition (he had, after all, contrived to leave the empire in the hands of a mere boy – Gemellus – who was not even old enough to enter the Senate). And soon enough Gemellus was dead (and the matter, implicitly, was laid to rest with him).

For Dio, Tiberius suffered something of a just fate in all this: he had refused to honour the prescriptions of his mother Livia's will in AD 29, and now his will was ignored – but only with respect to Gemellus.[3] The praetorians were paid what Tiberius had left them – and Caligula added much more on his own, in a clear effort to secure his succession by ensuring a happy soldiery. Copious awards were handed out to many others besides the Guard; indeed, Dio notes that if he had spent all his money in the same way, he would have been lauded as a generous ruler. But actors, gladiators and horses were also among the beneficiaries of the sudden age of largesse, and soon there was essentially no money left in the treasury. In his second year, he was already in need of additional funds to cover expenses.

What picture, though, do we have of the emperor as he begins his reign? Caligula is mentioned in passing by Dio in the narrative of the mutiny of AD 14, where the son of Germanicus and Agrippina is identified with the story of the *caliga*, or military boot, and the detail that Agrippina and the boy were initially both held hostage by the rebellious soldiers, with the wife released first at her husband's request, but with Caligula retained.[4] Dio records that Sejanus and Caligula alike were awarded priesthoods in 31, the same year that Sejanus was Tiberius' colleague in the consulship.[5] Tiberius is noted to have made Caligula a quaestor in 33, though not one of the first rank; he promised to advance him to the other offices of the *cursus honorum* five years earlier than usual, though he had told the Senate not to instill arrogance in the young man by giving him too many honours.[6] Tiberius planned for Caligula to succeed him, in part because he suspected that Gemellus was not a true son of Drusus, and also because of the boy's youth. He also assumed that Gemellus would soon enough be murdered by Caligula. Dio's Tiberius is all too well aware of Caligula's character, preserving the anecdote that when he witnessed an argument between Gemellus and Caligula, he admonished the latter that while he would murder Gemellus, others would murder him. For Dio, the point was indeed that Tiberius would seem all the better once Caligula was in power – and that a number of senators would no doubt be dead under the new emperor. Furthermore, there were simply not very many living relatives; the empire, after all, needed to remain a family affair.[7] Tiberius quoted a verse from Greek tragedy as well: ἐμοῦ θανόντος γαῖα μιχθήτω πυρί – 'Once I am dead, may the earth be mingled with fire.'[8] Tiberius was also in the habit of declaring the Trojan King Priam a fortunate and lucky man, since he was able to plunge both his country and his throne into ruin. Tiberius was not the only one to see through whatever pretences of respectability Caligula was able to put forth. Lucius Arruntius is said to have committed suicide in anticipation of Caligula's rule, noting that in his old age he was not able to become the slave of a new master like Caligula.[9]

The changing fortunes of Tiberius' health in his declining days are said to have caused Caligula and others predictable enough alternations between rejoicing and anxiety.[10] Caligula finally decided to hasten matters by refusing to give Tiberius food, arguing that the nourishment would actually harm him. He further argued that the emperor needed to be kept warm to avoid a chill, and wrapped him up in so many heavy bedclothes that it became all the easier to smother the old emperor (with the aid of Macro at least). Dio's Macro is a social and political climber, orchestrating Caligula's falling in love with his wife Ennia. Tiberius did not fail to notice the personality traits of Caligula, and he did not miss the intentions of Macro – he noted that the prefect was wise to follow the rising and not the setting sun.[11] Soon enough Tiberius was dead, and Caligula arranged both the funeral and the eulogy.

Dio's Caligula, then, is a young man of questionable virtue, though throughout the extant history from before the narrative of his reign, there is no detailed account of why Tiberius and others saw such prospect of harm in the young man. Once in power, however, the spendthrift ways of the new ruler are matched by other marks of deterioration. Caligula was at first assiduous in careful deference to the Senate – but soon enough became autocratic, going so far as to assume all of the Augustan titles in one day, postponing none except that of *Pater patriae*, 'Father of the fatherland'. He came to hate all the women of whom he was ever enamoured, with the exception of the last – and in Dio's estimation, he would have hated her as well had he lived long enough.[12] He was respectful towards Agrippina, Antonia and his sisters for a while at least. Antonia was saluted as Augusta and made a priestess of Augustus, with the privileges accorded to the Vestal Virgins granted to her. The same vestal honours were given to his sisters, and the privilege of witnessing the games from the imperial box; prayers and oaths of allegiance were made in their names. The bones of his mother and brothers were reverentially returned to Rome by his own hands; everything ever decreed against them was overturned.

But ere long, piety changed to monstrosity. In Dio's account, Caligula compelled Antonia to commit suicide after she had rebuked him for something or other.[13] All three sisters were violated by their brother, and two were exiled after the third (i.e. Drusilla) had died. Interestingly, Caligula is said to have demanded that the Senate honour Tiberius with the same tokens of esteem that had been bestowed on Augustus. When the Senate prevaricated, Caligula decided only to grant a public funeral to his grandfather, with the body brought to Rome by night. The eulogy delivered by the new emperor was not so much a panegyric in honour of Tiberius, as a tribute to Augustus and Germanicus – and a chance to present himself as a wonderful new ruler.

There was a flicker of senatorial independence: they could not bring themselves to honour Tiberius, and yet they were hesitant to act too boldly before they fully appreciated the character of Caligula.

Dio's Caligula surpassed Tiberius in all his wickedness, for all the licentious acts for which the young man used to criticize his predecessor – and he followed none of the virtues for which Tiberius was extolled.[14] The senatorial hesitation as to how to respond to Caligula's wishes regarding Tiberius was well-placed. Caligula soon enough punished those who indulged in criticism of his predecessor, though he also targeted anyone who praised Tiberius, as if they were a friend of the dead emperor (and thus, implicitly, no friend of his).[15] It was an age in which one was truly likely to face condemnation, no matter the act; both the enemies and friends of Tiberius were equally liable to be damned. He had allegedly burned the records that dealt with the treatment of his mother and sisters – but according to Dio, he had actually burned copies, retaining the originals so as to be able to charge potential victims.

Caligula's contrary nature was also reflected in his attitude toward his own cult. He initially banned statues and images of himself, only later to see to their construction and erection himself.[16] Soon enough there were temples and sacrifices in his divine honour, and he presented himself to the public as a god.

He was a lover of crowds, and also of isolation; he wanted requests to be granted, and also to be refused. He was wanton in the spending of money, and also stingy. He might like you if you flattered him – or he might despise you; he might appreciate your honesty, but he might also hate you for it.[17] Those who managed to succeed in their dealings with Caligula were the blessed children of Fortune, not of any intelligent action or forethought on their part. In short, it was impossible to plan ahead well to survive (let alone flourish) during Caligula's reign – all was left to random chance.

In Dio's appraisal, then, the reign of Tiberius appeared superior to that of Caligula, just as Augustus' did to that of Tiberius. Dio's Tiberius always acted through agents and other men, so that his own hands would not be dirtied, we might say, while Caligula was the servant of gladiators and charioteers, and those connected to the world of theatre. The tragic actor Apelles was always at his side, even in public.[18] The arts of theatre and the stage were cultivated to lavish excess by the new emperor, who was an avid spectator and once left a performance when the crowd did not seem to incline to his preferences. Eventually Caligula was unable to remain a mere member of the audience, and soon enough he was driving a chariot, engaging in gladiatorial combat and acting in pantomime and tragedy. Indeed, one night he engaged in a dance for the benefit of leading senators who had been called to observe the spectacle.[19]

The early days of Caligula, at any rate, were marked by courtesy to the Senate. The new emperor promised to share his power with that august body, and he called himself their son and ward.[20] Quintus Pomponius was freed from prison after seven years in custody. Treason (*maiestas*) charges were dismissed. Caligula's youth is thought to have worked in his favour, as no one believed that a 24-year-old could be capable of lies and crafty subterfuge. Extending the Saturnalia and lowering the price of grain only helped his initial popularity.

The Senate was initially willing to grant Caligula the consulship immediately, and to have him hold the office every year, but he waited until the incumbents finished their terms, and then accepted the office with Claudius as his colleague.[21] In his speech at the inauguration of his consulship, Caligula attacked Tiberius, promising a new age. The Senate, interestingly, is said to have decreed that the speech should be read every year, so that Caligula might be reminded of his assurances.

Caligula also saw to the honour due to his ancestor and predecessor Augustus; the dedication of a shrine to the *Divus Augustus* was celebrated by banquets and games. The first day of the horse races had twenty heats, and the second forty – for it was the emperor's birthday, 31 August AD 37. Four hundred bears were slain, and an equal number of Libyan wild beasts; the *lusus Troiae*, or Troy game, was observed. The emperor's own triumphal chariot was drawn by six horses – the first time such a thing had been seen. Business in the courts – and even private acts of mourning – were all abolished in favour of mandatory attendance at games and performances. For Dio, some of the first signs of real trouble and corruption in Caligula's reign came in the context of the theatre and the races.

Caligula surrendered the consulship in September – and after this, Dio notes the emperor's famous illness. Caligula recovered – instead of his death, the death of Tiberius Gemellus was ordered. The date is uncertain: it was either late in 37 or fairly early in 38. The charge was that Gemellus had prayed and wished for the death of Caligula during his illness. Others fell with the young man, accused of the same wrongdoing. Dio – ever the senator – notes that Caligula's actions against Gemellus were taken even without senatorial notification. The death was simply arranged, without much of anything in the way of comment or defence.[22]

Dio sees the death of Gemellus as another example of Caligula's contradictory nature, another facet of the puzzle for the historian's study of the emperor's arbitrary policy. He had given Antiochus the rule over Commagene,[23] and had restored Agrippa, the grandson of Herod, to power – but he saw to the death of his own brother and indeed son.[24]

The Antiochus in question is Antiochus IV, the last king of Commagene, an ancient kingdom of Armenia with its capital at Samosata in modern Turkey. Commagene had been reduced to being a part of the Roman province of Syria after the death of Antiochus' father in AD 17, and Caligula now restored its independence and enriched the new king.[25] As for Herod Agrippa, he was the son of Aristobulus IV and Berenice; his name was in honour of Marcus Vipsanius Agrippa.

Antiochus and Agrippa profited (at least at first) from the new order of affairs, but Gemellus perished. Another victim was Publius Afranius Potitus, who had vowed that he would die if Caligula might survive his illness. Atanius Secundus had boasted that he would fight as a gladiator if Caligula survived. Dio makes clear that these men had hoped to receive a present of money in return for their loyalty, yet instead Caligula compelled them to keep their vows, and both men died.[26]

His father-in-law, Marcus Junius Silanus, was also forced to take his own life, though he was not among those who had vowed their lives for the emperor's safety.[27] Silanus had been honoured under Tiberius; the new emperor subjected him to such insults and derision that he finally committed suicide.[28] Caligula divorced his daughter Junia and married Cornelia Orestilla, who had been seized by the emperor at the very celebration of her own wedding to Gaius Calpurnius Piso.[29] Both new wife and prospective old husband were banished within two months on suspicion of having resumed their liaison.

Dio marks the commencement of the events of 38 with the accession to the consulate of Marcus Aquila Julianus and Publius Nonius Asprenas. Now we learn that the oaths associated with the acts of Tiberius were not taken; the acts of Augustus and of Gaius were ratified. Dio records the strange tale that a slave named Machaon climbed up on the couch of Jupiter Capitolinus on the first day of the year, and that he uttered many baleful prophecies before slaying first a small dog and them himself.

Like Suetonius, Dio notes some praiseworthy actions of Caligula. He released financial accounts – like Augustus and not Tiberius before him. He assisted in the extinguishing of a fire, and compensated those who had incurred losses from the conflagration. He supplemented the flagging ranks of the equestrian order and permitted certain senatorial honours to those who seemed likely to become senators at a later date. These actions, at least, were praised by the nobility, and the crowd was happy when elections were put back into the hands of the people, taxes were remitted and presents were distributed at an athletic event.[30]

But then there were the wicked deeds. Caligula forced many men to fight as gladiators, some in matched pairs and others as if in lines of battle. Perversely, we might think, he asked the permission of the Senate to do this; evidently that body was cowed into consenting.[31] For Dio, the problem was not so much how many men died in consequence of the emperor's gladiatorial fancy, but how sanguinary was Caligula's passion: he delighted overmuch in the scenes of blood and gore. When there were too few criminals to feed to the wild beasts, he is said to have ordered some of the common rabble to be taken up to supplement the animals' diet.[32] Lest the victims be able to shout out or to protest their unjust fate, he had their tongues cut out. A prominent equestrian was compelled to fight in the arena on the charge that he had insulted Agrippina the Elder, yet when the man won his bout, he was handed over to be killed anyway. The man's father was confined to a cage and left for dead, though he was innocent of any wrongdoing.[33]

Macro and Ennia were forced to commit suicide, but they were merely two of the most prominent victims, among whom some were convicted of 'crimes', while with respect to others the emperor did not even bother to wait for an 'official' condemnation. For Caligula, the pretext was that the 'guilty' had all been in some way associated with the wrongs done to Agrippina and his sisters;

in reality, Dio notes, it was so that their property could be seized and financial ruin averted. Those who made the mistake of hosting entertainments, greeting each other or even bathing during the mourning enjoined after the death of Caligula's sister Drusilla were also subjected to capital punishment.[34]

Mention of the execution of those who violated the mourning period for Drusilla leads Dio to further commentary on Caligula's most beloved sister. She had been married to Marcus Aemilius Lepidus, but Caligula treated her as if she were his wife (or least his concubine). Lepidus gave the eulogy at her funeral, and Caligula ensured a public requiem. The *lusus Troiae* was performed about her tomb, and the Praetorian Guard and equestrians showed her special honour. The dignity that had been accorded to Livia was now extended to Drusilla; she was named a goddess, and a golden image of her was set up in the Senate. Her statue was added to that of Venus in the shrine of Venus Genetrix in the Forum, and she was honoured with the same liturgical rites as the great patron goddess of the Julian *gens*. Drusilla was given her own shrine, and priests of mixed gender. Women were to swear by her name in giving testimony. Her birthday was to be marked as if it were the so-called Ludi Megalenses – the games in honour of Cybele, the Trojan mother goddess. She was called 'Panthea' – the 'All-Goddess' – and was to be venerated in all the cities of the empire.[35] A senator testified that he had seen her ascending to the heavens and conversing with the other immortals.[36] His reward was a million sesterces. Once again Caligula was seen as being eminently contrary; those who seemed glad during her festival were punished as if they were not sufficiently in mourning at her death, while those who seemed to mourn were condemned for not appreciating her apotheosis and godhood. A man who sold hot water during Drusilla's festival was convicted of apparent disrespect for the period of mourning.[37]

Lollia Paulina was soon added to the emperor's list of wives; her husband, Memmius Regulus, was compelled to betroth her to Caligula. Legal fiction was thus maintained; Lollia was soon among the ranks of the divorced and discarded.[38] Memmius is mentioned, we might note, in Josephus as the official in charge of overseeing the transfer of the statue of Zeus at Olympia to Rome.[39]

From nuptial affairs, Dio returns to foreign policy. Various grants were made to minor royal potentates. Sohaemus received the territory of the Ituraean Arabians. Cotys (we might call him 'Prince' Cotys, since he was son of the Thracian King Cotys) took Lesser Armenia and other parts of Arabia. Rhoemetalces was ceded the lands of the late King Cotys; Polemon the son of Polemon his ancestral domains. The Senate voted on all of these measures.

In these briefly narrated details of Eastern dealings, we may well wonder if there is any evidence of a competent, indeed inspired vision of settlement in that distant area of the Roman world.[40] We know next to nothing about Sohaemus; he is also mentioned by Tacitus.[41] Cotys' takeover of Armenia Minor and part of Arabia (Dio is quite unspecific as to extent or provenance here) is equally mysterious. Rhoemetalces' territory was in Thrace; Cotys, his predecessor, had been murdered in AD 19.

There is a brief anecdote in Dio from the ceremony that was held to confirm the appointments of the eastern monarchs. Caligula is said to have noticed a lot of mud in an alleyway, and to have ordered that some of the dirt be thrown on the toga of one Flavius Vespasianus, who was the curule aedile in charge of maintaining sanitation and cleanliness. At a much later time, when the aedile would become emperor (the great Vespasian, who inaugurated the Flavian dynasty in AD 69), men would remember the incident of the mud in the alley, and comment that Caligula had entrusted the cleansing of the city to the man who would one day put an end to the horror of the so-called Long Year or Year of the Four Emperors, the man who would one day end the chaos of the civil wars that followed on the death of Nero in June 68.[42]

Caligula resumed the consulship in 39; his colleague this time was Lucius Apronius Caesianus. This time he was in office for but thirty days (his replacement as suffect consul was Quintus Sanquinius Maximus), but he allowed Apronius to hold his station for six months.[43] For Dio, the commencement of the year 39 meant the death of many of those who had been condemned, not excluding some who had been sentenced under Tiberius and then reprieved under Caligula – they were now back in line for death, facing the same charges for which Tiberius had damned them. Gladiatorial combats continued to take the lives of other prisoners. Dio states that there was, in fact, nothing but slaughter. The days of bounty and largesse were over (the money had no doubt run out). There was public outcry and protest at the killings, but the emperor would even have some people dragged out to prison and death as they watched the very games in which others were perishing.

Dio gives the reasons for the anger of Caligula. The people were accused of not being sufficiently enthused by the games; they were apparently bored because the emperor would make his appearance at unforeseen times, sometimes before dawn and on other occasions not until afternoon, so that those who dutifully waited for his arrival were frustrated by the unpredictable schedule he kept.[44] He despised being referred to as a 'young Augustus', because he thought the point of the salutation was that he was being insulted for assuming the command of the empire at such a young age. And he made his famous threat that he wished the people had but one neck.[45] Apparently the people were not inclined to tolerate the emperor's brutal speech any longer on this occasion, turning against his agents and informers and demanding that they be handed over for mob justice. Caligula made no response, but withdrew to Campania.

The emperor did return, of course, for the celebration of the birthday of the divine Drusilla. Her statue was brought forth on a chariot drawn by elephants, and a free exhibition of games was given to placate the people for two days.[46] This time 500 bears were killed on the first day, and as many Libyan wild animals on the second. Feasting was offered to all, while senators and their wives were given presents. Caligula had obviously realized that there were limits to what could be tolerated.

A lacuna of unknown length is marked by Xiphilinus at this point in the narrative. It is apparently not terribly long, since our text resumes with the note that while these murders were being carried out for the sake of enhancing the imperial treasury, the emperor set on a new course for raising cash quickly: selling the survivors of the gladiatorial bouts and increasing the prices at auction by sitting by the auctioneer and raising bids.[47] Dio notes that some people willingly participated in this charade because they wanted to appease Caligula and thus be spared, while others wanted to spend as much money as they could, since they assumed that the emperor would not target them for death if they were impoverished.

Such strategies for survival were in vain; the best and the most noteworthy of men were still marked down for slaughter, taken away by poison.[48] The horses and charioteers of rival factions were similarly killed – such was his partisanship toward the Greens. The favoured horse Incitatus was invited to dinner and encouraged to drink wine from golden goblets. Caligula promised that he would one day make him a consul, and Dio believes that he would have done so, had he lived long enough.

Those who had essayed to leave bequests to Tiberius were ordered to leave the same amount to Gaius. Another scheme was hatched with the aid of the senator Gnaeus Domitius Corbulo. It seems that Corbulo had made it his pet project to complain about the condition of the roads; he had made many speeches in the days of Tiberius to the effect that the highway system was in dire need of repair. Caligula now attacked anyone who had ever received money or a commission for road repair, arguing that they had, in fact, done nothing – as Corbulo's own repeated testimony had indicated. Fines were levied, and more money thus accrued to the imperial coffers.[49] Corbulo was honoured for his part in the whole affair by being made consul, and this detail is responsible for the problem of who exactly the consuls of the year 39 were.[50] Some simply note that Caligula had his thirty-day consulship, with Sanquinius taking over as suffect, while Apronius was in office for six months. We know from Dio 59.20.1-3 that Gnaeus Domitius Afer was in office from 2 September – but who was Corbulo's colleague in office?[51] The answer remains frustratingly elusive.

Dio notes that Caligula had up to this point regularly insulted Tiberius, and had taken delight in the insults that others had poured out against his predecessor.[52] Now he entered the Senate and made a eulogy in honour of Tiberius, condemning the Senate for having complained about the old man. We may think that there is some contradiction here with what Dio had said earlier in his account of Caligula's attitude toward Tiberius.[53] It seems that as time went on, criticism of Tiberius was less and less tolerated. Caligula was quick to note to the Senate that he was permitted the privilege of insulting and criticizing Tiberius – but they were not.[54] Caligula even endeavoured to take the enormous amount of time necessary to review the cases of those who had been condemned under the ever frequent treason trials of the last imperial reign, noting case by case how the Senate was to blame for the deaths of most of the condemned. Caligula insulted the Senate for their acquiescence in whatever Tiberius wanted, likewise heaping opprobrium on them for their indulgence of Sejanus. The lesson, the young emperor made clear, was that he could not trust or expect any better treatment from the Senate than that which had been shown to Tiberius and Sejanus. One day they would grant him all he desired, but the next they would demand his death, as in the case of the notorious praetorian prefect. Eerily, he imagined Tiberius speaking to him from beyond the grave, urging him not to spare any of the senators, eager for his slaughter as they were. The ghost of Tiberius offers philosophical advice to his young successor: the person who is afraid pays heed to the stronger man, while the courageous man avenges himself on the weaker – no man is ruled willingly.

And so the charge of *maiestas*, or treason, was restored to Roman imperial jurisprudence. Caligula at once left Rome for the suburbs after ordering that his commands be set up in bronze throughout the city.[55] There was considerable fear in the wake of Caligula's ranting – but soon enough there was a declaration of praise in honour of such a pious and honourable ruler. In a perverse outpouring of gratitude, the survivors were grateful that Caligula had not yet killed them. Annual sacrifices were to be offered to the clemency of the emperor. His golden image was to be carried to the Capitol in tribute to his abiding mercy and forbearance. Caligula was also granted the honour of celebrating an ovation.

But Dio notes that Caligula had no interest in driving a chariot (that is, as at an ovation) on dry land: he preferred to drive it on water – as in, by bridging the waters between Puteoli and Baiae.[56] The massive bridge of ships was so great in cost and expenditure that a famine resulted in Italy, and especially at Rome. Caligula donned what he claimed was the breastplate of Alexander the Great; a purple cloak (*chlamys*) was put over it, with precious stones from India to adorn it. Sacrifice was made to Neptune, and even to Envy (so that no ill-will of the other immortals would taint his day). He advanced with an armed retinue from Baiae to Puteoli on his engineering feat of a bridge, resting on arrival for a day. The next day he returned to Baiae, and spoils were led as if in triumphal procession, including the person of Dareus, a Parthian hostage in Rome. A speech was delivered by the emperor, while feasting followed and the giving of gifts to the soldiery. Fires were lit from the surrounding mountains, so as to illuminate the night. Caligula is said to have wished to conquer the nocturnal darkness, just as he had vanquished the sea.[57]

There was a dark side to all of this. In a state of intoxication, Caligula hurled many of his companions from his bridge into the sea. Some died, though others were able to save themselves – despite their own drunkenness. The sea was calm, which aided the efforts at survival. Caligula interpreted this as a victory over Neptune; he praised himself as being greater than those Persian monarchs who had bridged the Hellespont.[58] The dark side would seem to have been relatively minor in the catalogue of Caligulan atrocities. But in fact, many owed their deaths to that bridge of vessels. The whole enterprise had cost so much money, that the emperor had no choice but to target more men for death to secure legacies and property to pay the price.[59] There were trials and more trials; some were imprisoned and others were hurled down from the Capitoline. Others committed suicide to cheat the executioner. The exiled found death even in exile, and some were even slain on the road.

Dio notes that it would be tedious to catalogue all of the victims of this madness – and so he confined himself to some particularly important cases.[60] The senator Calvisius Sabinus was charged, together with his wife Cornelia.[61] Calvisius had been governor in Pannonia, while his wife was apparently accused of watching the soldiers on sentry duty and manoeuvres.[62] Husband and wife committed suicide before they were tried. Titius Rufus also committed suicide, having made the fatal error of noting that the Senate thought one way and voted another. The praetor Junius Priscus was arraigned on trumped-up charges. In reality he was reputed to be too rich to live in such an age; when Caligula learned *post mortem* that he was not, in fact, so very wealthy, he commented cynically that he had died for no reason, and could just as easily have lived.

Dio moves on to the case of Gnaeus Domitius Afer, who is praised as a survivor. Caligula despised him because during the reign of Tiberius, Afer had accused a woman who was related to Agrippina the Elder. Afer is said one day to have avoided Agrippina on the street out of fear or embarrassment. Agrippina quoted Homer's Achilles by noting that she was not angry at Afer, but at Agamemnon. Afer had apparently crossed Caligula by setting up an image of the emperor and noting that he was consul for the second time at the age of 27: Caligula assumed he was being mocked or otherwise insulted for his youth. Afer was brought before the Senate, and Caligula proceeded to deliver a lengthy speech against him. Afer offered no defence against the charges; instead he responded point by point to the oration, and he praised Caligula's oratorical skill. He finally threw himself down before the emperor, as if in fear of imperial eloquence more than any other hazard. Caligula assumed that he had actually overwhelmed Afer by the power of oratory, so he gave up his anger and allowed Afer to be reprieved.[63] Afer was convicted, as it were, of being a bad orator and no Caligula in the matter of speechmaking.

Lucius Annaeus Seneca, however, almost died – he was too good an orator, and thus incurred the resentment of Caligula. He was spared, Dio notes, only after a woman commented that he was suffering from an advanced state of consumption and would die soon anyway.[64]

Afer was made consul. The way to his new office was paved by the firing of the consuls who had failed to proclaim a thanksgiving on 31 August – the emperor's birthday. But they had made certain to observe the anniversary of Actium – and so Caligula noted that they had insulted his ancestor Mark Antony.[65] The wily Caligula did note to some of his confidantes, however, that the consuls in question could not win, regardless of their actions; either they would have insulted Augustus or Antony.[66] Caligula had the *fasces* of the consuls broken; one of them committed suicide.[67] Corbulo was almost certainly one of the deposed consuls, yet the identity of the suicide, as we have noted, remains uncertain. Afer, Dio is careful to note, was chosen by Caligula – the people had been granted the power of elections, but in Dio's account they had grown so unused to the duty of the franchise that in practice they were irrelevant to the equation. This sort of dereliction of duty led Caligula to abolish the popular elections once again, with matters in this regard restored to the practice of the Tiberian Age.

Envy and suspicion were the order of the day.[68] Carrinas Secundus was forced into exile because he had made the mistake of criticizing tyrants in a speech that he delivered as a rhetorical exercise.[69]

The case of Lucius Calpurnius Piso is interesting. He was the son of Gnaeus Calpurnius Piso and Plancina, the suspected agents of Tiberius in the murder of Caligula's father Germanicus. He became proconsul of Africa in AD 39, but the emperor was afraid that a rebellion against imperial rule would be all too easy in the richly apportioned province. Dio says that the military force and the Numidians of the province were assigned to another official, so as to reduce Piso's potential for working against Caligula.[70] The changes in African administration are among those foreign affairs decisions for which scholars have credited Caligula with an intelligent policy change, notwithstanding the ancient evidence that attributes such alterations to the emperor's irrational fears of possible usurpers and rebels.

Dio credits the increasing financial problems of the empire under Caligula's rule for the decision to launch a campaign into Gaul and Germany.[71] The pretext was given that the Germans were interfering in Gallic affairs and threatening Gallic security, but for Dio, the real reason was money, and Spain was also a prospective theatre for Caligulan revenue via the Roman war machine. The expedition was not announced in advance; soon enough, however, the emperor set out with gladiators, horses, women and other signs of decadence and luxury. He did cross the Rhine, though not very far – and then immediately returned to safety, indicating that he was now going to launch an attack on Britain. Here he proceeded to the edge of the ocean. He is said to have become annoyed at his commanders who won some trifling success (against whom is unspecified and unclear); enormous harm, however, was visited upon the population (including the allies of Rome). The point of the expedition, after all, was money – and money and resources, treasure and spoils are what Caligula seized wherever he went, and from whomsoever he wished. Deaths followed, and on the usual pretexts: some men were allegedly rebellious, others were said to be conspiring against him, but the real reason for the Gallic slaughter was the same as for the Roman – they were wealthy.[72]

Lest one imagines that Caligula plundered only the possessions of others, Dio notes that he also ransacked the imperial coffers for whatever he could sell – items that had been in the possession of Mark Antony from Egypt and other 'souvenirs' that might fetch a high price on the market.

None of these financial expediencies did anything to relieve the pressure on Caligula's economy, however, since the emperor continued to spend money recklessly. Games were exhibited at Lugdunum that were a significant expense. The armies were expensive to maintain – Dio notes that the he had assembled some 200,000 soldiers for his 'expedition', recording that some sources say he had 50,000 more besides. By means of trickery, Caligula is said to have captured some of the enemy – but the real victims of the 'war' were the many soldiers he ordered slain. Some prisoners were also killed, 'from bald head to bald head' – the famous and somewhat cryptic tale familiar from Suetonius.[73] When playing dice and realizing that he had no more money, he ordered the census lists to be brought out so that he could kill the richest of the Gauls so as to continue playing. Dio preserves the name of one of the victims – a Julius Sacerdos, who died 'by accident' because of a similarity of name with the intended victim.

Once again Dio notes that he need not record the names of all of Caligula's victims (there would be too many), but some particularly noteworthy figures deserve special mention. First is (Gnaeus Cornelius) Lentulus Gaetulicus.[74] The reason for his death (at least in Dio's estimation) was apparently simply that he was beloved of his soldiers, whom he commanded when he was governor in Germany.

Gaetulicus was said to have been involved in a conspiracy against Caligula.[75] There is precious little surviving evidence for whatever plot he may have been a party to (or a conceiver of). In the *Acta Fratrum Arvalium*, it is recorded that he died on 27 October AD 39, *ob detecta nefaria consilia in Gaium Germanicum* – 'on account of nefarious plans that were discovered against Gaius Germanicus'. The conspiracy is not detailed in Dio, and may well have been another invention of Caligula.[76]

Dio gives brief notice, too, to Lepidus, one of the emperor's lovers and favourites, the husband of Drusilla, who allegedly also had improper relationships with the other imperial sisters, Agrippina and Julia. Three daggers were sent to the temple of Mars Ultor – we may recall Suetonius' reference to the same story.[77] The sisters were sent into exile, and Agrippina was given the bones of her *quondam* lover Lepidus and made to carry them back to Rome. Thenceforth, Dio observes, honours were not awarded by Caligula to his relatives. The emperor informed the Senate of the allegedly great plot that he had survived. For the historian, however, it is abundantly clear that whatever happened was either a comparatively minor threat or more or less fabricated by Caligula's irrational fears. The Senate voted an ovation for Caligula in honour of his triumph over the conspirators, and Claudius was sent to be one of the bringers of the tidings of good news. The sending of his uncle seemed at variance with the imperial edict to show honour to his relatives; implicitly, there is also the fact that Claudius was seen as a bumbling fool and thus unworthy of such missions (even if Caligula had seen value in appointing Germanicus' surviving brother as his colleague in his first consulship).

Once again, Dio visits the question of contradiction. Caligula is said to have deplored small honours, since they seemed cheap – but large honours seemed to preclude any further glory. He was also resentful of senatorial honours, since the very act implied that the Senate was in some way superior to him. He would not receive all the emissaries sent by the Senate. Indeed, he even contemplated killing Claudius at this point, but felt such contempt for the man that he decided to spare him.[78] The ever capricious Caligula was more favourable in his response to a second senatorial legation, which was larger than the first, and this time he willingly received the honours that were lavished on him.

Caligula next divorced Paulina.[79] He now married Caesonia, who had already been his lover and was pregnant with his daughter at this point (Suetonius makes the same association between the wedding and the child). Dio records that the population was not happy about the imperial nuptial antics, or how those who had been friends with the emperor's sisters were now being accused of complicity in the alleged conspiracies. Rome was apparently also sweltering in a heatwave in AD 39, which only added to the frustration and general sense of unrest.[80] Ofonius Tigellinus was banished on a charge of having had an improper relationship with Agrippina.[81]

As the year 39 drew to a close, there was a general sense of apprehension in Rome that Caligula's behaviour could grow even worse, and he was associated in his tyrannical behaviour with his friends Antiochus and Agrippa. He assumed his third consulate in 40,[82] but had no colleague because the designated consul had died prematurely. The tribunes and praetors are said not to have convoked the Senate on the occasion of Caligula's entry into office – such was the apparent climate of fear. The Senate did meet, but essentially only to offer praise to Caligula. The emperor resigned his consulship on 13 January, with the men who had been chosen for the second half of the year then assuming office.[83]

Votes were soon enough taken in the Senate though, awarding Tiberius and Drusilla the same honours that had been granted to Augustus.[84] Images of Caligula and Drusilla were erected. Dio is careful to note that this was all done in response to communications from Caligula, who is said to have followed the practice of indicating to the consuls what he wished to see done.

Dio's history of Caligula's reign gives out here in its surviving text, just as Caligula summons Ptolemy of Mauretania, the son of Juba – only to have him killed once he learned that he was wealthy.[85] We are dependent on Byzantine epitomizers to glean some sense of what the rest of the historian's account contained. Especially given the relative brevity of Caligula's reign, it would be frustrating to lose any portion of Dio's account – but the loss in this case is especially keenly felt in the matter of the emperor's foreign affairs and expeditions.

From Xiphilinus we learn that Caligula reached the ocean, as if he were going to launch a campaign to Britain. He assembled troops on the shore and embarked on a trireme, but sailed for only a short distance before returning. He then gave the soldiers the signal as if for the commencement of battle, only suddenly to order the men to pick up shells. He took this all as a sign of the conquest of the ocean, and brought back the shells for exhibition in Rome as evidence of his great achievement. The Senate was quite unsure how to respond to this – the idea may have crossed some of their minds that Caligula was deliberately testing them to see if their praise and adulation were merely empty gestures, and by this point he had amply proven that any response whatsoever was fraught with peril. On this occasion, Caligula is said to have come close to killing every senator – divine honours had not been voted to him. The common people, however, were showered with presents; many are said to have died in the business of lunging for the treasure that was hurled down on them from a lofty height.[86]

From Zonaras we may read of another alleged plot against Caligula, namely that of Anicius Cerealis and his son Sextus Papinius.[87] Caligula is said to have uncovered a plot against him, and father and son alike were tortured for information. Cerealis would reveal nothing, while Papinius was assured that he would be spared if he denounced all the plotters. The father and many others subsequently perished. We shall return to this story later as it constitutes some evidence of the no doubt growing unrest regarding Caligula's reign.

The father of one of the men ordered slain was commanded to be present for his son's death; when he asked that he might keep his eyes closed, he was also sentenced to death. Xiphilinus gives a fuller account of the opening of this ghastly story of *pietas* perverted. Betilinus Bassus was the son, with Capito the father who was condemned after wanting to avert his eyes.

Zonaras records that Capito then pretended that he was, indeed, guilty of participation in the conspiracy, and that he would happily surrender the names of the other guilty parties, naming companions of Caligula who were partners in the emperor's wanton behavior. Capito became a bit too zealous in his prosecutions, naming the beloved freedman Callistus and Caligula's wife Caesonia among the conspirators, and was soon enough simply executed as Caligula had originally intended.

Caligula was said to have reacted to the threat against him, however, by summoning Callistus and the prefects of the Praetorian Guard. He noted that they were three in number and he was but one; if they wanted to kill him, they could since they were armed and he was not. He invited them to assassinate him if indeed they despised him. Though he was not killed on the spot, he was convinced that there was indeed great enmity toward him – and thenceforth he wore a sword for self-defence. He attempted to play one of his intimates against another, hoping to foster distrust among the men in whose presence he no longer felt entirely safe, and desirous of ingratiating himself now with one, and now with another.[88] Eventually his confidantes were well aware of that he was doing, and they abandoned their emperor to those who were indeed plotting against him.

In Xiphilinus we read that one Protogenes assisted the emperor in his condemnations and denunciations of enemies real and perceived. He was responsible for maintaining the books known as 'Sword' and 'Dagger'.[89] Protogenes entered the Senate one day and was greeted by all. When Scribonius Proculus approached with his salutation, however, Protogenes asked why someone who hated Caligula as much as he did would be extending his greeting. At that – as if by terrible signal – the other senators set upon him and killed him.[90]

Caligula is said to have been pleased by this sanguinary senatorial sacrifice in his honour; various awards were now voted to him by the subservient fathers. The emperor for once is reported to have been placated, and to have done several positive things. One Pomponius was freed despite the charge against him of alleged conspiracy - he had been betrayed by a friend, which apparently earned him a degree of sympathy on this occasion at least. Pomponius' mistress was tortured, but she would not reveal anything, so Caligula let her go with a monetary reward.[91]

Caligula was showered with praise for this – both out of fear, we read, and out of sincerity – and some began to call him a demigod or even a god. Xiphilinus records that the emperor had already been contemplating declaring his divinity, noting that he had had sexual intercourse with Selene, and that the goddess Victory had put a crown on his head.[92] Caligula affected to be Jupiter, with his incest with his sisters thus explained as like the actions of the god with Juno and Ceres. He also played the role of Neptune, noting his bridging of the sea, while others gods whose station he usurped included Hercules, Apollo and Bacchus.[93] Indeed, he impersonated all the immortals, not excluding the goddesses (Juno, Diana and Venus are cited). He played his part in theatrical fashion, donning the costume of the deity he was imitating. His only real concern was to appear to be something more than mortal.

Interestingly, the anecdote is preserved that one day Caligula was giving oracles in the dress and guise of Jupiter, playing the role of the supreme god with gusto and nerve. A Gaul started to laugh, and when Caligula asked what he thought him to be, the man replied bravely and directly that he thought Caligula was a raving lunatic. The emperor did nothing at all to the man, for he was only a cobbler – thus giving evidence to the idea that the insults of a common man can be endured more easily than those of a powerful one.[94]

Very few senators and officials of high rank were greeted by Caligula with a ceremonial kiss, but those who were took great pride in the fact – despite the fact, we are told, that the emperor used to kiss actors every day.

Caligula's divinity was acknowledged not only by the commoners, but even by senators and the nobility. Xiphilinus cites the case of Lucius Vitellius, the governor of Syria. We are summarily told of how Vitellius had been a most capable governor, successful in preventing the Parthian King Artabanus from invading Roman Syria the way he had entered Armenia. Vitellius surprised Artabanus near the Euphrates (the traditional border) and secured a conference with the king; subsequently he ordered him to sacrifice to images of Augustus and Gaius Caligula. Peace was secured, even to the point of the king surrendering princes as hostages.

But Vitellius faced death in Rome at the order of Caligula, given that the emperor was certain that so powerful and capable a man must be plotting against him. Vitellius abased himself and gave testimony to the divinity of the emperor; soon enough he was not only excused, but also admitted into the emperor's inner circle. Caligula told his new friend one day that he was having a conversation with the moon goddess Selene, and asked if Vitellius could see her. The wise Vitellius noted that only gods could see other gods.

Caligula reportedly sought to appropriate a temple that was being constructed at Miletus in honour of Apollo, intending it for his own worship, complaining that the other gods had their sacred haunts, including Augustus' at Pergamum – but nothing was left for him.[95] Two temples of Caligula were erected at Rome; one had been voted to him by the Senate, and the other was built at his own cost. He had seen to a sort of dwelling on the Capitoline, so that he might live with Jupiter, as it were – but he was angry that Jupiter had taken the hill first, and he loathed the idea that he was second to the supreme god. Thus he planned a Palatine temple to himself, with the statue of Olympian Zeus transferred there after having been redone as Caligula.[96] The ship sent to bring the statue was said to have been destroyed by thunderbolts, while anyone who tried to approach the pedestal of the statue heard laughter. Caligula consequently threatened the statue and had another set up in his honour.

The temple of Castor and Pollux was cut in two, so that an entrance to the imperial palace could run through the middle of the shrine, and the brothers could serve as sentinels for the emperor. He assumed the title of Jupiter Latiaris; Caesonia, Claudius and some others were named ministers of the cult, each paying ten million sesterces for the honour. He made himself a priest of himself (a unique honour in the annals of ancient religion?) – and named his horse to the office as well. He had some sort of contraption made that would respond to thunder and lightning in kind whenever there was a storm. He was also accustomed to throwing javelins at rocks when there was thunder and lightning, repeating the line of Homer about either lifting or being lifted.[97]

The fact that Caligula married Caesonia only soon before she was due to deliver his daughter Drusilla was advertised as further proof his divinity: he married her and then had an instant child. The infant Drusilla was taken to the statue of the Capitoline Jupiter and placed in his lap, as if she were his, and the goddess Minerva was assigned to be the child's nurse.

Caligula also adopted the name Jupiter, a name that even is said to have made it into documents from his reign.

The palace was turned into a brothel for the sake of making money.[98] A fair number of the populace was actually pleased with the 'entertainment' of the days of Caligula. He was popular among many for his sheer licentiousness and wanton conduct, and the lustful delights that were more readily available under his reign. This passion for his more 'amusing' and liberal side was counterbalanced, however, when they threatened to riot over the tax code and other laws that were set forth on tablets in such small letters that people could not easily read them, such that men were found guilty of violations of edicts and decrees of which they had no knowledge.

The surviving evidence of Dio as preserved by his epitomizers concerns the conspiracy that finally succeeded. Cassius Chaerea and Cornelius Sabinus are once again named. Callistus was apparently privy to the plot. Indeed, the membership seems to have been quite extensive; those who were not involved but who knew about it were happy to say nothing and to let history take its course, relieved if anything that someone was ending the nightmare.

Dio's Cassius Chaerea is said to have been rather old-fashioned, and particularly upset over the issue of the watchwords, 'Desire' and 'Aphrodite' being prominent among them.[99] Caligula was warned by an oracle to beware of someone named 'Cassius' - the emperor assumed that the reference was to Gaius Cassius (Longinus), the governor of Asia, because he was descended from the Cassius who had helped to slay Julius Caesar.[100] An Egyptian by the name of Apollonius foretold the fate of Caligula in Egypt; he was brought to Rome to answer for this prediction to Caligula, being brought before the emperor on the very day of the assassination – and so he managed to escape death.[101]

Caligula was celebrating a festival in the palace, and was putting on a spectacle for the public entertainment. There was copious food and a lavish banquet. The consul (Quintus) Pomponius Secundus was eating as he sat at the feet of the emperor, constantly interrupting his meal to kiss the imperial feet. We know that Pomponius was serving as suffect consul for Caligula, who had assumed his fourth and final consulship in AD 41.[102] The *Fasti Feriarum Latinarum* indicate that he assumed his office on 25 June (that is, well after the assassination).[103] Cassius Chaerea and Cornelius Sabinus are said to have waited for five days during the festival, chafing as they were at such proceedings as this. Caligula seems to have announced that he wanted to dance and act in a tragedy, and that the festival would thus be extended for a triduum (a period of three days). That was the limit of tolerance for the assassins, who waited until the emperor exited the theatre to see noble Greek and Ionian boys who were to sing a hymn in his honour.[104] Caligula was killed; even after he was dead, men continued to stab him in frenzy, and some of the assassins even tasted his flesh.[105] Caesonia and Drusilla were also soon slain. Caligula thereby learned, we read in Dio's epitomizers, that he was not a god.[106]

Caligula's memory was reviled. The soldiers of his German bodyguard began to riot, and there was bloodshed on account of their acts of violence. The people remembered the emperor's 'witticism' about wishing that they had but one neck, proving conclusively that he was the one in possession of one neck, while they had many hands. The Praetorian Guard was discomfited at the whole business.[107] When they ran about shouting after who had killed Caligula, the ex-consul Valerius Asiaticus shouted, if only I had – and this frightened the Guard so much that they were reduced to calm. The consuls Sentius and Pomponius Secundus moved to secure the treasury, transferring money to the Capitol and stationing senators and soldiers to guard it against plunder.

The evidence of the epitomic remains of Dio's Book 60 note that the consuls and Senate accomplished little to nothing on the day of the assassination and the ensuing night. They were in disagreement among themselves as to what should be done, with some preferring the restoration of the Roman Republic and others clamouring for this or that candidate for emperor. Claudius had been with Caligula when he exited the theatre, and was found hiding in the palace by guards. He was immediately saluted as the new emperor – his family connection was perhaps his greatest asset. He protested, in an apparent wish to avoid the burden of office, but the Guard was determined to be responsible for deciding who the successor of Caligula would be.

Claudius had Cassius Chaerea and some others executed.[108] Regicide was regicide, even if Claudius was happy with the act. Cornelius Sabinus committed suicide. Interestingly, Claudius did not agree with the Senate's wish that Caligula's memory be held in contempt – but secretly, on his own initiative, he did have all the images of his notorious nephew removed. Dio notes that the names of Tiberius and Caligula do not appear in the roll of the emperors by whom oaths are sworn, though neither suffered an official decree of disgrace. Protogenes was killed; the infamous books 'Sword' and 'Dagger' were burned, along with the records and books that Caligula had claimed to have destroyed. Caligula's poisons were disposed of as well, while exiles were restored to home, including Agrippina and Julia. Those charged with *maiestas* and the like were freed from prison. Those who had insulted Claudius as a way of ingratiating themselves with Tiberius and Caligula were prosecuted if, and only if, they were guilty of some other charge – such was the manner of Claudian revenge.

No one in AD 37 could have had much hope that Germanicus' much reviled brother would ever assume the principate. One might think that after the events of 37-41, even Claudius' accession seemed a return to something approaching normal.

Chapter Four

Tacitus on Caligula

The fact that we are missing the historian Tacitus' account of the reign of Caligula is a major loss for our investigation into the foreign and domestic affairs of the four years during which Gaius maintained his seemingly strange, increasingly mad rule.[1] Some tidbits of information, however, can be gleaned from the surviving portions of Tacitus' corpus, especially the *Annales*, or annals, of imperial Rome.[2]

Caligula is famously listed among the emperors in Tacitus' historiographical introduction to his work at *Annales* 1.1. He notes that those who essayed to compose histories on the reigns of Tiberius, Gaius, Claudius and Nero were afflicted by fear while those emperors lived – and by an all too recent hatred in the immediate wake of their deaths. Of possible note is that Caligula is not singled out for special treatment or negative consideration here; all of the successors to Augustus in the Julio-Claudian line are accorded the same fate with respect to historical composition.

Tacitus' first mention of Caligula in his actual narration of historical events harks to the story of the emperor's violent death.[3] Cassius Chaerea is identified as a fierce young man, violent and reckless (*tum adulescens et animi ferox*) during the uprising in Germany after Augustus' death. Tacitus notes that he would later earn his place in the memory of posterity by the slaughter of Gaius Caesar (*mox caede Gai Caesaris memoriam apud posteros adeptus*).[4] Rather fittingly for Tacitus' programme, we might think, the first 'appearance' of Caligula comes with the mention of his future assassination. Cassius Chaerea is depicted as being one of the officers in danger of losing his life, or at least suffering serious injury in the mayhem of the rebellion; he is presented as fighting his way through an armed multitude, saving his life by the power of his sword.

The first and only reference to Caligula as a child in the extant *Annales* comes in Book 1, Chapter 41. The year is AD 14, and Caligula was just over 2 years old.[5] The infant is introduced in the unforgettable scene in the wake of the rebellion of the legions in Germany. Germanicus' wife Agrippina was in peril, and her child – a son who had been born in the camp and raised among the soldiers. They had named him 'Caligula', since he often wore the *caliga*; Tacitus notes that he was dressed in this fashion to appeal to the rank and file soldiery. Germanicus is depicted as addressing the soldiers to respond to their mutiny; he notes that neither his wife nor his son is dearer to him than his father and his fatherland – and that he would happily devote his spouse and his offspring to death for the cause of the soldiers' glory.[6] Nevertheless, he declares that he is removing them from their fury (*nunc procul a furentibus summoveo*).[7] If the soldiers want blood, let them have his blood and not that of the great-grandson of Augustus and the daughter-in-law of Tiberius.

Germanicus' appeal worked; the soldiers begged that he recall his wife, and that Caligula – the *legionum alumnus*, or nurseling of the legions – not be handed over as some hostage to the Gauls.[8] Germanicus noted that Agrippina was on the verge of delivering a child; his son, however, would return.[9]

Later, Caligula is mentioned in Tacitus' account of the events of 15. Tiberius was complaining about Agrippina and her officiousness with the soldiers and attempts to ingratiate herself and her family with the military in Germany. Tiberius notes that she dressed the son of Germanicus in the garb of a common soldier, and that she wished that he be called Caesar Caligula,[10] or perhaps that she wanted a Caesar to be called Caligula (that is, a degrading and insulting name for a member of the imperial family).[11]

Book 5 of the *Annales* is terribly preserved, but we do find mention of Caligula having delivered the eulogy for Livia on the occasion of her funeral in AD 29.[12] Caligula was now 16 years old; we are unsure as to why exactly he was chosen to deliver the address (one possibility is that it was simply because he had been taken in by Livia after the exile of Agrippina - but it is not certain that she was banished before Livia died).[13]

We may proceed to Book 6, and in particular the events of 32.[14] Caligula is mentioned in passing as one of the many targets of the bloodthirsty Lucius Aelius Sejanus. One Sextus Paconianus is identified as the man Sejanus had decided to employ to assist in Caligula's destruction.[15] Nothing else is known about whatever is referred to in this passage. Sejanus wanted to destroy many people, of course, and Caligula was certainly on his target list as one of the sons of Germanicus.

We also learn that Cotta Messalinus was indicted for hinting more than once that the sex of Gaius Caligula was in question.[16] There were many who were willing to argue that Cotta was indeed guilty of this and other offensive remarks. Tiberius is said to have taken the position that such phrases and comments should not be turned into cause for condemnation.

More may be gleaned from the Tacitean description of Caligula that is found later, amid the historian's record of the happenings of AD 33.[17] Caligula accompanied Tiberius to Capreae;[18] he married Claudia, the daughter of the doomed Marcus Silanus. For Tacitus, Caligula was a study in concealment: he was monstrous in spirit, but he covered up his true nature by an affected modesty.[19] Caligula said nothing when Agrippina was condemned to exile, nor when his older brothers were destroyed. Caligula was a Tiberian weathervane, as it were; whatever Tiberius felt on a given day, that was what Caligula felt. Whatever Tiberius said on a particular occasion, that was what Caligula parroted. So it was later said by the orator Passienus, Tacitus notes, that there had never been a better slave, or a worse ruler.[20]

We may proceed to the Tacitean account of AD 37, the crucial year of the death of Tiberius and the succession of Caligula. The account begins in the forty-fifth chapter of the book, and is an invaluable record of the accession of Caligula and the waning days of his predecessor.

Tacitus notes that the last Tiberian consuls were Gnaeus Acerronius (Proculus) and Gaius (Petronius) Pontius (Nigrinus) – and that by this point in Tiberius' reign, Macro's power was excessive.[21] Macro is described as an assiduous cultivator of Caligula. As the days went on, he was all the more zealous to become a friend of the future emperor. After the death of Claudia, he is said to have encouraged his wife Ennia to pursue Caligula, and to bind him by a promise of marriage, protesting as she did her love for the young man. Caligula for his part is said to have refused nothing, so long as he could achieve the throne.[22]

The fact is that we simply do not know exactly what happened between Caligula, Macro and Ennia. What is certain is that Macro wanted to ingratiate himself with Caligula, and that Caligula saw that he would benefit immensely from Macro's help – at least in the matter of obtaining the succession. The fact that both Macro and Ennia would be dead before the end of the year 38 is telling. Tacitus notes – after his usual fashion – that Caligula was a master of the arts of duplicity;[23] the clear enough implication is that Caligula was not entirely the fool of Macro and Ennia – quite the contrary (as events would prove soon enough).

Tiberius is said to have been well aware of what was going on between Caligula and Macro – and he hesitated over the question of the succession.[24] Tiberius Gemellus is noted as having been the closer to Tiberius by blood and also by affection, but the problem with him was his youth. The son of Germanicus is said to have had the vigour of youth and also the favour of the crowd – an occasion for enmity on the part of Tiberius.[25] Tiberius is presented by Tacitus as being clearly uncertain as to what should happen after his death – even Claudius was considered a possible candidate.

Tacitus' Tiberius is portrayed as being worried that if a successor were sought from outside the family, that the name of Caesar – the *nomen Caesaris* – might soon enough be held in contempt and mockery. We might think of the later, successful (at least for a time) practice of the so-called Good Emperors of the late second century AD, men who utilized adoption in pursuit of the best man for the job, as it were.[26] Tiberius was determined that the principate should remain a family affair, so his choices for imperial candidacy were quite limited by 37.

Tiberius is also said to have worried more about the verdict of history than his immediate popularity.[27] Ultimately, he left the matter to fate (*fatum*). He was tired and unsure of what to do; in Tacitus' estimation, he was not up to the task – though he had some clear enough sense of what would happen if nature were allowed to take her course. And so he noted to Macro that he was abandoning the setting sun in favour of the rising one. As for Caligula, when one day the young man was reviling the memory of the infamous republican dictator Sulla, the emperor noted that he would have all the vices and none of the virtues of that man.[28]

Tiberius once also embraced Tiberius Gemellus, and when Caligula looked vexed at this, he noted that Caligula would kill Gemellus – and that another would kill Caligula.

Caligula is also referenced in the account of the prosecution of Lucius Arruntius. Arruntius was advised by friends to pursue a strategy of delay and prevarication – Tiberius, after all, was not expected to live so very much longer – but the ex-consul from the days of Augustus (AD 6) noted that while he might outlive Tiberius, how could he escape the youth that was already a threat – that is, Caligula?[29]

Tacitus' account of the dying Tiberius is as unforgettable as other purple passages of the historian.[30] The emperor was weakening in body, but his powers of dissimulation remained (Latin *dissimulatio*). He came to a villa at Misenum that had once been owned by Lucius Lucullus.[31] The doctor Charicles tried to take Tiberius' pulse surreptitiously (the gesture did not escape the emperor's notice, and incurred the anger of old man – though at this stage there was likely little energy for him to do much in response). Charicles is said to have told Macro that the emperor's respiration was poor, and he could not survive for more than a few days.

On 16 March, it was believed that Tiberius had died. Caligula was surrounded by fawning crowds as he proceeded from the villa, anticipating his assumption of power. At that point, word arrived that Tiberius was in fact awake, and wanted someone to bring him food. Panic ensued; some people appeared to be ignorant of what was happening, while others were in a state of grief and despair.

Tacitus tells us: *Caesar in silentium fixus a summa spe novissima expectabat* ('Caesar stood fixed in silence, and from his deepest aspirations he now awaited his end').[32] This is one of the rare instances where Caligula is depicted by any ancient source as being in a state of what we might think was something approaching fear. His greatest aspirations had been dashed, it would seem, and Tiberius would not be forgiving.

Macro, however, was not afraid – he was *intrepidus*. He ordered that the aged emperor be smothered with bedclothes, and that the people should exit the threshold of the villa. So Tiberius was finally dead.

There is another interesting appraisal of Caligula near the start of Tacitus' first book on the principate of Nero.[33] The historian notes that Nero was the first *princeps* who was in need of someone else's eloquence (*alienae facundiae*). Caesar and Augustus were skilled, while Tiberius had his own abilities in dissimulation and the mastery of ambiguous speech that was carefully crafted to accomplish what he wanted.

Etiam Gai Caesaris turbida mens vim dicendi non corrupit, Tacitus writes ('even the troubled mind of Gaius Caesar did not corrupt his power of speaking'). Caligula, in short, for all his vices, was a capable public speaker. So was

Claudius – only Nero was a failure in this regard. This is a consistent feature of the Caligulan tradition; even the palpable hostility of the sources did not deny Caligula this credit.

At *Annales* 12.22, we learn that in AD 49 Agrippina the Younger orchestrated a prosecution of Lollia Paulina on charges of magic. She was in reality jealous that Lollia had been a candidate for the role of wife of Claudius after the execution of Messalina. Claudius is said to have given a speech in praise of her illustrious character. He mentioned her marriage to Memmius Regulus, but, Tacitus notes, was silent about her union with Caligula.[34]

Caligula's reference to Junius Silanus as 'the golden sheep'[35] is mentioned in passing at *Annales* 13.1, as Tacitus notes that the lazy and despised Silanus was finally killed under Nero – earning, in fact, the dubious distinction of being the first murder of the new principate.

The alleged consequences of Caligula's many sexual misadventures is noted at *Annales* 15.72, where Tacitus notes that Nymphidius Sabinus was awarded consular insignia. The historian relates how Nymphidius was the son of a freedwoman who had been loose with her affections; her son went so far as to claim that Caligula had fathered him. He was tall and grim in appearance – in other words, not unlike his purported sire. Tacitus notes that this was either mere chance, or he was indeed the son of Caligula, who even, after all, lusted after whores.[36] Nymphidius would aspire to the purple in the wake of Nero's suicide in June AD 68, but successful aspirant Galba would not suffer his rival to live for long. The implication one receives from Tacitus' narrative is that Caligula's legacy continued to endure for less than edifying reasons.

Lastly, at *Annales* 16.17, amid the grim catalogue of Neronian casualties of 66, Tacitus records that Cerialis committed suicide, though without much popular lament since he had divulged the details of a conspiracy to Caligula, and the people apparently had long and good memories.[37]

All of these Tacitean passages deal more or less with various aspects of Caligula's domestic life. They offer some insights into the historian's appraisal of Caligula. There is one significant extant Tacitean reference to the foreign policy of the emperor: *Annales* 11.8, which mentions Caligula with respect to Armenian and Parthian affairs.[38] The simple detail given in brief, passing note is that Mithridates had been named king in Armenia, and had later been arrested by order of Caligula. Tacitus notes that he had already alluded to the appointment of Armenia; the reference is to *Annales* 6.31-37, where the historian devotes attention to Parthian and Armenian affairs as part of his discussion of the events of the year 35.

By the time Caligula had assumed the principate, relations with Parthia (and, by extension, the buffer state of Armenia) were at a critical juncture.[39] We do not know why Caligula ordered the incarceration of Mithridates, who had been appointed by Tiberius and had perhaps outlasted his usefulness.[40]

We may turn to Tacitus' *Historiae* and the references there to our emperor.[41] The first, at *Historiae* 1.16, is a mere recollection in a speech of the new *princeps* Galba that the empire was once the province of a single man; Caligula is named in order with Tiberius and Claudius. With this mention of Caligula we may join the similar comment at 1.89, where Tacitus observes that under Tiberius and Caligula, the country knew only the 'evils of peace'.[42] The reference is admittedly interesting in terms of its comment on the times. Caligula was undeniably wicked, as was his predecessor – but there was a general peace, though not necessarily a peace under which one would like to live.[43]

A more valuable historical allusion, however (at least in terms of corroborating details from the record of the emperor's reign), comes at 1.48, where we learn of the scandal of AD 39 occasioned by the behaviour of Cornelia, the wife of Calvisius Sabinus, the legate to Pannonia under Caligula. She had been guilty of inappropriate activities in a military camp, not excluding adultery in the commander's own quarters.[44] Titus Vinius was convicted of wrongdoing in this episode, and was arrested by order of Caligula, but was soon freed (a fortunate redemption thanks to the assassination of the *princeps*), only to be a casualty of the civil wars of the Long Year of 69.

At *Historiae* 3.68, amid the account of the fall of the doomed Emperor Vitellius, Tacitus notes that Julius Caesar had fallen victim to sudden violence, while Caligula had been felled by *occultae insidiae*, or 'hidden treachery' – a secret plot, as it were. The passage does not much improve our knowledge of the circumstances surrounding the death of Caligula, though it does offer an interesting contrast between the fates of the two Gaiuses. One might think that both Julius Caesar and Gaius Caligula suffered from *repentina vis*, or sudden violence; there were certainly *occultae insidiae* (hidden plots) that doomed both men. The reason for Tacitus' distinction is not clear. Perhaps the point lies in the number of plots that were afoot in the case of Caligula, against the circumstances that surrounded the Ides of March.

Whatever Caligula managed to do with respect to the Britons is shrouded in mystery. One clue is found at *Historiae* 4.15, where a certain Brinno of the Canninefates is mentioned. His father is said to have shown absolute contempt for Caligula's so-called expedition against Britain. It is not entirely certain what the father did to show how little he valued any threat from Caligula.[45]

We have already alluded to the problem of the administration of the province of Africa Proconsularis that is referenced at *Historiae* 4.48, where Tacitus notes that under Augustus and Tiberius, the governor in Africa had one legion and several auxiliary units to guard his territory (which was a frontier of the empire, though usually a fairly quiet one). Caligula is said to have been restless by his very nature – in other words, he favoured innovation for innovation's sake – and to have been suspicious of the governor Marcus Silanus. He withdrew the command of the legion from the governor's prerogative and assigned it to an imperial legate. He purposely created tension between the men by not clearly defining their respective spheres of influence, indeed by assigning overlapping responsibilities and equal amounts of patronage and support. Tacitus notes wryly (and very much in his usual style of historical commentary) that the imperial legate had the better of the situation, given that his tenure was more assured than that of the governor – but balancing this was the fact that the most outstanding governors, in the historian's estimation, worry more about their safety than their authority.[46]

At *Historiae* 4.68, there is a detail about how the father of Arrecinus Clemens had been a commander of the Praetorian Guard under Gaius Caligula, and had served with great distinction. Arrecinus Clemens had a sister who married the emperor Titus,[47] and he would eventually be one of the many victims of the tyrannical Domitian.[48] The elder Clemens was a conspirator in the assassination of Caligula, as we shall discuss in our examination of the evidence of Josephus for the emperor's assassination.[49]

Lastly, at *Historiae* 5.9 there is a mention in the historian's summation of the history of Roman involvement in Judaea of how Caligula had ordered that his image be erected in the Temple. The Jews had refused to obey such an abominable edict, preferring war to blasphemy – but Caligula's death offered a timely intervention.[50]

We may turn finally to Tacitus' so-called *opera minora*, or minor works.[51] The reference at *Agricola* 4.1 to Caligula has already been noted; Julius Graecinus was the father of Tacitus' father-in-law, Gnaeus Julius Agricola, and had incurred the enmity of Caligula – he was ultimately killed for refusing to prosecute Marcus Silanus.

At *Agricola* 13, Tacitus notes that Caligula had planned an invasion of Britain – indeed he notes that this fact was well known.[52] Caligula is said to have been constantly swift and prone to change with respect to his thoughts. He soon abandoned the plan (*velox ingenio mobili paenitentiae*) – and, besides, his ambitious undertakings with respect to Germany had come to naught (*et ingentes adversum Germaniam conatus frustra fuissent*).[53] We may recall just how little the Canninefates were said to have regarded Caligula. Augustus had decided to leave the island of Britain more or less alone, and Tiberius had followed him in this foreign policy – Caligula's claim to British fame would seem to rest at best on the claim of paving the way for what would happen under his successor Claudius.

The final reference to the emperor in the *Agricola* comes at chapter 44, where it is noted that Agricola was born on 13 June, in the year of Caligula's third consulship – that is, AD 40.

In the *Germania*, whatever Caligula did or intended to do is reduced to the level of farcical memory.[54] The context is the same as for the British reference; Tacitus is giving a brief summation of Roman involvement with the Germans. The language is reminiscent of the earlier passage: *mox ingentes Gai Caesaris minae in ludibrium versae* ('the great threats of Gaius Caligula were turned into an object of mockery').[55] Everything that Caligula had boasted of planning to achieve, one might think, had been reduced to fodder for jokes at the imperial expense.

The only reference to Caligula in the *Dialogus* is a mere note about the nearly four years of his reign, amid an account of how long the different emperors ruled.[56]

Snippets, then, of evidence abound for what Tacitus thought of Caligula; the bulk of the surviving material concerns the period just before the accession of the emperor in 37. There is no reason to believe that Tacitus had a positive view of Caligula; the historian who was so hostile to Tiberius would never have found much of anything positive to say about Gaius. Whatever the emperor accomplished in Germany and Britain is reduced to the level of bad comedy. He is seen as either mentally unhinged or prone to sudden changes of mind and intention, thoroughly unpredictable and a failure in most of his grand endeavours. While we would give much to have access to Books 7-8 of Tacitus' *Annales*, the main thrust of the content is reasonably clear enough to imagine.

Chapter Five

Josephus on Caligula

While those interested in the life of Caligula are perhaps most likely to turn first to Suetonius' biography – and, perhaps, second to Book 59 of Dio, and what of relevance remains from Tacitus' work – one of the most valuable extant sources of information is the great writer Josephus, who was born, coincidentally, in the year Caligula assumed the principate. Born in Jerusalem, Josephus had an incredible career under the Flavian emperors, and is known as Flavius Josephus after having assumed their family name. He died sometime after AD 97, perhaps spared seeing whatever Rome suffered under the last of the Flavian rulers, Domitian.

Caligula was perhaps of special interest to Josephus, given that the historian was born in the year in which Tiberius died and was succeeded by the future scourge of Jew and Roman alike.[1]

The *Jewish Antiquities* is a massive work in twenty books, the scope of which extends from the very creation of the world until AD 66.[2] The mammoth compendium is of inestimable value for the history of Judaism, as well as for a wide range of other topics in history and ancient studies. Book 18 mentions the accession of Caligula and the administration of the oath of loyalty to the new emperor by the Syrian governor Lucius Vitellius.[3] The friendship of Herod Agrippa with Caligula is noted; Agrippa was received as a friend by Antonia, and is said to have begun to court the favour of Caligula, who was held in the greatest esteem on the strength of the reputation of his father Germanicus.[4] Agrippa had financial problems, but he was able to borrow successfully and use money to aid in his attempt to ingratiate himself with Caligula.

The anecdote is related that once while riding, in the year 36, Agrippa expressed the wish to Caligula that Tiberius would abdicate in favour of the young man, since Caligula was so very much more competent than his adopted father.[5] Eutychus, the freedman and charioteer of Agrippa, overheard the remark, but at first he prudently kept it to himself. Later, however, guilty of having stolen some of Agrippa's clothing, he fled and eventually indicated that he had a secret message for Tiberius and should be permitted sanctuary to deliver it. He was sent to Capreae and held as a prisoner for some time.[6]

Agrippa eventually asked Antonia to intercede for him – he had come to know what Eutychus was going to report to the emperor. Antonia approached Tiberius, who replied in classic Tiberian fashion – essentially that what mattered was the truth or falsehood of what Eutychus had to tell him.

One day, however, while Tiberius was reclining on his litter, Caligula and Agrippa were in front after lunch. Antonia approached and ordered Macro to bring forth Eutychus. The freedman reported what he had heard Agrippa say to Caligula on that fateful day when they had been riding. Josephus records that Tiberius believed the story; he had held an old grudge against Agrippa, not least for the fact that Agrippa had befriended Caligula and so disregarded him.

Tiberius ordered the arrest of Agrippa and the young man began to remonstrate with him. Agrippa was taken away; the day was very hot and he had had wine but no water. A slave of Caligula named Thaumastus offered him water, and Agrippa promised to secure the servant's freedom if things turned out well for him.[7]

Antonia, meanwhile, saw to it that Agrippa's imprisonment was as comfortable as possible, and things went on for six months. In the meantime, Tiberius became ill. The emperor was concerned about the succession. Of his family there seemed to be only two left as possible heirs: Tiberius Gemellus and Gaius Caligula. Caligula is said by Josephus to have received a very good education, and to have been held in high esteem by the populace on the strength of Germanicus' reputation. The army in particular was inclined to support Caligula, so popular and greatly respected was the young man's father.

Josephus offers the story that the indecisive Tiberius decided to leave the question of the succession to augury: he would wait and see which of his sons was the first to visit him on a given morning.[8] It would appear that Tiberius was inclined to favour Gemellus, and had decided to orchestrate oracles to his own wishes by ordering that Gemellus be summoned to appear early in the morning. The boy had not finished his breakfast, however, and Caligula was the first to behold his emperor. Tiberius soon enough was lamenting the fact that Gemellus was likely doomed; Caligula would be hostile to him, and there would be no powerful people willing to risk the new emperor's displeasure and wrath to intercede for Gemellus. Gemellus, for his part, would be unable to resist plotting against Caligula.

Josephus' Tiberius is made to announce to Caligula that he would be the next emperor, and he was urged to remember Tiberius' kindness in bestowing the succession on him, and to remember his bond of kinship with Gemellus. Tiberius noted that Gemellus would be a strong aid to Caligula's survival if he was allowed to live, and a prelude to ruin if he should be slain.

Caligula pretended to accept Tiberius' advice, yet in reality he planned to kill Gemellus and did so, though he himself also met his ruin soon enough.[9] Tiberius lived for but a few more days, and then met his death. News was brought to Agrippa in prison of the death. There was some controversy as to the truth of the reports, and some risk to Agrippa.[10] Caligula soon sent two letters: the first, to the Senate, announced the death of Tiberius and his accession; the second, to the prefect of the city, ordered that Agrippa be sent from the camp where he had been held prisoner to the house in which he had previously lived.[11] Caligula returned to Rome with the body of Tiberius, and a splendid requiem was observed. Caligula was meanwhile eager to free Agrippa. Antonia warned the new emperor that he should beware of too hasty an act, lest it seem inappropriate. In a few days, then, Caligula summoned Agrippa, freed him and gave him the tetrarchy of Philip and that of Lysanias.[12]

Josephus proceeds to note that in the second year of Caligula's reign, the emperor gave his permission to Agrippa to return to the East to settle certain affairs, and then to come back to Rome. Herodias – the sister of Agrippa and wife of Herod – was jealous of her brother's newfound fortune and favour. She urged her husband to set out to Rome to seek the same honours. Finally, after repeated entreaties, Herodias succeeded in convincing Herod to plan for a lavish entourage to accompany a journey to Rome and Caligula.

Agrippa made his own preparations once he heard of what his sister and brother-in-law were doing. He sent a freedman to Rome with presents for Caligula and negative things to report about Herod – and the promise that he would tell more when he was next in Rome. Both the Herod party and Agrippa's freedman found Caligula at Baiae. Caligula literally read the letters from Agrippa while meeting with Herod. Agrippa's claims were vast: Herod had cooperated with Sejanus to overthrow Tiberius, and was now involved in a conspiracy with the Parthian King Artabanus to overthrow Caligula. Herod allegedly had arms reserved for some 70,000 infantry.

Caligula inquired of Herod as to the truth of the report about the arms. Herod admitted it – Josephus notes that he could hardly do otherwise given that the arms were in fact stored away. Caligula immediately deposed Herod and gave his tetrarchy to Agrippa. Herod was sent into exile to Lugdunum in Gaul.

Herodias was offered the privilege of keeping her property on the strength of whom her brother was; she indicated that she was loyal to her husband. Caligula is said to have been angered by this defiance, and to have sent her into exile as well – with her property assigned to Agrippa.[13]

Josephus is clear that the first two years of Caligula's reign were noble. This accords more or less with the report from other sources, though with perhaps a somewhat longer 'good' period than we find elsewhere attested. Josephus' 'early' Caligula was a moderate ruler, and in consequence was extremely popular both in Rome and abroad. The change in Caligula is attributed to his eventual arrival at the conclusion that he was divine, so great, after all, was the empire that he governed.

Josephus' next topic follows in natural sequence: what happened between the Jews of Alexandria and the Greeks of that storied city of Egypt.[14] This major episode in the history of Judaism in early imperial Rome is amply attested not only by Josephus, but also, notably, by the writer Philo (whose works will be considered in our next chapter).

Delegations were sent to Rome to appeal to Caligula to settle the civil strife in Alexandria. One of the Greeks was Apion, who attacked the Jews viciously in his words. The Jews were accused essentially of a monotheism that did not countenance the honours due to the emperor. Philo, the leading Jewish delegate, tried to refute the arguments of Apion. He was interrupted by Caligula and not permitted to finish his response; he was expelled from the emperor's presence and threatened with violence. Philo is said to have told his fellow Jews not to worry, since Caligula was now essentially declaring war on God.

Caligula sent a new governor to Syria to succeed Lucius Vitellius; Publius Petronius set out to take up his new office.[15] Petronius was ordered to take troops into Judaea and to set up the image of Caligula in the Temple. Petronius took two legions and many auxiliaries, and prepared for action against any Jewish rebellion in the face of his attempted desecration of the Temple. Petronius was approached by Jewish delegations, but the negotiations between the Romans and the Jews failed on account of the refusal of the new governor to disobey Caligula, and the refusal of the Jews to consent to a violation of their law.

Threatened with war and a military response to their perceived intransigency, the Jews indicated that they preferred death to dishonour, and that they would not fight, but were ready to die. They neglected their agricultural life and prepared for an end. Agrippa's brother Aristobulus interceded for the population at this juncture, urging Petronius to write to Caligula about the impasse. Petronius was moved by the appeal, and agreed to contact the emperor. Josephus notes that he was essentially deciding to risk the emperor's wrath by this action. He indicated to Aristobulus that perhaps the letter would work – and he is said to have spoken to the multitudes with appreciation for the honour and reverence they displayed toward their ancestral traditions. A timely shower of rain seemed to indicate that divine providence was on the side of the Jews, Petronius including mention of this portent in his letter to Caligula. Petronius argued that the death of tens of thousands of Jews would lead to reduced financial revenue, and might well incur the displeasure of the gods.

Josephus shifts the focus of his history to events in Rome, where Agrippa was feasting Caligula at a lavish banquet. Caligula offered to enrich Agrippa in any way he could as a sign of gratitude. He expected, Josephus notes, that Agrippa would ask for more territory to rule. The wily Agrippa at first indicated that he did not wish any present, but Caligula persisted. And so at last Agrippa requested that the emperor not persist in demanding that Petronius be ordered to erect the image of Caligula in the Temple of the Jews.

Josephus' story offers fascinating insights into the psychology of Caligula. The emperor is depicted as being willing to grant Agrippa's request, and ready to write to Petronius. His letter – which was sent before he saw Petronius – indicated that the governor should relent from the erection of the statue, but should leave the statue in place if it had already been set up in the Temple.[16] Agrippa was given the credit for the change in Caligula's mind and mood regarding the whole matter.

But soon enough Caligula read Petronius' own letter, and he was now in a very different circumstance. He felt that the Jews were threatening a rebellion, and that the governor was not revealing himself to be sufficiently dutiful in the exercise of his loyal responsibilities to his *princeps*. Caligula wrote back and essentially ordered Petronius to commit suicide.

Fortunately for Petronius, he received a different letter first – namely the one informing him that Caligula had been assassinated.[17] For Josephus, the death of Caligula is evidence that God favoured Petronius, the righteous Roman. The governor soon received the second letter, and marvelled at how divine beneficence had protected him (from, we might say, the false god).

We may turn now to Book 19 of the *Jewish Antiquities*, which provides one of our most valuable sources for the life of Caligula – and in particular for the conspiracy that resulted in his assassination.[18] Josephus had indicated that the first two years of Caligula's reign were marked by moderate rule, but from the commencement of his commentary in Book 19, the emperor is noted for his madness and insanity – not only toward the Jews in Judaea and Jerusalem, but throughout the Roman world. Simply put, Josephus presents Caligula as being the bringer of the worst ills to Rome that the city and empire had ever known.[19] Caligula did not favour Rome, but treated the capital of the empire as if it were like any other place in the world – a city ripe to fall victim to his wanton actions.

Caligula is said to have deprived the equestrians of the privileges peculiar to their rank, to have killed them and taken their property. Financial greed was the motivation for his prosecutions and executions.[20] He intended to pursue his own deification, and once addressed the Capitoline Jupiter as his brother. His attempt to turn sea into land with a bridge of ships is also noted.

One problem in appreciating Josephus' account is the familiar one with some of our ancient sources: chronology. Josephus prefaces his account of Caligula's assassination with details of the emperor's insanity, such as the story of the Xerxes-like action whereby Caligula attempted to emulate (if not surpass) the god of the sea. This might be taken to imply that Caligula's action was taken late in his reign, whereas Suetonius and Dio date it from the earlier, more rational part of his rule (and Suetonius even includes it among the actions of the *princeps*, not the *monstrum*). Indeed, some have been led to conclude that the entire incident was fabricated.[21]

Caligula plundered the temples of the Greeks, ordering that works of art should be brought to him, on the pretext that the loveliest of *objets d'art* should be housed in the loveliest of cities, that is, Rome. Orders were given to bring back to the capital of the empire even the legendary statue of the Olympian

Zeus by Phidias. In Josephus' account, the reason the transfer of the statue never occurred was that workmen reported to Memmius Regulus that it would be ruined if there were an attempt to move it.[22] Josephus records that Memmius was deterred too by certain portents. In any case, he is said to have written to Caligula that he was not going to execute the orders – thus risking his own execution.[23] Once again, Caligula's assassination saved the day for another Roman official in foreign lands.

On the birth of his daughter, Caligula brought the infant to the statue of the Capitoline Jupiter and deposited her on the knees of the god, noting that the child had two fathers – and that the question of which father was the greater was in dispute.[24]

The general tenor of Caligula's reign was one of fear and terror, not least because slaves were permitted to bring charges against their masters. Claudius' slave Polydeuces brought such an accusation against Claudius, and there was an expectation that Caligula's uncle would be slain.[25]

Josephus' particular interest in the assassination of Caligula is associated with the fact that in his estimation, the killing of the mad emperor was important in terms of the general human pursuit of the protection of security and the rule of law – in other words, a Caligula must be dispensed with if order and justice are to be preserved. Further, for Josephus the destruction of the Jewish nation and the ruin of the Jewish people was likely, should Caligula have survived and been allowed to continue on his mad path. Further, the historian takes the story of Caligula's end as proof of the abiding power of the true God, a tale that even provides comfort and assurance to those in difficult circumstances.

The general reason for what happened is a familiar one in our sources: Caligula was so awful that it was inevitable that there would be many conspiracies and plots to do him in by violence.[26]

Josephus identifies three separate plots to overthrow Caligula. Aemilius Regulus was in charge of one conspiracy.[27] He was from Cordoba in Iberia, and hoped to kill Caligula either by the hands of others or even by his own. A second group was apparently formed to aid the first; the familiar Cassius Chaerea, the military tribune, was the leading force of this contingent. And finally there was Annius Vinicianus.[28]

Josephus details the reasons for the individual lead conspirators' dislike of Caligula. Regulus was apparently a man of principles and free, independent spirit – he was so free and independent, in fact, that he was not a good conspirator in terms of keeping affairs secret, but was all too willing to reveal what in his view needed to be done, and done swiftly. Vinicianus had the personal vendetta of avenging Marcus Aemilius Lepidus, the former husband of Drusilla and would-be successor of Caligula. Vinicianus was also afraid for himself; he realized that anyone was in peril for as long as Caligula was allowed to remain in power.

Cassius Chaerea was upset with the emperor because of slurs on his manhood. Of all the conspirators, he saw the most of Caligula; he felt that he was consequently in the most danger – and besides, he also had a spirit of liberty about him, and a disdain for tyranny.

All three men are said to have been willing to slay Caligula, even if it meant the forfeiture of their own lives. All three were willing to lay bare their wishes before anyone who had been privy to the madness of the emperor. Of the three, Josephus identifies Cassius Chaerea as the most zealous to do the deed, in part because he saw Caligula so often – and in part to redeem his own reputation.[29]

Josephus says that there were chariot races at this time – he gives the observation that the Romans are particularly obsessed with this sort of contest. Traditionally, the chariot races were the time to appeal to the emperor for favours; on this occasion, the people begged Caligula to remit some of the heavy tax burden under which they laboured.[30]

The emperor had no patience for the popular uprising. He ordered his subordinates to proceed to arrest those who were shouting in protest, and to have them killed. Countless individuals lost their lives in the ensuing slaughter; the crowd finally grew silent when they saw the fatal hazard. Cassius Chaerea, for his part, was all the more determined to kill Caligula – the spectacle of the death of so many was for him intolerable.

Caligula grew angry with Cassius Chaerea, meanwhile, when he realized that his tribune was being too slow in carrying out the duty of collecting taxes and other financial impositions. Caligula associated his officer's compassion for the people with effeminacy, and so we have the assignment of obscene passwords and other marks of revilement of the guard's allegedly womanly nature.[31]

Josephus notes the irony inherent in Caligula's taunts of Cassius Chaerea. He relates how Caligula was a transvestite in his practice of certain religious rites, wearing women's robes and wigs. The password mockery caused the tribune untold troubles. The emperor was insulting him, and there were the other soldiers to whom he had to pass on the obscene watchwords. Chaerea thus began to look for associates with whom he might prepare his plot to end the Caligulan nightmare.

Josephus identifies one 'Pompedius' – a senator – as the man Chaerea approached.[32] Pomepdius was of high rank and had enjoyed a distinguished career; he was also an Epicurean and thus given to living a leisurely life. He was accused by a certain Timidius of having insulted Caligula. The actress Quintilia was called as a witness; she had had an affair with Pompedius and others, and was renowned for her loveliness. Quintilia would not betray Pompedius, so her torture was ordered. Chaerea was Caligula's usual torturer, Josephus notes, because the emperor assumed that he would want to be crueller and more savage in tormenting prisoners, so that he would be less liable to accusations of effeminacy. Quintilia is said to have stepped on the foot of someone who was privy to the conspiracy, as if to indicate that no matter what they did to her, she would not betray the plot. Chaerea tortured her savagely – but she yielded no information. She was finally brought to Caligula, in a terrible state of abuse. Even the emperor was moved by the horrible sight, and he ordered the acquittal of both the actress and Pompedius. Quintilia was awarded financial compensation for her severe physical abuse.

The Quintilia episode caused even more anger in Chaerea toward Caligula, so he widened the circle of his conspiracy, including now (Marcus Arrecinus) Clemens and Papinius; the former a praetorian prefect and the latter another tribune. Clemens is said at first to have been reticent and hesitant to agree with Chaerea's assessment of Caligula (he blushed in obvious shame, however, at having followed the orders of the madman). Chaerea pursued the strategy of arguing that officers like the three of them were guilty of tormenting humanity when it was within their power to do something about Caligula. There was also the fact that sooner or later, the three of them would all fall prey to the same Caligulan insanity that had already claimed so many victims.[33]

Clemens urged Chaerea to remain quiet about the whole plan. He was worried about detection, and urged trust that there might be some stroke of luck that would intercede to aid in the conspiracy.[34] Clemens invoked his advanced age as an issue, noting that while Chaerea's plan was not the path of safety, it certainly was marked by honour. Chaerea meanwhile approached

Cornelius Sabinus, another military tribune, eager to enlist his aid.[35] Chaerea was eager to be quick about the whole matter, worried that Clemens might say something, and he felt that delay only favoured Caligula.[36]

In Sabinus, Chaerea found a man after his own heart. The second tribune had been planning his own conspiracy, and had only lacked for someone in whom he could place his trust to divulge his secret. So the two men approached Vinicianus, whom they knew well: Vinicianus had been friends with Lepidus, and was thus both angry with Caligula and fearful for his own longevity.

The three men met for an impromptu conference, and Vinicianus was allowed to speak first out of deference for his higher rank. He asked Chaerea what the password for the day was. Chaerea responded that the password was 'Liberty', and that he needed to hear nothing more from Vinicianus – that indeed he had one sword, a sword that would work for both men. Chaerea urged that what needed to be done should be done swiftly.

Josephus notes that when Chaerea thereafter entered the Senate, a voice was heard that told him to proceed to his task with the support of heaven. The tribune initially assumed that his conspiracy had been betrayed, but soon realized that he had the support of divine providence – once again, a hallmark of Josephus' account of the Caligulan nightmare. But everyone seemed to know about the plot – Josephus makes clear that there was essentially no one who did not realize that life would be better off without Caligula.

Josephus also gives attention to the case of the freedman Callistus.[37] Thanks to the patronage of Caligula, Callistus had risen to a notable, high rank, but was smart enough to realize that he was in grave danger himself precisely because he had profited so appreciably from his friendship with the emperor, and was now too wealthy to survive for long in such an age. He is said to have begun to show special favour even to Claudius, surmising that if Caligula were to be removed, Claudius would be the successor. He even claimed that he had been ordered to poison Claudius, but had found various excuses and subterfuges by which to delay the murder.[38]

The conspirators were cautious and hesitant; nobody was very much in favour of finally agreeing to a date and place for the deed – except for Chaerea. Chaerea was willing to kill Caligula instantly, on the first occasion that offered itself, and only his fellow plotters were able to restrain him. Chaerea grew increasingly frustrated and even angry with the others, but they meanwhile continued to urge him to take all proper precautions to avoid detection and trouble. The Palatine Games, in their estimation, afforded the best chance for success.[39]

Josephus notes that these games were in honour of Augustus, and that a stage was set up a little in front of the imperial palace. The original plan was to kill Caligula as he entered – on the first day of the games. For unspecified reasons, Josephus notes that again and again there were delays, yet finally, on the last day of the games, Chaerea is said to have tried to rouse his co-conspirators to action.[40] Chaerea also noted that Caligula was planning to depart for Alexandria. Chaerea indicated that he was ready to act now, alone and without any further thought of caution – after all, he might otherwise be cheated of his opportunity to do something about Caligula, given that some Egyptian might kill the emperor on the forthcoming trip.

And so in the morning – having finally inspired his fellows that this would be the day – Chaerea proceeded to the Palatine, armed with the sword of his equestrian rank. The crowd had already assembled for the last day of the games. The seating was a mess of disorder and confusion. Caligula finally appeared and made sacrifice to Augustus. The robe worn by (Publius Nonius) Asprenas was sprinkled with blood from a sacrificial victim.[41] Caligula laughed at the sanguinary accident that had marred Asprenas' clothing; it was an omen that he would be struck down that day over the body of Caligula.

Josephus alone among our surviving sources records that Caligula was actually for once in a very good mood on his final day. Josephus provides a brief but invaluable description of the temporary theatre that was traditionally erected for the games.[42]

Caligula was seated in the right wing of the theatre, while Chaerea was with the other tribunes. One Balthybius – a man of senatorial rank who had held a praetorship – asked Cluvius, another consular, if he had heard about an impending revolution – taking care not to be overheard. Cluvius indicated that he had no idea about this, and Balthybius replied that the programme for today's spectacles included the assassination of a tyrant. Cluvius urged Balthybius' silence, quoting Homer's *Iliad* – lest some other of the Achaeans overhear him.[43]

Fruit and rare birds were scattered among the people as presents. Caligula was amused as he watched the crowd dart about for the prizes and treats. A mime was presented meanwhile, in which a chieftain was crucified.[44] The tragedy *Cinyras* was performed, in which both father and daughter were killed.[45] Fake blood drenched the stage from the crucified man and Cinyras. It was also the same day on which Philip of Macedon had been killed by Pausanias as he entered a theatre.

Caligula hesitated over the question of leaving the show to bathe and dine, so as to return refreshed. It was the last day of the games, and there was a sense of not wishing to miss anything. Vinicianus rose to leave, worried that Caligula would never get up to depart, and that the whole matter would need to be abandoned. He saw that Chaerea was already proceeding to the exit, and urged the tribune to take courage. Caligula was still in an apparently friendly mood, pulling at Vinicianus' clothes in a casual manner and asking where he was going. Vinicianus proceeded to resume his seat, more out of fear than anything. But soon enough he rose again as if to depart, and the emperor did and said nothing – assuming, one might think, that Vinicianus needed to relieve himself or some such thing. Asprenas was aware of the plot, and urged Caligula to depart as well, recommending a bath and meal, and then a return for the last bit of the games.

It was now about the ninth hour, according to Suetonius – sometime after two in the afternoon, given the time of year.[46] Chaerea was becoming ever more impatient; he was ready to re-enter the theatre and simply slay Caligula where he sat. He was willing to do this even though he knew that many senators and equestrians might be killed in the fray. Throughout the narrative, he is possessed of an absolute zeal to act. Indeed, Josephus indicates that Chaerea and others were actually in the process of re-entering the theatre, when the signal was given that Caligula was exiting. The conspirators returned to the places they had taken up in anticipation of slaying the emperor – and now they began to push back the crowds, arguing that Caligula would be irritated if there were a rabble and din as he made his way back to the palace.[47]

Walking ahead of Caligula were Claudius, Marcus Vinicius and Valerius Asiaticus. Josephus notes that no one could have stopped the exit of these men, even if they had wanted to do so – their dignity guaranteed their safety.[48] Caligula was walking with Paulus Arruntius.[49] Once inside the palace, Caligula is said to have eschewed the usual, direct route that was lined by slaves – the path Claudius and the others had just taken. He preferred to use a deserted alley that provided a short path to the baths. Boys had also arrived from Asia as a choir to sing, with some ready to take part in Pyrrhic dances.[50]

At this point, Chaerea stepped forth and asked Caligula for the watchword. As usual, the emperor gave a mocking, insulting reply. Chaerea then began to abuse Caligula verbally, drew his sword and struck him severely, though not fatally. Josephus records that some authorities argue that Chaerea deliberately delivered a non-mortal wound, hoping thus to make Caligula suffer all the more by the infliction of many blows. However, Josephus discounts this, arguing that fear would have precluded any such action.

The wound was between the shoulder and the neck; Caligula was stunned. The emperor did not cry out, nor did he cry for help. Josephus speculates that he was either in a state of shock, or else in some manner out of his mind.[51] He moaned, however, in serious pain – and tried to escape. Cornelius Sabinus blocked his way, pushing Caligula to the ground, down on one knee. Now all of the assassins were on Caligula, thrusting their swords at the helpless target. Aquila delivered the death blow – Josephus says that there is no disagreement about this fact.[52]

Aquila was responsible for the death – but Josephus assigns the credit for the assassination to the mastermind, Cassius Chaerea. The tribune was the one responsible for bringing together other would-be conspirators, his eloquence steeling their nerves for the audacious deed.

Josephus proceeds to the chaotic aftermath of the assassination.[53] Caligula's killers knew that they needed to fear both the Guard and the mob, as Caligula was the object of irrational affection for some (no doubt on account of such sops to public opinion as the spectacle entertainments). The passageways were narrow, and there was danger on all sides, it seemed, from soldiers and bodyguards – in short, no easy path of secure egress. They took a path that led to the house of Germanicus – a certain irony given his paternity of the man they had just slain. Josephus notes that the imperial palace had been enlarged, and the different sections bore the names of significant members of the 'royal' family.

Caligula's German bodyguards were the first on the scene. Josephus offers the ethnic commentary that the Germans are given over more than any other of the barbarians to the habit of acting first and asking questions later; they are also physically impressive in power and size, and thus a significant threat. The

Germans were now incensed at the death of Caligula, for the simple reason that he paid them generously for their service. A contingent of the Germans was led by one Sabinus, a tribune who owed his rank to his appreciable strength as a gladiator. They found the unfortunate Asprenas before anyone else, and he was slaughtered in the ensuing violence.

Norbanus was the second to die.[54] His death was more dramatic than that of Asprenas. He was also physically powerful, and is said to have wrestled away a sword from one of the Germans, and to have put up something of a fight against hopeless odds.

Anteius, the third in the grim line of casualties, was another senator of some fame, though history has consigned him to something like oblivion.[55] Anteius was guilty of the phenomenon of slowing down to see the traffic accident, as it were; he had ventured close to gaze on the body of Caligula for himself, and had thus run foul of the Germans. Anteius' father had been driven into banishment by Caligula; soon enough, soldiers had been sent to kill him. Now the son was also a casualty of Caligula, though in a very different manner from his father.

The news of the death reached the masses in the theatre.[56] Those who secretly welcomed the news of Caligula's end were moved by fear and apprehension. Those who were displeased by the report did not believe it, assuming that no one would be bold enough to strike down the emperor so audaciously. There were soldiers who were disconcerted by the news, because Caligula paid them so well, while there were also women who were happy to watch the gladiatorial shows, and who favoured the emperor because he indulged them with these sanguinary spectacles.[57]

Slaves were said to have enjoyed Caligula's rule, simply because he provided them with something of an escape from their masters – in Caligula they had found an emperor who would happily welcome any reports that indicted their *domini*. Slaves could profit from participating in the condemnation of their masters; they could secure property and even freedom.

As was the case after the death of Tiberius, there were those of the nobler classes who pretended not to believe the news, worried that any false reports would engender premature sentiments of rejoicing that would doom them. Reports were confused (as would be expected) in the immediate aftermath of the slaying. One story said that Caligula had survived and was receiving medical treatment. The most frightening rumour was that Caligula had actually managed to escape the assassination, and was now covered in blood and giving an effective speech to the mob in the Forum.[58] People were actually afraid to leave the theatre. No matter the intention that prompted their exit, they were worried that their actions would be misconstrued – a sad but altogether predictable commentary on the times.[59]

The Germans now surrounded the theatre, and the audience expected to be slain on the spot. Immediately the crowd began to remonstrate with the soldiers, begging that they not be killed. The soldiers were apparently ready to start killing anyone they even remotely suspected of complicity in the plot. The pleadings of the crowd calmed them, though they proceeded to mount the heads of Asprenas and the other victims of their wrath on the altar of sacrifice. The grisly sight created even more dread among members of the audience, as they contemplated their own possible imminent fate.

At this juncture in his narrative, Josephus introduces one Euarestus Arruntius, a professional auctioneer who had a voice appropriate to his career. He entered the theatre in the garb of mourning, and announced the death of the emperor – the rumours of Caligula's survival were thus dispelled. The crowd was calmed as Arruntius recalled the Germans. According to Josephus, the wrath and rage of the loyal bodyguard was quelled as soon as they learned that Caligula was in fact dead. The spell, as it were, had been broken. The historian notes that the Germans were afraid that if they persisted in threats or acts of violence, the Senate might fire them should they come to power in some restored republican government.[60]

Cassius Chaerea was worried for the safety of Vinicianus (he should have also been concerned for his own future). Vinicanus was brought to Clemens, who made clear that he would acquit him. Clemens gave testament to the fact that Caligula had been a tyrant, and that all tyrants eventually fall victim to their own designs – in short, if anyone killed Caligula or was responsible for his death, it was Caligula himself.

The crowd in the theatre at last began to depart, the doctor Alcyon arranging the fortuitous exits. He had been taken away to treat some wounded men, and he had sent away those with him on the pretext of securing medical supplies, though the real point was to safeguard them.[61] The Senate was soon convened, and the popular assemblies also met in the Forum. Josephus notes that the people were quite serious about tracking down those responsible for the death of Caligula, while the Senate only pretended to be interested in the question. Valerius Asiaticus (the ex-consul) was presiding over the popular assembly, and when there was a demand to know who was involved in the imperial assassination, he indicated that he wished he had been complicit.[62]

The Senate in the end decreed that Caligula was deserving of charges, and that the people and the soldiers should return to the business of their normal lives – with the promise of financial and other incentives to keep the peace. Those who had been involved in the assassination were now buoyed up in spirit, even assuming that the government would soon be in their hands.

Claudius, however, was kidnapped from his home.[63] The Praetorian Guard, after all, was just as capable as the imperial Senate of holding a meeting – and they saw no possibility of any sort of republican restoration. That meant a continued principate – and they had no intention of letting anyone else decide the question of who would be the *princeps*. So Claudius was the praetorian candidate – he was suitable to the interests of the Guard both by virtue of his family lineage, and because he was considered a noble member of the Senate. Claudius was essentially kidnapped by the soldiers – the Praetorian Guard had their would-be emperor.

Josephus proceeds to relate a speech to the Senate that was delivered by Gnaeus Sentius Saturninus.[64] Sentius noted that at long last freedom had been restored to Rome. There were many, he observed, who had never lived under republican rule. Sentius traced the coming of wickedness to Rome with the attempts of Julius Caesar to destroy the democracy – the founder, as it were, of the Julian dynasty was thus lambasted in the Senate in the aftermath of the death of his Julian descendant. While not naming Augustus or Tiberius, Sentius proceeded to argue that step by step, the traditions and regulations of the old republican system had been stripped away; in short, all the Julio-Claudians were tyrants, but Caligula had outdone them all in tyranny and horror.

Sentius proposed that Cassius Chaerea should receive the highest honours, the senator dramatically declaring that he was greater than Brutus and Cassius, since their slaying of a tyrant had inaugurated a civil war, while Cassius had removed both the tyrant and the horrors that were engendered by him.[65]

The Senate and the equestrians shouted their approval of Sentius' words. Trebellius Maximus rose and grabbed Sentius' ring, on which was engraved an image of Caligula – the senator had been so carried away by his speech that he had forgotten he was still wearing this sign of subservience to the old tyrant. The image was smashed.

It was now far into the night (24/25 January), and Cassius Chaerea asked the consuls for the watchword. The response was simply, 'Liberty'. The giving of the watchword had been restored to the consuls, it was noted, for the first time in a century.[66] Chaerea passed on the watchword to the soldiers who were loyal to the Senate – some four cohorts. Chaerea was soon the darling the people as well.

Chaerea next sent the military tribune Julius Lupus to kill Caesonia and the infant Drusilla.[67] Lupus, who was related to Clemens, had not been involved in the conspiracy to kill Caligula, and it was thought that he might now be allowed to have some share in the glory of the hour.

Some were concerned that the killing of the emperor's wife and infant child were ignominious deeds, but others said that Caesonia was to blame for much of Caligula's horrid rule, arguing that she had given him a love potion that had driven him insane. Those who wanted Caesonia dead carried the hour, and Lupus was sent to see to the murder.

Josephus' death *tableau* for Caesonia is suitably dramatic. Lupus found her stretched out by the bloodstained corpse of her beloved husband, spattered with the sanguinary evidence of the assassination. The daughter was at her side. Caesonia was heard to cry to Caligula that he had ignored her predictions of his death. Josephus notes that opinion was divided as to what exactly Caesonia meant; some thought that she had been encouraging the emperor to tone down his craziness and tyrannical behaviour, while others believed that she had learned of the conspiracy, and had urged her husband to kill all the plotters at once, even if they were innocent.

Caesonia is said not to have realized initially what Lupus intended. When she saw that he meant to kill her, she exposed her throat to his blade willingly. The wife was slain, then the daughter, and Lupus brought news of the killings to Chaerea.

Josephus proceeds to a summation of Caligula.[68] He was a monster of perversity; avaricious and sadistic; greedy for pain and profit alike. He wished to be viewed as greater than either religion or the law – in fact he was a pawn of the fawning adulation of the crowd. Virtue was his true enemy. He engaged in incest with his sister; for Josephus, this more than anything else was what caused Caligula to lose the favour of the crowd.[69]

Josephus further notes that no building project of Caligula can be cited that was beneficial either to his contemporaries or to posterity, except the planned harbour near Rhegium and Sicily for the intake of grain imports from Egypt.[70]

Caligula is said to have been a splendid orator, with excellent knowledge of both Greek and Latin; he was a master of extemporaneous speechmaking. For Josephus, Caligula was a product of the competition that was engendered by the mere fact that he was the successor to Tiberius and the grandson of Tiberius' brother – Tiberius, after all, had also been distinguished in literature and oratory.

None of Caligula's educational benefits, however, availed him in his life as emperor. For Josephus, the point is that Caligula had to answer to no one – and so the life of virtue was exceedingly difficult for him to pursue (even were he so inclined). At first, we are told, Caligula made every effort to cultivate the friendship of men of the highest rank. Later, they were discarded in the face of the sadistic brutality of the tyrant – and they formed the core of the conspiracy that finally ended Rome's long nightmare.

Claudius had gone into hiding as soon as he learned of the assassination of his nephew.[71] Josephus notes that he was worried because of his noble rank, though not for any particular reason beyond that, since he had always conducted himself if anything as a scholar, especially of Greek. The Praetorian Guard, meanwhile, was debating what to do. Several of them openly admitted in their meeting that Caligula had more or less deserved what had happened to him. The guardsman Gratus found Claudius, and proposed that he be the candidate of the praetorians for the purple. Claudius thought that he was being led away to his death. Gratus immediately laughed at him and noted that on the contrary, he was the desired successor to Caligula.

And so Josephus commences his account of how the Senate, Claudius and the Guard were soon involved in a more or less delicate political ballet.

Agrippa meanwhile tended to the body of Caligula.[72] After dressing the body and preparing it on a bier, he went out to the bodyguards and announced that Caligula was still alive, and that doctors had been summoned since the wounds were serious. On hearing of what had happened with Claudius, Agrippa made his way to visit him and urge him to accept the principate.[73]

Confusion – after a fashion at least – was the hour of the day. The Senate was urged on by the assassins of Caligula not to surrender their hard-won, newly regained prerogatives; the Praetorian Guard was staunchly arrayed in defence of Claudius, and there were several senators who were willing to cast their lot for a chance at the principate. Chaerea was incensed at the demand of the soldiers for an emperor, and sarcastically promised that he would bring them an emperor, if someone would bring him the watchword from Eutychus – the favourite of Caligula and charioteer from his beloved faction of the Greens. Chaerea insulted them for their slavish devotion to Claudius, and urged them to bring forth the head of Claudius.[74] He noted that after seeing Rome ruled by a madman, the Guard was essentially willing to hand it over to an imbecile.[75]

Cornelius Sabinus threatened to commit suicide rather than see Claudius installed as Caligula's successor.[76] Sabinus insulted even Chaerea, since his co-conspirator was at least willing to talk to Claudius to see what he intended to do in the face of his promotion by the Guard.

In point of fact, neither Chaerea nor Sabinus was ultimately permitted to approach and engage in dialogue with the future emperor. They were prevented from doing so by (Rufrius) Pollio, the new praetorian prefect (whom Claudius appointed – one of his first 'imperial' acts, we might think). Claudius ventured under guard to the Palatine, raising the question of what should be done with Chaerea. The general sentiment was that Chaerea had done a noble and honourable thing, but that the regicide, as it were, needed to be slain in turn as a deterrent against future such acts.[77]

And so Chaerea was taken off to be killed, and Lupus and others with him. Lupus (who had taken his orders from Chaerea in the matter of the death of Caesonia and the child, we might note) is said to have started to cry at his impending fate. Chaerea insulted him for his weakness, and met his end with bravery and fine bearing. Chaerea asked his executioner if he had experience in swordsmanship; at any rate he was slain by the first blow. Chaerea also asked that he be killed with the same weapon with which he had killed Caligula. The unfortunate Lupus took several blows to die, and kept nervously moving his neck.[78]

A few days later, the people made offerings to the shade of Chaerea, beseeching his ghost now to be vengeful against the apparently ungrateful

Romans. Sabinus was set free by Claudius and even allowed to maintain his rank – but guilt at the fate of his comrades in the conspiracy drove him to commit suicide. Claudius meanwhile confirmed what Caligula had decreed in the matter of Agrippa's rule, even adding the territories that his grandfather Herod had ruled – Judaea and Samaria.

Not surprisingly given the focus of his history, Josephus turns at once to the question of the conflict between the Jews and the Greeks in Alexandria, noting that under Caligula the Jews had suffered humiliation.[79] Claudius addressed the problem, acknowledging the insanity of his imperial predecessor in demanding that the Jews abandon their monotheistic traditions and worship him as a god.[80] Claudius essentially decreed that he wished for none of the Caligulan prescriptions to be maintained, and for order to be restored on the basis of the restoration of the *status quo ante*.

In addition to his *Jewish Antiquities*, Josephus also authored a *Jewish War* in seven books, which provides an account of the Jewish wars against the Romans from 170 BC to his own time.[81] Some of the material for this work naturally overlaps with the events covered in the *Antiquities*. The *Jewish War* is the earliest work of Josephus that we possess.

At 2.178-79, Caligula is referenced in the context of how Agrippa paid court to the young man on his trip to Rome in AD 36. We find the story of how one day at dinner Agrippa prayed that Caligula might replace Tiberius – and soon. One of Tiberius' household servants mentioned the comment, and Agrippa was cast into prison for the next six months, until the death of the aged emperor. Caligula freed Agrippa on his accession, and gave him the title of king and the tetrarchy of the late Philip.

The story of how Herod's wife Herodias was much vexed at the signal honours shown to Agrippa is also related. Herod travels to Italy to appeal to Caligula, but is banished for his greed to Spain. The Spanish detail is a good example of frustrating historical inconsistency on admittedly fairly minor points; in the *Antiquities* the Herodian exile is to Lugdunum.[82]

Caligula's insane desire to be made a god is next. There were executions and dismissals of the leading men of Rome, and the dispatch of the governor Petronius to Jerusalem to see to the erection of images of Caligula in the Temple. Caligula ordered that if there were any resistance to his edict, the Jews were to be killed and the nation reduced to a state of slavery. And so Petronius took three legions as well as Syrian auxiliaries, and prepared to march on Jerusalem.[83]

There were confused and disparate reactions among the Jews; some simply did not believe that war was imminent. Petronius soon reached Ptolemais in Galilee.[84] Here Josephus provides a brief digression on the geography of the place and certain curious properties associated with the locale (i.e. vitreous sand). Petronius left the statues of Caligula and the soldiers in Ptolemais, and proceeded deeper into Galilee, to Tiberias, where he addressed the people and noted the folly of resistance to what had already taken place in the other territories of the empire. The Jews protested that the traditions and laws of their ancestors would not permit the setting up of images of Caligula in the Temple, but Petronius noted that he too had his law, and that war would be the consequence of defiance of the emperor's new edict.

The Jews noted that they already sacrificed twice daily for the emperor and the Roman people, but that the injunction regarding the statues was impossible. Negotiations continued for some time. Petronius impressed on the Jewish authorities and people just how insane Caligula was, and how ruinous the whole prospect of rebellion would be for the Jewish people. But finally, Petronius indicated that he would try to reason with Caligula; either he would succeed and it would be for the benefit of all, or he would fail – in which case, he was ready to surrender his own life on behalf of the Jews.[85]

Petronius returned to Antioch, the capital of his Syrian province, where he wrote to Caligula.[86] Caligula replied that Petronius could be put to death for being dilatory in carrying out the orders. Fortunately the message was delayed for three months by storms at sea; meanwhile the ship bringing the news of Caligula's assassination was not delayed.

Caligula was dead after a reign of three years and eight months.[87] The army favoured Claudius as his successor, while the Senate was inclined to make war against Claudius, on the grounds that Caligula had been so brutal a ruler that they could not tolerate another *princeps*.[88]

What we find in the *Bellum Iudaicum*, then, is a mere outline or sketch of what Josephus expanded on in his *Antiquitates*. The details of the story are not exactly in order between the two works, but the general progress of the story is the same.

Josephus presents a detailed picture of certain aspects of Caligula's life and death. His record of the assassination of Caligula is of immense value in determining the exact course of events on that fateful January day, not least in the question of the topography of the temporary theatre for the Palatine Games, the players in the drama of the conspiracies and the immediate aftermath of the killing. The historian's examination of Caligula's foreign policy is largely confined to the problems in Judaea and Alexandria, where important kernels of information can be gleaned from his works despite the abiding sense that everything that went well for Judaea and Rome in this period happened because of the divine providence that saw to it that Caligula was justly punished for his insane presumption of divinity.

Chapter Six

The Evidence of Philo's *De Legatione ad Gaium*

From Josephus, we may move to the Alexandrian Jew Philo, a great scholar and contemporary of Caligula, who was born in about 20 BC.[1]

For the study of Caligula, Philo is valuable for his work on the embassy to Caligula concerning the problem of the relationship between the Alexandrian Greeks and Alexandrian Jews, an embassy in which he himself participated as a Jewish representative.[2]

The state of Rome after the death of Tiberius was one of immense prosperity and blessing, and the early days of Caligula were times of unrivalled majesty and splendour beyond words.[3] Rome enjoyed untold wealth, as well as a dominion that could rightly be said to stretch from the rising to the setting of the sun. The first part of the reign of Caligula was a veritable reborn Golden Age, the age of Saturn come again to Italy.[4]

In the eighth month of his reign, Caligula fell sick. This would be the autumn of AD 37, and the illness of the emperor is once again cited as the dividing line between the 'good' and the 'bad' divisions of his reign. Philo associates the sickness with the beginning of the autumn/winter closure of the sailing season; people were now confined to their homes, as it were, and a depressing atmosphere ensued. Everyone was worried that the darling emperor, the son of Germanicus and replacement for the cruel and savage tyranny of Tiberius, would be carried off by his illness. The world was afflicted by the bad news and evil tidings of the emperor's health, since Rome, after all, was mistress of the world.

The report that Caligula had recovered spread quickly through the realm, and the mood of the people changed for the better. For Philo, the happiness of the world on the occasion both of Caligula's accession and of his restoration to good health was like nothing heretofore. Humanity, in short, was fooled and foolhardy.[5] The blindness of men did not allow them to see that in reality, their lot in life had taken a dramatic turn for the worse, and that the time of their oppression and experience of horror was at hand.

For Caligula was now hopelessly insane, either because of the illness, or because he was no longer willing or able to mask furious and insane tendencies that had long been present.[6] The first sign of the new and horrid state of affairs was the death of Gemellus. Philo notes that Gemellus had more right to the principate than Caligula on account of his closer family tie to Tiberius; he was accused now of complicity in a conspiracy, though the historian notes that he was too young to have participated in such a venture.[7]

Philo cites the evidence of unspecified sources for the fact that had Tiberius lived but a little longer, he would have seen to the death of Caligula and the succession of Gemellus. For Philo, the evidence was already present that Caligula was unsuitable for rule. Caligula meanwhile strategized how he might manage to escape any blame for the death of Gemellus.

The subterfuge that Caligula is said to have employed was to announce publicly his close bond of affection and kinship with Gemellus. For Philo, Caligula took advantage of the sacred Roman tradition of the rights of a father over a son; nobody could question the authority of Caligula over Gemellus, and Caligula was also responsible for the state (as well as for his own imperial household). Philo uses the metaphor of a fighter in the arena who casts down his last opponent – a splendid image given the obsession of Caligula for the games and spectacle entertainments.

And so Gemellus was ordered to commit suicide. Philo notes that the officers assigned to oversee the enforced death were not able to touch the young man, given that it was considered sacrilegious to kill someone who descended from emperors. Caligula was respectful of tradition – a bizarre element of his depraved personality. Gemellus needed to be put out of the way, in short – but Caligula would maintain the solemn obligation of Roman *pietas*, we might say, by not having anyone directly kill the imperial youth.

Gemellus, unfortunately, was a bit too young. He had never seen anyone killed, and was apparently untrained in the military arts and thus ignorant of how to take his own life with the sword.[8] Gemellus thus initially asked for the soldiers to kill him; when they refused, he asked for advice on exactly how best to stab himself in the throat. After instruction, the grandson of Tiberius was at last able to take his own life – and Caligula had achieved his purpose, though with strict adherence to custom if not to law.

From Gemellus, Philo's Caligula proceeds to target Macro.[9] Philo recalls how Macro had been instrumental in helping to secure the principate for his new master. Tiberius is said to have been displeased with Caligula, given that the young man seemed overly attached to the family of his mother Agrippina, and that he knew that as soon as Caligula should take over the empire, Gemellus' days were numbered.

Beyond this, Tiberius recognized that Caligula was unfit and unqualified to rule, given his personality and temperament. Above all, Caligula was noted for his inconsistency.[10] Macro, if anything, was Caligula's tutor and *aide-de-camp* in working on his negative qualities, in order to assuage Tiberius' opposition. Macro even tried to argue to Tiberius that Caligula was in reality so modest that once Tiberius died, he would no doubt gladly yield to Gemellus in the matter of rule; modesty, after all, is often mistaken for guile, and in this Caligula had been unjustly prejudged.

Tiberius would believe none of it (the arguments could only have sounded preposterous) – but Macro resorted to a simple attestation of his loyalty to the regime. He had helped to destroy Sejanus, after all, and so Tiberius could trust him in this matter.[11]

Philo reports that Macro was more than willing to help Caligula, given that he was interested in currying the favour of the young man (whom he saw as the likeliest successor to the purple) – and there was also the question of Macro's wife. In Philo's version of events, Macro's (unnamed) wife is not involved in any seduction of Caligula at the behest of her husband; the whole matter is entirely her doing. Macro's wife was involved in advising her husband to do all he could to assist in defending Caligula. The praetorian prefect had no idea that he was aiding in his own mockery by an unfaithful wife by interceding for her paramour.

Philo provides snippets of evidence of how Macro became the tutor and aide to his would-be master. If Caligula fell asleep at a banquet, it was Macro who would wake him up, both because it would be rude to indulge in slumber on such occasions and because it was an easy way for someone to try to kill the young man unawares. If Caligula became overly excitable on account of the performance of mimes or some other cheap and vulgar entertainment, it was Macro who would try to restrain him.[12]

Macro's psychology was admittedly impeccable. He argued with Caligula that he should not behave like everyone else around him in the audience, since he was different from the crowd, far above all others in prosperity and good fortune. Macro presented to Caligula the image of the shepherd of the Roman flock, the leader and guardian of the people who must always find the noble elements in whatever he observed. The best art is that of government and the maintenance of the political order of the greatest empire the world has ever known. For Caligula to indulge in empty, unmanly and contemptible pursuits is beneath the dignity of the future prince and ruler of the world. Caligula – the inheritor of the Augustan mantle – is the helmsman whose hand is on the tiller of the ship of state.

Philo's Macro speaks in honorific platitudes and employs commonplace metaphors. One can almost imagine that the prefect really did try to use such arguments on a young man he thought incorrectly was impressionable and able to be manipulated.

Needless to say, Macro failed utterly in his attempts to rein in and to civilize his emperor.[13] Caligula would do the opposite of what Macro urged. When the prefect drew near, the rebellious young man would comment to his friends that Macro did not appreciate that Caligula no longer had any need of a teacher. For Caligula – who is made to deliver a lengthy address about the philosophical and biological underpinnings of his position – the soul of an emperor is in need of no education or improvement from the advice of a commoner. And so little by little, Caligula divorced himself from the authority of Macro and began to assert his independence. False charges followed, and were readily accepted. Caligula began to spread the report that Macro had boasted of how Caligula owed his life to him, of how on three occasions Tiberius had wished to kill Caligula, but Macro had saved his life. Caligula's charges against Macro included the claim that on the death of Tiberius, it was Macro to whom Caligula owed his successful claim to the throne.[14]

There were those who believed Caligula's charges against Macro, given that they were unaware of the duplicitous and conniving nature of the new emperor. Macro was soon compelled to commit suicide and his wife did the same, notwithstanding the fact that she had once been Caligula's mistress. In Philo's estimation, Macro had been sincere in his efforts to Caligula, but beneficence and goodwill are wasted on those who are plagued by ingratitude and a wicked disposition.[15]

From Macro's enforced suicide, Philo proceeds to the destruction of Marcus Silanus, the ill-fated father-in-law of the *princeps*. Once again, Philo's emphasis is on unrequited behaviour. Silanus acted like a father to Caligula, more than a father-in-law, continuing to court the emperor's favour and seeking to ingratiate himself with Caligula, even after his daughter had died. Caligula was not flattered by Silanus' attempts to advise and assist him – he was, on the contrary, insulted. Caligula hated his would-be teachers more than those who openly declared themselves to be his enemies – another interesting detail for those seeking to obtain something akin to a psychological portrait of the man.[16] And so Silanus was slain by treachery.

Philo notes that men began to speak about Caligula's atrocities and his penchant for murder and enforced suicide – though only quietly and in secret at first, out of a climate of fear.[17] There was also a general sense of disbelief that the emperor could have changed so quickly. In this, Philo presents a side of the Caligulan enigma that we do not find in our other extant sources. Men were confused by the transformation from beneficent bringer of a neo-Golden Age to monster, so they began to search for explanations – more specifically, for evidence, rationalization and justification that would excuse Caligula.

In the case of Gemellus, the argument was made that power cannot readily be shared, and that Caligula merely exercised the power of the stronger over the weaker – lest he himself be done in by an inferior, since clearly Gemellus would have tried to kill him given the chance. If Gemellus had been allowed to live, Rome might well have been plunged into yet another civil war – always the spectre that haunted both the Republic and the Empire. Government cannot function with factions and discord, with internecine strife and other signs of civil chaos. So Caligula was right to see to the untimely exit of Gemellus; it was for the good of the state. Philo's mob is made to serve as apologist for the regime. Had Caligula wished to justify his actions by public relations service, he could not have done better than hire the very crowd Philo presents as so eager to defend their new *princeps*.[18]

The case of Macro was easier for the general population to accept. He was thought to have risen too high above his station, to have behaved arrogantly and not to have understood his own self. Philo alleges that there was even talk of how he had ignored the Delphic maxim about self-knowledge.[19] Caligula was clearly the ruler, and Macro the subject, but the praetorian prefect had confused the natural order of things, so his fate was just. For Philo, the man in the street had forgotten that giving someone advice is not the same thing as trying to rule them.

Silanus was likewise dismissed as someone who had taken on haughty airs and had fatally misread his relationship with Caligula. The father-in-law had assumed that he was a father; the fathers of the powerful are usually content to step back and let their sons exercise their proper rule, but Silanus had dared to usurp the rights of a guardian and sire over the new emperor.[20] The death of Silanus' daughter should have spelled the end of the old man's attempted interference in Caligula's affairs, but instead it brought with it an increase in efforts to manipulate the new *princeps*.

With every effort of the mind and will, then, the people tried to argue that Caligula was a reasonable man and no tyrant.[21] The sudden change in Caligula's nature was otherwise inexplicable to them - they were possessed of a wish to excuse him at all costs.

Philo's Caligula had triumphed over the Senate, the equestrian order and in his own private life. Silanus had been a powerful senator, while Macro had been the most noteworthy of the equestrians in terms of authority and *gravitas* since the waning days of Tiberius. And Gemellus was of course a family problem. For Philo, the triple triumph of Caligula is what motivated the young ruler to seek to transgress all natural bounds and checks on mortal behaviour, and to consider himself to be a god. Early victory emboldened Caligula, and the people were complicit in the emperor's continuing spiral into insanity by virtue of their heartfelt desire to find excuses for everything that he did. It is a picture of inexorable, inevitable subversion of the order of the state, leading naturally to Caligula's intention to demand that he be venerated as a god even in the holy Temple in Jerusalem.[22]

Caligula is presented as rationalizing his divinity by noting that when men assume a pastoral office over sheep and goats, they are not themselves animals – they are men, a different class of being altogether, who have been entrusted with the responsibility of caring for (implicit) inferiors who are in need of protection and defence. Caligula is in charge of the herd of man, of the flock of humanity, and so he must himself not be a man, but some higher being – a god.

For Philo, Caligula first worked out this quasi-theological system in his head – and then, once he was satisfied that his reasoning was logical and sound, he began to share his findings with the public. Thus he compared himself to Dionysus, to Heracles, Castor and Pollux, while religious festivals and solemn occasions of commemoration of the deeds of demigods were taken as trivial compared to the power of the man who now controlled the vast Roman Empire. Caligula began to dress like a god, assuming the lion pelt that was associated with Heracles, and the club with which he had slain the Nemean Lion as one of his canonical labours. He also donned the fawn's hide and took up the ivy and *thyrsus* of the wine god.[23]

In an interesting twist on the polytheistic system of classical mythology, Caligula did not simply appropriate the iconography of one of the gods – he assumed the ornaments of them all. He was the *pantheos*, as it were – an 'all god' who assumed in himself and for himself all the rights and privileges of the many deities of Olympus, and of the lesser gods who populated the earth and sea. Philo notes rather amusingly that he was not like Geryon, the triple-bodied beast Heracles had defeated – he was more akin to Proteus, the marine god and shapeshifter. Whatever immortal he wanted to be on a given day, that god he emulated.

For Philo's strong moral sense, the emperor should have imitated the virtues of the gods, not their costumes and props.[24]

From the demigods and great heroes of mythology, the insatiably arrogant Caligula proceeded to rival even the most powerful of gods. Hermes, Apollo and Ares were all imitated. Once again he adopted the dress and costume of his desired divine role models. Soon enough there was confusion among the people, as they saw their emperor aspiring to be like a god, and yet in no way practicing the virtues that distinguished these immortals.[25] Philo outlines in detail how gods like Hermes brought great blessings to man, gifts that are symbolized by the traditional raiment and ornaments of the god – nothing of which pertained to the irrational Caligula.[26] At length, Philo rails against Caligula; the emperor was a laughing stock and worthy of derision for how he had done the opposite of what the great immortals had achieved for the betterment of their human charges.

Not surprisingly, then, Caligula was opposed to the Jews, since the Jewish people are monotheistic and devoted to the traditions of their elders.[27] The other nations and peoples of the world sought to gratify the insane aspirations of Caligula by currying his favour with every possible act of degradation and homage. Some in Italy even began to practice prostration before him.[28] For Philo, the Jews developed a unique status in the wake of Caligula's mad appropriation of divine airs. They preferred death to dishonour, and so they – the noble and great people of Abraham and Moses – were willing to sacrifice even their lives rather than to betray the traditions of their forefathers.

The Jews were ruled as slaves by Caligula's predecessors, since subject nations are always servants of their imperial masters.[29] But Caligula's predecessors are said to have ruled with a moderation that was quite absent from the young man's manual of governance.

Philo argues that the Alexandrians recognized that the Jews were now the object of hatred and enmity on the part of the emperor. The Alexandrians are said to have taken advantage of Caligula's attitude to give vent to their own disdain for the Jewish people, and they opportunistically began to persecute the Jews of that city. Jewish property was plundered, with riches and valuables stolen away.[30]

The possessions and real estate of the Jews was stolen, while the Jews themselves were confined to ghetto-like sections of the city. It was expected that the population would die through famine and unsafe, cramped living conditions that were prone to disease. Stifling heat and overcrowding contributed to the immense suffering of the Alexandrian Jews. Some tried to escape to the beaches. Jews who were found in now 'illegal' sections of Alexandria were stoned and assaulted with tiles and branches from trees, and men died from head wounds. Those Alexandrians with nothing better to do would surround a group of Jews, preventing their egress. Others waited in the harbour district to rob their easy prey. Some Jews were immolated in the very centre of the city, set on fire by mobs. Others were torn limb from limb, their bodies ravaged so terribly that no parts could be found for burial.

The governor did nothing, preferring to pretend that the riots and pogroms were not happening.[31] The Alexandrians knew that Caligula would not intervene, since he shared their hatred for the Jews, so they went so far as to set up images of the emperor in the public places of Jewish meeting and worship.[32] A bronze statue of Caligula was erected, with the emperor in a four-horse chariot.[33] For Philo, the point was not so much to honour Caligula as to humiliate the Jews (though certainly the emperor's appreciation of their adulation would be a wonderful fringe benefit).

Philo notes that the Alexandrians were not so eager to press for the display of divine honours and images of the Ptolemies in the temples and other public places of the Jews; the practice started only with Caligula.[34] Philo says that Tiberius ruled for twenty-three long years in Rome, and that Greece and Egypt were at peace under his reign – and yet there were no images of Tiberius set up in the Jewish temples of Alexandria, no divine honour shown to the adopted son of Augustus, no recognition of nearly a quarter century of prosperity in the East.

Philo proceeds to a long panegyric of Augustus.[35] Once again the emphasis is on all that Augustus did: he pacified and quelled the tides of civil strife throughout the Mediterranean world; he brought the blessings of serenity to men far and wide in the dominions under Roman sway. Augustus was sovereign ruler over Egypt for forty-three years, and yet never did the Alexandrians honour him with a portrait, an image, a painting or anything of the like. He was ignored, just like Tiberius after him. For Philo, if anyone deserved what the Alexandrians decided to award to Caligula, it was the great Augustus.[36] Augustus was acknowledged as a god after his death, the object of veneration and apotheosis, and Alexandria is filled with beautiful works of art in his honour – but never was there any effort to install his image in Jewish precincts.

Philo argues that the reason the Alexandrians were respectful of Jewish sensibilities was because Augustus understood that respect for the traditions and rights of individual nations was a hallmark of justice and peaceful exercise of power. Augustus knew that the Jews recoiled from any claim that a man was a god – and indeed, Augustus never wanted to be called a god by any individual.[37] Augustus respected the rights of the Jews who lived in Rome, and never forced any sort of dishonourable edict on them. Philo argues that Augustus even respected the Sabbath, noting that when there was a distribution of grain that happened to fall on the Sabbath (when no Jews could engage in the work necessary to retrieve the dole), Augustus would ensure that some grain was reserved for the Jews to acquire on the morrow.

Tiberius continued the tolerant practice of his predecessor, though Philo alludes to charges made against the Jews under the tyranny of Sejanus.[38]

Tiberius is said to have understood, after the fall of Sejanus, that the Jews were innocent of the calumnies spoken against them by his disgraced praetorian prefect.

But then there was Caligula. For Philo, the new emperor first said he was god – but then he actually began to believe it. In the Alexandrians, Caligula found the perfect people to indulge his whims. Philo condemns the Alexandrians for being master of abject flattery and abasement before would-be gods. He mocks their inclination to worship snakes and other sacred animals of traditional Egyptian religion and mythology.[39] Caligula assumed that the Alexandrians really did venerate him as a god and consider him to be divine, not appreciating that they spoke in the same way quite readily of any number of creatures.

Certain Alexandrians began to notify Caligula of what was being done in his honour in the city; with time, Caligula began to associate the Alexandrians with the best practices of homage and reverence to his honour. One great supporter of the Alexandrian Egyptians was the slave Helicon, for Philo a thoroughly disreputable and disgusting individual who had served under Tiberius, but who truly came into his own in the reign of Caligula.[40] Philo's Helicon seems all too aware that in Caligula, the pretentious slave had a ready audience for his quick wit and agile mockery of his targets – of whom the Jews were his principal concern.

Helicon began to impress upon Caligula how deplorable the Jews really were.[41] He was aided in his efforts by the bribes that the Alexandrians were said to have sent him to aid their cause. Helicon meanwhile exercised with Caligula, joining the emperor at leisure, in the baths and at meals. He was invested with enormous responsibilities and authorities in the imperial household. Most of all, he was the recipient of the gift of time – he had plenty of opportunities in which to speak to the emperor and to indulge the emperor's fancies. Helicon was a master of satire; his charges against the Jews were especially appealing precisely because of how wittily and craftily he constructed them.

The Jews, meanwhile, were at a loss as to what to do in their own defence. They had no idea if Helicon was actually working out of anti-Semitic prejudices or merely opportunistic whims.[42] The decision was at last taken that the Jews should prepare a document that outlined their position with respect to the charges and actions of the Alexandrians. The proposed document is said to have been a shorter version of one sent by Agrippa, who had visited the Alexandrian Jews en route to take up his new rule in the East.[43]

The Jewish representatives met with Caligula in Rome. They were at first gratified by the seemingly warm and affable reception they received from the emperor, but Philo was distrustful and worried that Caligula was practicing his signal characteristic of dissimulation. Philo and some few others of the embassy were worried that Caligula had already decided to agree with the Alexandrians, and that he was being duplicitous with the Jewish contingent.

Philo recalls that the Jews travelled from Rome to Puteoli with Caligula. Soon word arrived that the emperor had decided to demand that his statue be set up in the Temple in Jerusalem, a statue dedicated under the name of Jupiter.[44] Philo and his compatriots were immediately plunged into a state of uncertainty as to the best course of action in the face of this shocking and unexpected news, fearing for their lives and the fate of their nation. They learned that the emperor was convinced of his divinity, and that he considered the Jews to be the only people in the empire who would resist the proclamation of this godhood.[45]

Philo notes further that Caligula was stirred up by reports from the publican Capito.[46] A thoroughly unscrupulous sort in Philo's estimation, Capito had taken advantage of his position in Judaea in the wake of controversy concerning divine honours for Caligula. A makeshift altar had been erected to the emperor at Jamneia by troublemakers,[47] and the Jews had torn it down in a rage over the insult to their religious traditions. Caligula, informed of the whole affair, had ordered that an even more impressive altar should be constructed. Helicon encouraged him in this, as did the tragic actor Apelles. For Philo, Helicon was simply a scorpion masquerading as a slave, and Apelles a Greek from Ascalon whose inhabitants were notoriously anti-Semitic.[48]

So Caligula sent his notorious order to the Syrian governor Petronius to see to the erection of his statue. Petronius was ordered to bring half the armed forces from the Euphrates to be prepared to kill anyone who tried to interfere with the plan. Philo's Petronius is reminiscent of Josephus'; the governor was aware that he was caught between the seriousness of Caligula's orders and the implication of a threat to his own life should he fail to execute them (and quickly), and the fact that the Jews were highly unlikely to consent to any such degradation or abomination as that envisaged by the emperor.

The Temple was too sacred a Jewish site for any tolerance of what Caligula was demanding.[49]

Philo's Petronius, however, has an aspect of his character that is not found in Josephus (at least not to any great degree). Petronius in the *De Legatione* is worried at the vast power of the Jewish diaspora. If the Jews of the world should unite, he fears Rome would face a quite serious military threat. He was worried about the Jews beyond the Euphrates, in Babylon and elsewhere, and anxious about the Jews who came to the Temple for offerings and sacrifices, and who might rise up against Roman arrogance in the face of Caligula's demands.

Petronious ultimately came to the conclusion that if he acceded to Caligula's wishes, there was the likelihood of war with the Jews, and the outcome of the war was at least in doubt. Yet if he disobeyed Caligula, it was certain that he would face death. The Roman officials with Petronius agreed that there was really no recourse against Caligula – but there was a respite.[50] Caligula had, after all, not sent a statue from Rome for the Temple – and he had not ordered the selection of a statue from Syria. He wanted a new statue, and that would take time and effort to construct – time that could be spent in delay and prevarication. One could ask for only the best craftsmen to be assembled – and that would of course engender even more delay. There were myriad ways to slow down the whole process – and in this Petronius settled on his, at least temporary, salvation.

Petronius also began to try to remonstrate with the leading men of the Jewish state. His efforts failed, as the Jewish authorities were in no way prepared to argue the Caligulan (or Petronian for that matter) cause to their people. Soon enough, a great number of Jews were advancing on Petronius' position in Phoenicia; the Romans were stunned at the great number of Jews – Philo says that they woefully underestimated the population.[51]

The Jews made their appeal to Petronius. They noted that when the news had been delivered to his gubernatorial predecessor Vitellius that Caligula was emperor, the Jewish Temple was perhaps the first site to witness sacrifices being made on behalf of the new *princeps*. The message now is clear: the Jews will willingly face slaughter before they will tolerate any desecration of their most sacred precinct. Philo offers another of his highly rhetorical speeches: there will be no need of any army for Petronius to conquer the Jews; they will willingly become a living Greek tragedy, as family members and priests conduct the sacrificial killings of those who prefer death to dishonour.[52]

Death was a welcome alternative to disgrace – but the Jews do make a request to Petronius that he permit them to make an embassy of appeal to Caligula himself. The governor was by nature disposed to kindliness; he appreciated the reasonableness of the petition. Philo's Petronius allegedly had some knowledge of Jewish philosophy and culture – or at the very least, God was directing the course of events. He consulted with his officers and counsellors, and everyone was now in a more tolerant position regarding the rightness of the Jewish cause. Petronius ordered that those working on the statue proceed in a slow and painstaking manner; it was easy, after all, to claim that he merely wanted to ensure that the finished product was worthy of the emperor.

Petronius, however, was not willing in the end to grant the petition for an embassy to Caligula.[53] Considering the idea to be fraught with peril, his alternate course was to send his own letter to Caligula. He would note that there were delays in the construction, and that he was concerned that the Jews be occupied with the work of the harvest and agriculture. Petronius knew that the emperor was planning to visit Alexandria, and that because of the difficulties of winter sailing, he would be inclined to travel not by the most direct route, but by a circuitous path that would involve hugging the shore as he travelled by sea and land alike down the Syrian coast. Food and provisions would be needed to supply the journey, and surely Caligula would appreciate this and recognize the forethought of his governor.

The missive was sent to Caligula, but Petronius' idea backfired. The emperor became angrier as he read the letter. Caligula derided Petronius as being arrogant as well as cowardly, clearly having more regard and compassion for the Jews, and fear for the possibility of their uprising, than he had respect and reverence for his emperor.

Philo's Caligula is crafty: he orders that a letter be prepared for Petronius in which the governor is carefully praised and ordered not to worry so much about harvest, but to focus on the completion of the statue.

Fortuitously, Agrippa soon thereafter visited Caligula, and he immediately recognized that the emperor was furious and greatly vexed with someone.[54] After a time, Caligula finally confided in him, revealing to Agrippa that he was angry at the Jewish people who alone among men were obstinate in their refusal to accept his divinity.

Agrippa's reaction was dramatic, essentially fainting away and having to be carried home by his attendants on a stretcher. Caligula was made even angrier at the Jews by this development, wondering what the reaction to his edicts among the Jews would be if even Agrippa had such a dramatic response to the idea of the erection of the emperor's statue in the Temple.

Agrippa remained in a coma; when he recovered, he prepared to send a letter to Caligula with his own petition.[55] Agrippa pleaded the cause of the Jewish people and nation, noting that from the start of the new emperor's reign, they had been among the first to recognize and pay homage to the new master of Rome. The Jews, Agrippa argued, loved Caligula both in spirit and in truth – not merely in empty and fawning words.

Agrippa praises the glories of Jerusalem, noting the splendour of all the Jewish colonies that originated from that storied, great capital. He notes that he has never asked for Roman citizenship to be conferred on the Jews, or even for remission of taxes and tribute – and this despite his great loyalty to and close friendship with his beloved emperor. But this one thing he will ask: the safety and security of the Temple, free from images of anyone. Agrippa notes that Caligula's grandfather Agrippa visited the Temple, and that Augustus had also praised it.[56] Reverence for the sanctity of the place had ensured that no one should in any way transgress the traditions and customs of that holy place and sacred locale. Neither Augustus nor Tiberius violated the rights and customs of the precinct.

Agrippa recalls the arrogance of the governor Pilate in demanding that shields be set up in Herod's palace in the holy city, shields that did not even have the imperial image on them.[57] Pilate was beseeched by the Jewish authorities to remove the provocative emblems, but he refused and was threatened with an appeal to Tiberius. Worried that his myriad faults would be laid bare before the emperor, he was furious with the Jews. Tiberius was in the end made aware of what Pilate had done, and in anger he ordered that the shields be transferred to Caesarea Augusta on the coast.[58]

Agrippa's point was simple: if the Jews had reacted thus to the mere shields that Pilate had erected in Herod's palace, how would they respond to a colossal statue of the divine Caligula in their very Temple?

Agrippa praises the example of Tiberius and especially of Augustus, the latter at length. Even Livia offered the example of Roman respect and honour for the Jewish customs and traditions regarding their worship of the one true God.[59]

We might think that Philo's lengthy account of Agrippa's alleged appeal to Caligula offers a daring portrait of a brave man taking enormous risks. There is almost an implicit quality of defiance to the address. For if Caligula were the supreme god, then there would be no point in showing any honour at all to the supposed 'one true God' of the Jews.

Agrippa reminds Caligula that the new emperor saved him from the bonds and fetters of Tiberius – but that if he were to persist in his insistence on the erection of the statue of in Jerusalem, it would be a soul-killing gesture against the Jewish Agrippa. The king pledged that he would surrender all his honours and titles, and willingly so, were the emperor to desist from this one course of action.

The letter was sent, and Agrippa was plunged into a state of unrest and concern about the outcome of the matter. Caligula was filled with bitterness about the possible loss of his statue, but he began to soften.[60] The emperor was of two minds about Agrippa: on the one hand he seemed too subservient to his Jewish heritage, while on the other he had at least been honest with Caligula.[61] But in the end, Caligula wrote to Petronius and advised him to abandon the statue project.

However, there was a codicil.[62] If anyone outside Jerusalem wished to set up an image of Caligula, any attempt at obstruction or counter-intervention should result in Petronius' punishing them or sending the culprits to Caligula. The emperor had a simple plan: those who wanted to discredit the Jews and to foment civil discord would begin to erect statues of Caligula everywhere they could; the Jews would not tolerate the presence of so many images in their ancestral domains. Caligula would punish the Jews who tried to prevent the execution of imperial honours, and one possible penalty (depending on how out of control the situation became) would be to change his mind about the statue in the Temple.

Philo attributes it to divine providence that what Caligula assumed would happen, did not.[63] That said, Caligula was already of a mind to alter his decree, and already planning to disregard his concession to Agrippa and his new orders to Petronius. He ordered the casting of a colossal statue of himself in Rome, a statue that could be transported to the East. He intended that he would deliver it while en route to Alexandria for his planned imperial sojourn in Egypt. For Caligula, Alexandria was the very home and fountain of the image of divinity that he craved.[64]

Philo digresses at this juncture in his narrative to comment on the instability and unpredictability of Caligula. He notes that if ever the emperor did anything of a kindly or beneficial nature, he at once had an abiding sense of deep regret. On one occasion he freed several prisoners, only soon thereafter to have them arrested again, this time with a stiffer sentence and more dire punishments precisely because he had given them hope of release and liberty. Others who expected to be killed, he sent into exile, yet soon enough soldiers were sent to slaughter them all.[65]

If Caligula gave money to someone, he expected to be repaid at ruinous costs to the beneficiary of the original largesse. Lavish expenditures ruined the finances of those who felt that they needed to entertain the emperor in the highest style.

No one suffered the calamitous reign of Caligula more than the Jews.[66] Starting in Alexandria, he ordered all the holy places of the Jewish religion to be filled with the image of Caligula. He prepared to carry out his plan to have the Temple in Jerusalem transformed into the Temple of Caligula under the title of Jupiter Manifest.[67]

Philo proceeds to the description of the actual embassy in which he took part.[68] The account is meant to create suspense and a feeling of dread. At first things seem quite at variance with the author's earlier mention of the embassy.[69] The judge (that is, Caligula) is depicted as glowering with the scowling visage of a tyrannical despot. But then Philo surprises his audience by noting that nothing of the sort (that is, nothing of the sort that one usually expects in a *de facto* kangaroo court) took place. Caligula had been spending several days in nearby gardens (some of which had once belonged to Augustus' courtier Maeceneas). Philo and his associates entered with respectful, bowed heads and addressed Caligula as Augustus. The emperor responded with mildness and kindness, affability and warmth – such that Philo and the others were immediately in despair not only for their case, but also for their very lives.

For then, Caligula asked if these were the haters of god, the only men on earth who did not acknowledge his divinity.[70] He proceeded to curse them, with language that Philo indicates it was sinful even to hear, let alone to recall or quote.

The Alexandrian Greeks, in contrast, were in a state of absolute joy as they beheld Caligula insulting the Jewish ambassadors. They danced and blessed the name of the emperor and god. One of the worst of the lot, a certain Isidorus, addressed Caligula and noted that the Jews could not even countenance the idea of sacrificing in honour of the emperor.

The Jews objected at once, noting that they had conducted three solemn sacrifices: the first when Caligula assumed the throne, the second when he had recovered from his serious illness and the third in hope of the emperor's victory in Germany.[71]

Caligula noted that even if the Jews had ordered such sacrifices, they had made them to another god and not to him. In the meantime he continued to inspect garden villas, leading the Alexandrian Greeks and Jews about as the former heaped opprobrium and insult on the latter.

At one point, the emperor suddenly and with no contextual basis asked Philo and the Jews why they abstained from pork. The Greeks began to laugh. Their laughter was so obnoxious that Caligula's own servants sought to quiet them, feeling that the whole attitude of the Greek contingent was disrespectful to the imperial dignity. The Jews answered that different people had different customs. Someone interjected that there are those who do not eat lamb, though it is easily obtainable – at which Caligula laughed and indicated that he was no particular fan of lamb himself.

Philo records that Caligula then asked about the question of citizenship and what claims the Jews asserted on this point.[72] When the replies were dignified and the arguments sound, Caligula began to interrupt the proceedings with orders for this or that detail of the furnishings of the rooms of the villa he was just then inspecting. Distraction and lack of orderly focus in the conversation were the order of the day. Philo and his associates all expected death; they could do no more than to pray to God almighty that they might be spared to see another day. And to God does Philo credit their salvation, as Caligula is said to have reached the conclusion that the Jews were nothing more than fools, and that he was done with the whole proceedings and was departing – and that the Jews should make their exit as well.

Philo concludes his account of the 'Legation to Gaius' by noting that for a moment, at least, the very fate of the Jewish people was in the hands of the five men who represented Jewish interests before the emperor. He sums up by noting that he has provided a study of why Caligula hated the Jews – but that he must also provide a 'palinode'. The term is mysterious, but has been taken to refer to another work of Philo, in which he would offer the 'reversal' of the present treatment of the emperor's anti-Semitism. This would either be a work on the better fortunes of the Jews under his successor Claudius, or, perhaps, on the assassination of Caligula. There is no evidence that Philo ever wrote his 'palinode', so the *De Legatione* ends on a note of mystery.

Chapter Seven

The Evidence of Philo's *In Flaccum*

The *De Legatione ad Gaium* that we have just examined closely is generally considered to be rather unhelpful in terms of providing a clearer portrait of Caligula than that which is found in, say, the works of Suetonius, Dio Cassius and Tacitus. It offers a testimony, however, to the impact of Caligula on a representative of a foreign people, a Hellenized Jew from Alexandria who was learned in both philosophy and history, a great scholar and luminary of his day. At the very least, we catch a glimpse of Caligula from the pen of someone who had actually met him and known fear in his presence.

Besides the *De Legatione*, there is another work of Philo of significance for our examination of the *princeps* Caligula: the treatise against (Aulus Avillius) Flaccus.[1] Scholars cannot determine exactly what the relationship is between this work and the *De Legatione*, though it seems that we have pieces of a composite work, some of which is either missing or was never composed. We do well to note that despite the voluminous remains of Philo's work, there are a number of significant unknown details in his life, not least fixed dates – in fact only the famous embassy to Gaius provides a reasonable chronological marker, and even that is of imprecise timing (AD 39-40 is the generally cited time frame).[2]

We owe much of what we know about Philo to the fourth-century ecclesiastical historian Eusebius, who provides a convenient catalogue of what he knew to be the works of the Alexandrian Jewish scholar.[3] Eusebius notes that in addition to a large number of texts that he cites by title, there were single works, including one on the Jews – but it is not entirely certain to which works of Philo Eusebius' reference should be applied.[4]

Eusebius records that Philo came to Rome in the time of Caligula – this would be the embassy – and that during the reign of Claudius, he recited before the Senate an account of the misdeeds of Caligula.[5] Philo's work was so highly regarded that he was accorded a place in the libraries of Rome.

It is possible then (if not plausible) that there was originally a three-part work, of which the first part is entirely missing (this would have focused on the mistreatment of the Jews under Sejanus, *inter alia*). The second part is the present work under consideration, the *In Flaccum* that bridges, if one will, the period between Tiberius and Caligula – and then there is the *De Legatione*.[6] The *In Flaccum* is of less relevance to the study of Caligula than the account of the legation – but it does preserve some interesting references to the emperor.

Aulus Avillius Flaccus was appointed prefect in Egypt by Tiberius. Philo records that he was in office for five years under Tiberius, and one under Caligula.[7] Philo details at some length how competent and indeed laudable Flaccus' administration of Egypt was, especially in the first years of his prefecture. He identifies the death of Tiberius as the break between the admirable and the execrable portions of Flaccus' rule; he speculates that the prefect may have been profoundly saddened by the death of his patron, essentially 'never the same' thereafter.

What is of particular interest for a study of Caligula, however, is the report that Flaccus was a supporter of Tiberius Gemellus.[8] This partisanship makes sense in that Flaccus was unquestionably loyal to Tiberius, and so he might well have been expected to support the emperor's grandson – but we hear very little in our extant sources of any support for Gemellus.

Flaccus is also cited as having been one of the voices in a chorus of attack against Agrippina. Philo indicates that Flaccus may well have worried that he would be persecuted after the accession of Caligula, but how this legitimate fear of persecution accounts for a dereliction of his duties as prefect is unclear.[9]

We have a picture, then, of a loyal Tiberian in power in Alexandria, who hears first of the death of his beloved emperor, and soon thereafter of the death of Gemellus.[10] Philo's description of Flaccus' reaction to the news is reminiscent of what we saw with Agrippa's response to the report that Caligula intended to erect his statue in the Temple in Jerusalem. The prefect is stunned and in profound silence, convinced that he too would soon follow in some elimination of all the perceived enemies of Caligula.

Flaccus had one source of hope, however: he was friends with Sutorius Macro. Macro had helped Caligula to assure his succession, and could perhaps be trusted to ensure the survival of Flaccus. Philo echoes the report that Macro defended Caligula to Tiberius when the emperor wanted to eliminate the young man. Tiberius is said to have thought that Caligula was ill-suited to rule, and that Gemellus would be dead soon after Caligula came to power.[11] Macro argued that Caligula would surrender or yield power to Gemellus. If this was truly an argument the prefect raised, how Tiberius could ever have believed this is difficult to grasp.

Macro tried to treat Caligula post-purple in the same way as he had treated him before – with fatal consequences. Macro, his wife and his children were all slain.[12] A reported quote of Caligula is preserved - when he would be with his friends and see Macro approaching, he would urge that everyone immediately start to look dour, since Macro was such a critic of alleged wanton and careless behaviour.

The death of Macro, then, propelled Flaccus into an even more dismal state of despair.[13] For Philo, the consequence of this despair was an increasingly perilous and desperate situation for the people of Alexandria.[14] Flaccus began to act as inconsistently as Caligula in his worst moments: former friends were now regarded as enemies, and former avowed enemies were now treated as friends. The latter, seemingly favoured group, however, took no pleasure in their sudden reversal of fortune – they remained as hostile and untrusting of Flaccus as before.

In short, Flaccus was soon manipulated by those around him. Men took advantage of the situation to put forth their own proposals and to compel Flaccus to support them and to act on them in his power as prefect.[15]

The point of the attempted takeover of the government, as it were, was the persecution of the Jews. For Philo, the Greeks in Alexandria had long been hateful of the Jews, and now they took advantage of the weak position of the prefect to launch their attack. The logic used by the Alexandrians against the Jews was as follows: the prefect had lost the support of Tiberius; Gemellus was dead; Caligula was now in power and Macro was also gone. The only recourse Flaccus had was to rely on the support of his Alexandrian subjects, and they would assist him in presenting a virtual sacrifice to Caligula – the Jewish population.

Philo records that Flaccus was at once moved by the argument. He initially proceeded slowly, moving against the Jews only in passive aggressive displays of hostility – but later proceeded openly against them.[16]

Meanwhile, Caligula had enriched Agrippa with the honours and expansions of his territory that we have already seen detailed in other sources. Agrippa was preparing to travel back to the East from Rome, so as to see his new territories and to organize them and consolidate his rule. Caligula advised him to travel through Alexandria for the sake of an easier and more pleasant journey from Brundisium, and so Agrippa headed for Alexandria – though he was aware that the Alexandrians were hateful of the Jews, and he feared that they would especially resent the news that Caligula had so favoured a Jew in the monarchy and administration of Eastern territories. As for sightseeing, he had seen Alexandria already in the days of Tiberius – for now, he wished to come in and exit as quickly as possible.

The Greeks immediately informed Flaccus that the arrival of Agrippa was a sign of the prefect's own undoing. Here was a king, accompanied by an armed retinue. Here was a king who was intruding on the territory of another potentate, and there was no good reason why Agrippa had to make a sojourn to Egypt en route to Syria. Even if Caligula had ordered the journey, a reasonable man would have protested that such a course of action was disrespectful to the prefect.

Flaccus was easily persuaded that all of these comments were valid and true, and he began to grow quite intensely hateful of Agrippa, though in public and to his face he dissimulated.[17] Flaccus did nothing, however, to prevent a heap of abuse from being poured on Agrippa by the Alexandrians, and the Jewish king was soon the object of all manner of derisive and inappropriate comment and insult. Flaccus was a party to it all by his very silence; he was clearly encouraging the mistreatment of his honoured guest.[18]

Philo provides one memorable and noteworthy example of the bitter treatment to which Agrippa was subjected – the strange story of the lunatic madman Carabas.[19] Carabas used to spend day and night raving in the streets naked. A mob decided to drive him to the gymnasium at Alexandria and to dress him up in mock royal robes, all to put him forth as a pathetic imitation of Agrippa whom they could insult and abuse openly in lieu of any direct attack on the king.

Flaccus did nothing when he learned of this incident. He did not reprimand anyone for it, and he most certainly did not order an end to the spectacle. And so soon enough, the Alexandrians proceeded to what we might call the next stage of their plan – they made a call for setting up images of the emperor in public places, as well as meeting houses and other precincts and dwellings. Philo's Flaccus was well aware that the Jews of Alexandria would never stand for such a course of events to unfold. He also knew that anything he permitted or encouraged in Egypt would soon be liable to spread throughout the vast regions of the Roman East, where the Jewish population was considerable.

Flaccus sanctioned what amounts in Philo's report to the start of anti-Semitic pogroms. The Jewish rights that had been protected since the days of Augustus were suddenly in turmoil, and the Jews of Alexandria were now in a decidedly second-class state of citizenship. Their public places were seized, and even their very citizenship was called into question.[20] The exact legal specifications of what did or did not happen in Alexandria at this time are uncertain, but what is clear enough from Philo's account is that whatever happened *contra Iudaeos*, Flaccus did nothing to prevent it and in fact aided and abetted the Alexandrian attacks on the Jewish population. Jewish property was pillaged, the Jews were driven out of even their ghettoes in the city and flocked to the beaches to escape persecution; the Jewish workshops that had been closed for the sake of mourning the death of Caligula's sister Drusilla were ransacked.[21] Poverty ensued because of unemployment, as the Jews were driven from both home and livelihood.

Conditions of famine were artificially induced, and Jewish women and children perished.[22] Men were slaughtered in the streets of the city and torn limb from limb, deprived even of burial rights. Families were immolated in the streets. Philo's description is vivid and unrelenting in its recollection of the savagery of the persecutions.[23] Those who mourned the death and suffering of friends and kinsmen were arrested, tortured and finally crucified.

Jewish leaders were detained and subjected to scourging by order of Flaccus.[24] The prefect was now quite open in his alliance with the Alexandrian terrorizing of the Jews. The mask had come off, and the complicity of Flaccus in the whole affair was now laid bare.[25] There was no respite or respect for Roman holidays and civil observances. The torture and execution of the Jews continued, even during such normally relaxed and sacred times. From dawn to the third or fourth hour there was a spectacle 'entertainment' in which Jews were scourged and otherwise tormented, all before dancers and mimes began their perverse show.

Flaccus is also said to have claimed that the Jews were stockpiling weapons as if to aid rebellion.[26] There was an immediate search of the residences in the Jewish sections of the city, but no weapons were found, either offensive or defensive – not even kitchen utensils.

Jewish women were subject to all manner of outrages; dragged into the theatre, they were compelled to eat pork.[27] Those who submitted to the porcine outrage were freed, but those who maintained the traditions of their people were mercilessly tortured.

Flaccus was deceptive with the Jews.[28] When they had appealed to him for the right to send a letter to Caligula, he indicated that he would testify to their loyalty to the emperor and to the Roman state, promising by solemn assurance that he would aid in the promotion of the Jewish cause in Rome.[29] The prefect's intentions were certain, however: he had no intention of aiding the Jews, and on the contrary, he intended to support the Alexandrian argument that the Jews were the only nation on earth that was hostile to Caligula and Rome.

The Jews had a saviour, however, in the person of King Agrippa. When he was informed of what Flaccus was doing and countenancing, he agreed to support the grievances of the persecuted community with Caligula.[30] There was divine providence as well, which favours the cause of justice. Flaccus would not last long in office under Caligula.

Flaccus had been engaged in abject flattery of Caligula, sending letters filled with praise and encomiums to his new master. But soon enough, a centurion by the name of Bassus arrived in Alexandria with an armed contingent from Caligula. Bassus exercised the greatest secrecy on landing and disembarking, wanting no knowledge of his arrival to reach Flaccus. Bassus inquired as to the location of the local military commander; he wanted to be certain he had the support of as many soldiers as he needed for his task.[31] The centurion learned that commander and prefect alike were dining with Stephanio, a *libertus*, or freedman, of Tiberius. He set out for the place, sending one of his men dressed as if an attendant to go ahead to maintain the subterfuge. The soldier reconnoitred the place and determined that Flaccus was barely defended, with something like ten or fifteen slaves and not much more in his retinue. And so the signal was given, and Bassus' men swooped in to make their arrest.

At once, Flaccus realized that Caligula had ordered his doom.[32] The companions of the prefect were frozen; they could not leave the spot, and it was uncertain just how extensive the raid was in the matter of victims. Flaccus was led away. Philo notes that the whole scene was one of complete justice – from the comfortable setting of hearth and dinner, the wicked prefect was led off to his amply merited end – Flaccus had, after all, destroyed the hearths and cozy home life of so many Jews.[33]

Philo attributes the arrest of Flaccus to his mistreatment of the Jews.[34] The time of the arrest, he notes, was the autumn season of Jewish festival.[35] When the word arrived in the Jewish community that Flaccus had been arrested by order of Caligula, no one at first believed the report (we may compare the similar instances occasioned by the death of Tiberius and Caligula). It was assumed that this was all a trick of the prefect to provoke and instigate still further charges against them.

But soon it was clear that the report was true, and prayers of thanksgiving were offered to God in grateful appreciation for his apparent deliverance of the Jewish people.[36]

Flaccus had a difficult sea voyage back to Rome. It was autumn/early winter and a bad time to sail – more evidence for Philo of the enduring justice of God. In Rome, he was prosecuted by the same Isidorus and Lampo who recently had been so friendly with him in Alexandria, and so instrumental in the persecution and pogroms against the Jews.

Lampo, Philo notes, had been tried in Alexandria for impiety against Tiberius.[37] He was acquitted, but the memory of his difficult straits and alleged mistreatment under Flaccus' rule rankled, so he had scores to settle against the disgraced prefect.

Isidorus is described as a rabble-rouser and drunkard, a general opportunist and seeker of advancement by the fomenting of trouble and discord.[38] He was annoyed and irritated with Flaccus simply because he thought that he had been held in high esteem by the prefect, only to learn that he was considered to be of little importance. And so crowds were suborned to launch accusations against Flaccus.

The change of attitude on the part of Isidorus came as a complete shock to Flaccus, and to others. It was assumed at the very least that someone had paid the mob to trump up charges against the prefect. The tide eventually turned against Isidorus, who fled Alexandria in fear of Flaccus. The prefect fatally did nothing to move against him, convinced that once the scoundrel was out of the city, there would be no further trouble from him.[39] But Isidorus made his way to Rome, where he found a readier audience for his complaints about Flaccus.

Throughout his narrative, Philo is moralistic. He seeks to illustrate the justice of the divine providence by which Flaccus was condemned, and elaborates at rhetorical length on the appropriateness of the whole sequence of misfortunes. Flaccus was deprived of his property; Philo takes care to detail that this was an especially hard blow for him to bear, given the vast wealth that he enjoyed.[40] He was sentenced to be exiled to the Aegean island of Gyaros, though Lepidus is said to have interceded successfully to have his prison island exchanged for the comparatively more pleasant locale of Andros, the much larger island close by to Gyaros.

Again, in classic Philonic style, the narrative describes how Flaccus went from Rome to Brundisium into exile by the same route he had traversed years before when he had been appointed prefect in Egypt. Now in disgrace, all his arrogance had led to this moment, one both pitiable in the human sense and eminently just in the divine. He was subjected to incessant mockery along the entire path of his travels, the once mighty man now an object of insult and derision, especially for those who remembered his earlier parade in glory.

The journey to Greece and past the many islands of the Aegean was of course difficult; everything Flaccus experienced was a discomfort and source of grief.[41] Flaccus is said to have begun to weep as he saw the island of Andros, contrasting his fate in exile to his upbringing in Italy, noting that he had been a schoolmate of Gaius and Lucius Caesar, and one entrusted with the oversight of Egypt for six years.[42]

It seemed at first that Flaccus had gone insane. He began to rave like a lunatic after his Roman escort had dropped him off on the island, and he poured out his laments in fevered speeches to anyone who would listen.[43] This is again Philo at his rhetorical best, as he imagines the disgraced prefect in a hell of his own making, punished justly for what he had dared to do against the undeserving Jewish people. It is a vivid portrait of the fate of an exile under Caligula, though for once the banishment is of someone who would appear eminently deserving of his fate.

Some months later, Flaccus was living in solitude on Andros when it is said that around midnight, he arose with a frenzy that was like the Corybantes (they were associated with ecstastic rituals in honour of the Phrygian/Trojan mother goddess Cybele; armed dancers with drums and all manner of loud revelry in honour of the goddess). He raised his voice to heaven, and declared the justice of his fate, enumerating his wrongs against the Jews. He was stricken with palpitations, and a trembling throughout his body, shaken to his very core with anticipatory dread of the end that he knew was soon at hand. He feared that everyone who approached him was a potential bringer of death, but he was not able to bring himself to commit suicide, however, for the perverse reason that he knew that he still had more to suffer, to atone and expiate for his manifold maleficence.[44] Again, it is a memorable portrait of torment and despair, but is the sort of narrative that justly renders historians sceptical of its value as evidence of any fact regarding the Caligulan reign – yet it does provide insight into several facets of life under the new *princeps*.

Caligula is said to have hated Flaccus more than other men whom he had condemned. He instantly regretted that he had granted the former prefect exile on a Greek island rather than death, and blamed Lepidus for having persuaded him to substitute Andros for Gyaros as a prison. Lepidus was subsequently afraid that he would face punishment for having interceded on behalf of Flaccus. Philo attributes to this episode the effective cessation of any efforts on anyone's behalf to try to mitigate the punishment of another.

Caligula began to spend his nights thinking about just what exile meant for high-ranking Romans.[45] He came to the not unreasonable conclusion that 'exile' was really 'residence abroad', that the men who were condemned to these islands were in fact now at true liberty and peace, free from having to worry about political and other affairs and sources of turmoil. Those in banishment were essentially living like philosophers, at complete repose and in possession of serene calm and reflection.

Death was therefore the answer: a list would be prepared of all the leading exiles, and Flaccus' name was first.[46] We may think naturally enough here of the evidence from other sources for how Caligula thought to kill all of those who were in exile, for example on hearing that a released prisoner from the days of Tiberius had reported that he had spent his entire foreign sojourn in prayer for the death of Tiberius and the accession of Caligula. Whatever the reason on this occasion, the story is the same; Caligula decided that capital punishment was warranted.

Officials were sent to Andros to see to the death of Flaccus as part of their no doubt grisly round of the Greek islands. Flaccus by chance was travelling from the country to the town when he encountered the party of Romans. He was filled with fear when he saw them, divining that they intended to kill him. He fled in terror, Philo noting the pathetic detail that Flaccus seemed unaware that he was on an island, and that escape was quite impossible. The description is once again an example of Philo at his prolix best (or worst); he notes that one can either journey into the sea, or else be arrested at the very edge of the water. Men were assigned by nature to live on the land, and so Philo argues that it is better to die on land than at sea; the environment that witnessed the birth of men should also provide witness to their death.[47]

The assassins were soon on Flaccus, and the story is told with drama and verve by Philo.[48] Some went to grab the ex-prefect, while others already busied themselves with digging a pit. Flaccus went to his death not with the serene reflection of the philosopher, but with vicious resistance and frenzied protest. The result was that he ran into and upon the blows that rained down upon him, just as is the manner of wild animals. Because of his attempt to grapple with and to struggle against his killers, his death was all the harder. They had no easy place to apply their wounds, and so he suffered all the more grievously. He was, in short, slaughtered like a sacrificial victim.

Divine justice, Philo notes, wanted Flaccus to suffer multiple wounds to atone for the very many, indeed countless number of Jews whom he had stabbed, as it were, in his anti-Semitic administration of Alexandria and his prefecture. The whole locale was filled with the blood of Flaccus, which flowed from his veins as from a fountain. The corpse was dragged to the pit that had been prepared, but most of the body fell apart before it could reach its final resting place. Flaccus died just as did another;[49] in the end, the death of Flaccus was proof positive of the help and succour that God provided to the Jewish people.

The *In Flaccum* does not add much to our knowledge of the principate of Caligula – but it does provide further vivid testimony to one aspect of his reign, namely his involvement with the Jewish nation, not least to the enduring impression that Caligula made on Philo. The works of Philo and Josephus are in substantial agreement with each other in the matter of the uprising in Alexandria and the disturbances in Judaea occasioned by the attempts of Caligula to set up his image in the Temple – but the inconsistencies and discrepancies between the accounts are noteworthy.[50] Both authors focus on the obsessive madness of Caligula as would-be god. Politically, it is reasonably clear that Flaccus was doomed for his support of Gemellus and significant wealth. The fact that Alexandria was the scene of street riots and pogroms would not have commended him to his Roman masters. Whatever the rhyme or reason, he had failed to maintain order in his prefecture – always the most signal failing of a Roman official.

Flaccus was replaced by Gaius Vitrasius Pollio. We know from inscriptional evidence that Pollio was in Alexandria before the end of April AD 39.[51] He would live to see the downfall of Caligula.

Chapter Eight

The Evidence of Seneca the Younger

P hilo was a contemporary of Caligula, and had a fateful encounter with him in the matter of the embassy on behalf of the Jews of Alexandria. Lucius Annaeus Seneca is another contemporary source of information about Caligula's reign.[1] Seneca's life was a study in providence and fate. Born around 4 BC in Corduba, Spain, he would come to the attention of Caligula, suffer banishment at the behest of Messalina under Claudius and eventually be rehabilitated and, in turn, condemned under Nero.[2] He was arguably the greatest philosopher and writer of his age, and his life was a testament to the world engendered and orchestrated by the reigns of the Julio-Claudian emperors. Philo provides lengthy evidence of the experience of the Jews under Caligula – but to Seneca, too, we owe valuable contemporary evidence of Caligula from a man who knew him. As with all of our sources, we must exercise careful control over our assumptions about the reliability or plausibility of this or that detail from the ancient record – but first, we must examine what Seneca says about our imperial subject in his surviving work.

We may begin with the so-called *De Constantia Sapientis*, or treatise on the firmness or constancy of the wise man. The date for this work is much disputed; some would put it early in the reign of Claudius, others at some later point.[3] Seneca suffered exile in AD 41, and was not freed until 49, spending those miserable years in Corsica. The treatise is one of the ten Senecan works that are usually referred to as the *Dialogi*, or 'Dialogues' – a problematic title insofar as one will not find in Seneca's work the sort of 'dialogue' we associate with Plato's Socratic works, for example.

The *De Constantia Sapientis*, then, was written not long after the death of Caligula. It reveals the sort of philosophical mindset that we would certainly expect to read of in the wake of the madness of the Tiberian and Caligula regimes.

Caligula appears near the end of Seneca's Stoic treatise on constancy.[4] The emperor is cited as a prime example of someone who was quick and eager to insult other people, when in reality he was quite worthy of insult and mockery himself. Caligula's very appearance is given as evidence of his madness: he had a pale face, wild eyes, the brow of an old woman – grim and foreboding – a bald head with a few hairs here and there,[5] a neck overgrown with bristles, abnormally thin legs and large feet.[6]

Some critics might well note that Seneca opens his attack on Caligula strictly on physical grounds; the recent memory of the tyrant undoubtedly clouds this savage indictment. Seneca proceeds to note that it would take an endless amount of time to review all the things that Caligula actually did to bring disgrace on his family, all the things that Caligula was responsible for that brought ruin to men of every rank in Rome – and so he will focus only on what transpired that related to the downfall of the monster.

Seneca begins with the emperor's friend Valerius Asiaticus.[7] Valerius was a proud man, unlikely ever to endure the sort of insults that Caligula was fond of employing. At a public banquet, Caligula embarrassed Valerius by very loudly criticizing his wife for her sexual performance and inadequacies. The emperor was therefore confessing his adultery, and this with the spouse of a consul and man of noble years and bearing.

And then there was Cassius Chaerea. Though quite masculine in his abilities and bearing, his voice was apparently weak and effeminate, and thus the source of mockery and insult for the emperor. And so sometimes the watchword was 'Venus', at other times 'Priapus'.[8] Caligula openly asserted the womanly nature of Chaerea, while all the time it was the emperor who was wearing the clothes and adornment associated with women.

Not surprisingly, then, it was Chaerea who was the first to strike a blow against Caligula at his assassination. The one who seemed least like a man in the derogatory attacks of Caligula was the *primus vir*, or first man, to attack the emperor's neck.

There was also the case of Herrenius Macer.[9] Macer earned Caligula's scorn because he called him 'Gaius'; a centurion was attacked because he dared to use the nickname 'Caligula'.[10] Seneca attests to the familiar story of how the name had been given to Caligula as an infant, when he was raised in the camp of his father Germanicus; the soldiers were apparently in the habit of always

(*Above*) Ancient Aquae Sextiae, modern Aix-en-Provence, a storied location in the history of Roman relations with Gaul.

(*Below*) Modern Cassis, France, a Ligurian site and significant maritime route through southern Gaul.

(*Above*) Cassis, France.

(*Below*) Vulnezia, the modern Vernazza in the Cinque Terre region of Liguria.

(*Above*) Manarola in the Cinque Terre, so-called from the 'magna rota' that marked the mill works of the town.

(*Below*) Modern Valensole, France, in ancient Gallia Narbonensis.

(*Above*) The amphitheatre in Arelate (modern Arles), France.

(*Below*) The necropolis of Arelate.

(*Right*) Eleusis, Greece.

(*Below*) Cassis, France.

(*Above*) The island of Melita in the Adriatic, a favourite location for exiles in the imperial period.

(*Below*) Arles, France.

(*Above*) Sunset in eastern Cyprus.

(*Below*) Sunset at modern Ayia Napa, Cyprus.

(*Above*) The coast of eastern Cyprus.

(*Below*) Abbey near Gordes, France, an area rich in the archaeological remains of Roman imperial transportation networks and settlements.

referring to him by this moniker. By now, however, as emperor, Caligula was quite displeased with the name, precisely because he was now in the habit of wearing the tragic buskins associated with stage actors.[11]

For Seneca, the wise man may remain in a state of constancy precisely because even if he decides to forego revenge for some slight or another, there will always be another who will do the deed for him. There will always be a Cassius Chaerea who is ready to strike down the tyrant. There will always be someone who is willing to take the drastic action of eliminating the monster.

We may proceed to Seneca's dialogue *De Ira*, or his treatise on anger. The date of the essay is again quite uncertain; Caligula is dead, but there are few clues by which to divine the time of its composition. It is also a lengthy work, divided into three 'books', and Caligula appears near the end of the first.[12]

The angry, Seneca advises his audience, are prone to impressive sounding appeals and loud, bombastic assertions; essentially the angry man is a coward, and one can rest assured that while the speech and voice may be threatening and menacing, internally the man is pusillanimous and afraid.

As in the case of Gaius Caesar. He was once watching a pantomime, when there was thunder from the heavens that disrupted the proceedings. He became angry at the auditory intrusion on his pleasures – though Seneca notes that he was more interested in imitating the action on the stage than in merely watching. The thunder and lightning, Seneca observes ruefully, were too uncertain in their aim (*parum certis*) – Caligula, after all, was not struck down.

The emperor proceeded to challenge Jupiter, urging the god to fight him to the death, citing the line of Homer we have seen mentioned before about either lifting up or being lifted.[13] Seneca associates the madness of Caligula on this occasion with his eventual assassination. The future conspirators, after all, had just heard their emperor challenge the supreme god himself – and if Caligula could not tolerate Jupiter, how could they continue to tolerate Caligula?

Caligula reappears later in the dialogue.[14] The emperor is said to have been irritated by the son of Pastor, a noteworthy Roman equestrian. Pastor's son was apparently a bit too elegantly coiffed for Caligula's taste, with a splendid quality of dress and appearance that incited the emperor's irritation.[15]

The son was imprisoned on account of Caligula's affronted vanity, and the father begged that he might not be killed. Caligula at once treated the plea as a reminder; he ordered that the son be slain immediately. He also invited the father to join him on that day for dinner.

Pastor was no fool, accepting the invitation and giving no indication at the meal that anything was amiss. Caligula toasted the health of the man, and had already enjoined one of his attendants to watch closely for any reaction from the bereaved father. Seneca reports that Pastor went through with the wicked charade, though he felt as if he were drinking the very blood of his son.

Caligula's game had failed so far to elicit the reaction the emperor wanted. He therefore sent perfumes and garlands to Pastor – and once again, it was reported that the man behaved as if nothing were wrong, using the presents as if he were in no state of mourning or grief. On the day scheduled for his son's funeral, Pastor appeared among 100 dinner guests, and again acted as if nothing were at all amiss. On the contrary, despite his age and his gout, he drank more wine than would have been appropriate for a birthday celebration.

For Seneca, the reason that Pastor was able to maintain this front in the face of Caligula's savagery was that he had a second son (whom he wished to protect, certainly, and in whom he could maintain hopes for his family's future success). Seneca compares Pastor to Priam from the last book of Homer's *Iliad*; the father was willing to embrace the killer and desecrator of the corpse of his son Hector – the mighty Achilles.

And yet, Seneca is careful to note, Caligula was no Achilles. Caligula did not permit Pastor to leave his banquet to see to the gathering up of the bones of his slain son. He tormented his guest by urging him to forget his sorrows with wine and celebration. The father behaved in the way he knew he needed to act in order to save his other son from the wrath of the despot. Seneca thus employs the memorable story of Pastor as a cautionary *exemplum* of how to deal with tyrants and their anger.

The next reference to Caligula comes in the treatise's third and final book.[16] After discussing the horrors visited upon men in the days of the civil strife of Marius and Sulla, Seneca turns to more recent events. He notes that Caligula ordered the scourging and torment of Sextus Papinius, whose father was consular, and of Betilienus Bassus, who had been quaestor under Caligula, all in the same day – and not for the sake of interrogation or of discerning answers to questions important or trivial, but rather for the sake of amusement.[17]

Caligula is said to have been so unwilling to postpone the pleasure he took in savagery, that he decapitated some of his victims by the light of lamps (that is, at night), as he was taking an evening walk with senators and Roman matrons in his mother Agrippina's gardens. Seneca wonders what could have been so important and pressing that these men could not be spared until morning, lest men of senatorial rank be killed by an emperor in dinner-dress.[18]

Seneca takes advantage of these anecdotes about Caligula's savagery to launch into what he admits is a sort of digression from his main argument.[19] It is true, Seneca notes, that Caligula ordered the scourging of senators – but it was also Caligula who made it possible for people to say, this was business as usual.[20] Caligula tortured his victims by all manner of devices – including his own face.[21] Three senators were treated as if worthless slaves, and yet this was the man who wanted to kill the entire Senate, and who wished that the Roman people had but one neck.[22] In other words, yes, there were three victims of senatorial rank on one occasion – yet this was the monster who envisioned the death of everyone.

Seneca is especially bothered by the notion of nocturnal executions. Theft and brigandage, he notes, occur by night so as to conceal the crimes – but punishments are normally conducted in the light of day, so as to serve for the public edification and warning. And yet once again, the point is that for Caligula, the violence and savagery was merely habit. He needed to have executions by night, because he was so obsessed with punishment and torture that he could not endure to sleep or rest without it.

Caligula was also angry and savage to so great a degree that he ordered that sponges be shoved in the mouths of the condemned, so that they could in no way utter a last word. He was afraid, Seneca notes, that the dying might speak some final message that would discomfit him. He knew that the dying had nothing to lose, and that some of his victims might reproach him for this or that criminal act. And if there were no sponges handy, he even ordered that the condemned man's clothing be torn up, so that strips of fabric might be used as a muzzle.

Seneca's rhetoric is high-flown: let the dying man have an outlet for his voice other than his wounds.[23] Some men were sent for to face death, and on the same night Caligula would order the deaths of their fathers, ostensibly out of compassion and pity, so that the older men might not have to mourn the deaths of their children.

Non enim Gai saevitiam, sed irae: Seneca notes that he is not so much interested in detailing the savagery of Gaius, as he is in reflecting on the very nature of anger and wrath. Anger is that which destroys not just one person here or there, but entire nations. Implicitly, though, we might conclude, for Seneca the Emperor Caligula – the master of the vast Roman world – was the very incarnation of anger. He was madness incarnate: the embodiment in purple robes of the spirit of wrath that threatens to overwhelm the world.

Madness and anger are ultimately to no purpose, though, at least to no purpose for which they are exercised and employed by tyrants. For Caligula is also said to have ordered the destruction of a villa near Herculaneum, a lovely villa in fact – all because his mother Agrippina was once imprisoned there.[24] And yet, Seneca notes, while the villa stood nobody who walked by it ever remembered anything about Agrippina's imprisonment – though now, everyone asks why the villa was destroyed, and so the memory of the insult to Caligula's mother is alive and well, rekindled, as it were, by the emperor's counter-productive action.

We may turn to Seneca's *De Brevitate Vitae*, his essay on the brevity of life. Again, precise dating is impossible. It is thought by some that the work dates to the period after Seneca returned from his Corsican exile, but before AD 50 (AD 49), while others prefer a year as late as 62.[25]

Seneca refers herein to the allegedly mad wish of Caligula to build his infamous bridge of boats, with specific reference to the dire straits to which his exorbitant expenses in that initiative drove the Roman people.[26] The text is somewhat vexed, and the logic of the passage is not always pellucid – but the general thrust of Seneca's argument is easy enough to glean. Caligula squandered the resources of the empire on his attempted imitation of Xerxes, so that those who were in charge of the city's grain supply had to face not only the wrath of a hungry people on the verge of riot because of their starvation diet, but also the anger of Caligula, who wanted no delay in his expensive construction plans. The managers of the grain supply (i.e. the *praefectus annonae* and his staff) had to face the stones, fire and sword of the mob – and their emperor as well.

Seneca vividly imagines that Caligula might still be exercising his wrath even beyond the grave, angry at learning that there was still seven or eight days of provisions left in Rome, and that the Roman people were, after all, still alive.[27]

In the *De Tranquillitate Animi*, Seneca records the name of Julius Canus,[28] who was allegedly involved in a longstanding dispute with Caligula of uncertain provenance, but is otherwise unknown to history. Caligula had indicated that he would have him killed, but Canus is said to have remained unshaken in the face of the threat, and to have thanked Caligula. Seneca wonders what he meant by this: possibly that Caligula's cruelty was so great, with the result that death was a blessing. Canus is said even to have been removed from any fear that Caligula might have spared him – for Caligula was always a man of his word in threats of execution (one might call it his one example of constancy). Canus spent ten days at peace before his death, playing a board game, and chastising his opponent with the admonition not to claim after his death that he had won (i.e. he urged his partner not to steal a victory by cheating).[29] Canus went to his death uncertain as to whether the soul was immortal. He indicated that he would soon find out, and promised to inform his friends as to what the truth of the soul's fate was. Seneca promises that the memory of so great a man would never be forgotten, indeed would be made immortal – and in this the philosopher kept his word.

Canus, we should note, is also cited in a fragment of Plutarch's *Moralia*.[30] Caligula is said to have executed the Stoic philosopher Julius Canus. Plutarch notes that the Greeks invented a story about him – he clearly doubts its veracity – that when Canus was being led away to die, he prophesied to Antiochus of Seleucia that on the very night after his death he would come to discuss an important matter (cf. the Senecan reference to the promise to return to talk of the immortality of the soul, if it were possible) – and that he predicted that his friend Rectus would also die by Caligula's order, in three days. Rectus is indeed said to have died, and Antiochus is said to have been visited by the ghost of Canus, who discoursed to him about the lasting nature of the human soul.[31]

We may turn to the *De Consolatione ad Polybium*, the essay on consolation to Polybius, which is certainly a work from Seneca's period of exile. Here Caligula furnishes an example of grief, if only to serve as a model for how not to behave in the face of trauma.[32] After the death of his sister Drusilla, Caligula behaved in the same way in which he managed his pleasures – namely, like a prince (Latin *principaliter*). He fled away from the sight of all, and did not attend her funeral, indulging in dicing and other games at his villa at Alba to escape his sorrow. Caligula was an object of shame to the Roman world, then, by playing board games when he should have been respectfully conducting the rites appropriate to the requiem for his sister.

Caligula proceeded to wander aimlessly down the coast of Italy and Sicily, sometimes letting his hair and beard grow in his state of 'mourning', and sometimes not allowing them to grow.[33] The emperor was uncertain as to whether he wanted his late sister to be lamented as a casualty of our mortal nature, or worshipped as a new goddess. Temples at any rate were erected to her memory, and those who did not seem to mourn her sufficiently well were punished for their 'crime'. In short, Caligula responded to the death of Drusilla in the same way in which he responded to everything – excessively and without moderation.[34]

The treatise *Ad Helviam Matrem de Consolatione* is another of Seneca's exilic works. The consolation in this case was for death of a particular sort: namely a mother's grief occasioned by the banishment of her son.[35] Caligula is once again lampooned for his numerous vices and foibles. He is said once to have dined at the cost of ten million sesterces; though everyone helped him in every way they could, he was scarcely able to figure out how to spend the tribute revenue from three provinces on one dinner.[36] For Seneca, the *rerum Natura*, or nature of things, had produced Caligula so that man might know how far vice could go. Caligula is an example to Seneca of the pathetic state of those whose appetite demands expensive and indeed outlandish cuisine. Once again, the Senecan portrait of Caligula is unremittingly hostile.

We may proceed to the last of Seneca's dialogues, the so-called *De Beneficiis*, or 'On Benefits'. This work is generally taken to be an example of late Seneca, and once again Caligula figures here as a villain from recent Roman history.[37]

At *De Beneficiis* 2.12.1 ff., Seneca cites the case of Pompeius Pennus, who was granted his life by Caligula – if, Seneca notes, you can consider the failure to kill Pennus as an example of giving him life. After he spared the man, Caligula offered his left foot to be kissed in grateful homage for the benefit he had bestowed. Some, Seneca notes, tried to defend Caligula by arguing that the emperor merely wanted to display his golden slipper, studded with pearls – in short, that no insult was meant toward Pennus.

For Seneca, Caligula wanted to turn Rome into Persia. It was not enough for Caligula that Pennus should have to kiss his feet; the emperor found a way to cast down *libertas*, or freedom, even lower – the old consular was obliged to kiss a golden slipper, and one adorned with pearls besides. In Seneca's estimation, the arrogance of the *princeps* defied all bounds of reasonable conduct.

And then there was Julius Graecinus.[38] Caligula had him killed simply because he was a better man (*quod melior vir erat*) than the tyrant thought was profitable. Julius Graecinus, as we have seen, was the father-in-law of Tacitus' father-in-law Agricola; he had refused to prosecute Silanus, and thus incurred the undying wrath and enmity of Caligula.

Seneca also considers the question of how providence could have thought it right to give the world a Caligula.[39] After all, the emperor in question was so bloodthirsty that he ordered blood to be shed in his presence as if he intended to catch the sanguinary stream with his own mouth.[40] And yet the honour was given not to Caligula *per se*, but to Germanicus and his other ancestors. Seneca here echoes the judgment of those who explain why Caligula was as popular as he was in his early days; the favour that had been shown to his father redounded to him in abundance.

There is one final reference to Caligula in the treatise.[41] He is said to have considered giving Demetrius 200,000 sesterces.[42] Demetrius considered Caligula to be mad,[43] and noted (to Seneca's approval) that if Caligula had wanted to test or bribe him, he should have offered him his entire empire (*totum imperium*).

We may turn to Seneca's letters to Lucilius, literary epistles that date to the last years of the author's life.[44] Caligula's assassination is associated with the changes of fortune that stalk the lives of men; Caligula had ordered Lepidus to extend his neck to the tribune Dexter, but the emperor himself put forth his throat to Cassius Chaerea.[45]

A macabre example of black humour is preserved at *Epistulae* 77.18. Caligula was walking by on the Via Latina, where there was an assembly of condemned prisoners. One old man, with a long, unkempt beard that stretched out over his chest, implored the emperor that his life might be spared and that he might be permitted to live. Caligula sarcastically asked him if he was alive now. Seneca notes that this is precisely the answer to give to those for whom death would be a blessing, and proceeds to note that what matters in life is not how long one lives, but how well one manages the last portion of this mortal coil. One might note that this is an exceedingly rare example of a Senecan reference to Caligula where the author agrees with the madman; the context, of course, is harrowing.

To the closing years of Seneca's life we may also date his *Naturales Quaestiones*, a scientific work in seven books.[46] A passing reference is made herein to how Caligula's influence did not ruin Seneca's friendship with Gaetulicus.[47] Seneca soon thereafter also observes that in the reign of Caligula he saw tortures, burnings and the act of mercy of merely killing men rather than tormenting them savagely and cruelly. And yet he maintained a constancy that did not permit him to rush headlong into some course of desperate action; he did not commit suicide, he did not leap into the sea to drown – indeed, he pursued no course that would have been a mere death for *fides*, or loyalty.[48] He was, we might say, an exemplar of Stoicism, as he was not deterred from his path by any fear or excessively emotional reaction to the horrors around him.

The portrait of Caligula that may be seen in Seneca's extant works is certainly a hostile one. There is not much that contributes to the solution of any problem of the reign of the *princeps* – but we are fortunate in having any testimony so close in time to Caligula's own life, indeed by someone who came close to closing his life in the madness of that quadriennium of his rule. By the unnatural end of his life, Seneca may have been remembering Caligula all too well as he dealt with Nero.

Chapter Nine

The Evidence of Pliny the Elder

P liny the Elder is the author of a mammoth encyclopedia known as the *Historia Naturalis*, or *Natural History*, a vast and richly fascinating compendium of lore on a plethora of subjects.[1] The *Natural History* is one of the great treasure troves of classical antiquity, a miscellany that provides access to an astonishing range of material on everything from geology to metallurgy, botany, zoology, anthropology, painting and the art of sculpture, geography and cosmology.

Pliny was born in AD 23 and died a casualty of the eruption of Vesuvius in 79; literally to his death he was an indefatigable scientific investigator and thinker. His nephew was the celebrated Pliny the Younger, most famous today for his extensive correspondence (including letters with the Emperor Trajan).[2]

Pliny's work does not, of course, provide a detailed history of the reign of Caligula – but the *Historia Naturalis* does contain interesting references to the emperor that help in our attempt to elucidate certain aspects of his principate. And Pliny is another reasonably contemporary source.[3]

The celebrated attempt to dig a canal through the Corinthian isthmus is cited by Pliny as an example of the sort of engineering enterprise that is frowned upon by the gods. Julius Caesar contemplated it, as did Caligula and Nero – and all three met with violent ends.[4]

We may proceed to Book 5 of Pliny's work, which is part of his extensive survey of the geography of the world. Pliny opens his book with a study of Africa, and commences his treatment of the continent with a look at the 'two Mauretanias'. Pliny notes that the two Mauretanias were kingdoms until the time of Caligula, only then to be divided into provinces on account of the emperor's savagery.[5] This is the sort of valuable reference that historians are keen to cite. As we have seen, we are in fact quite ignorant of Caligula's arrangements in Africa on account of the loss of Dio's narrative, and remarks such as Pliny's offhand comment are thus all the more important in gleaning some historical chronology from the extant evidence.

One problem with interpreting Pliny's reference to Caligula's work in Mauretania is another reference to the West African region that our author makes soon thereafter.[6] Pliny observes that the first time that Roman military units fought in Mauretania was during the principate of Claudius, after the death of King Ptolemy. Ptolemy was killed, and his freedman Aedemon sought to avenge him; the rebellion did not succeed, however, and Roman forces pursued the enemy as far as the Atlas Mountain range. In Dio's account of the early reign of Claudius, he notes that there was fighting in Mauretania, and that only after the suppression of the rebellion was the former kingdom of Ptolemy divided into two administrative regions.[7]

Pliny's two references to Mauretania are not necessarily internally inconsistent. Caligula could have reorganized the territory, with armed rebellion coming only after the accession of Claudius (or, perhaps, only after the start of Claudius' rule did the Roman military respond to the threat). We cannot be sure of what happened here; certainly Pliny may be wrong in his dating, but there is every chance that there was not enough time for Caligula's orders to be implemented before his sudden assassination.[8]

Caligula is mentioned incidentally amid discussions of breech births.[9] Marcus Vipsanius Agrippa was said to have been a successful such birth. The bad luck that attends on such a delivery is said to have been visited upon him in the destiny of the two Agrippinas (his daughter and granddaughter), who gave the world Caligula and Nero.

Caligula's wife Lollia Paulina is cited as example of decadence.[10] At an ordinary betrothal banquet, she was said to have worn emeralds and pearls in an alternating pattern, all in a sheen over her hair, head, ears, neck and fingers – to the sum total of forty million sesterces. The jewels were not even the gift, Pliny notes, of an extravagant emperor – they were ancestral possessions of her family, acquired from provincial rapine and wealth. Pliny notes that for anyone who doubted the price or provenance of the emeralds and pearls, Lollia actually carried certificates of authenticity and letters of attestation with her, for consultation by the doubtful.[11]

An interesting discussion of human sight and 'imperial eyes' leads to a brief comment on Caligula's vision.[12] Pliny notes that Tiberius had some interesting night vision abilities, while Augustus had grey eyes like those of a horse, with unusually large whites (he is said to have become annoyed if anyone stared too long at them). Claudius was often bloodshot in appearance, while Caligula had fixed and rigid, staring eyes.[13] The passage has been cited as part of the medical, clinical discussion of possible evidence of physical ailment.[14]

A picnic that Caligula attended is cited as one of Pliny's innumerable incidental anecdotes.[15] The emperor was on an estate at Velletri for the event, and he was impressed by a prodigious plane tree that served as the setting for the meal, with benches that were set up on beams that were fashioned out of the branches of the tree. Caligula himself was a noteworthy part of the shade, or *umbrae*, that was provided by the sylvan setting.[16] The emperor referred to the *tableau* as his *nidum*, or 'nest' – a memorable example of the eccentricity of the *princeps*.

Caligula's notorious luxury is cited among the examples of those in history who have gone the route of olfactory decadence by scenting their bathrooms; the emperor Gaius is said to have scented his bathtubs with perfume.[17] A slave of Nero is said to have done the same thing – and so Pliny observes that not only princes engage in such (implicitly ludicrous) behaviour.

Caligula's judgments on wine are also referenced. Tiberius is said to have dismissed wines from Sorrento as being little more than 'noble vinegar' (*generosum acetum*), recommended and praised only because doctors endorsed them. Caligula, for his part, referred to them as *nobilem vappam.* or 'noble flat-wine'.[18]

The famous obelisk that Caligula brought to Rome from Egypt is cited by Pliny, in the context of his discussion of especially noteworthy trees. The ship that conveyed the obelisk and stone shafts for its base is said also to have carried an impressive fir tree.[19]

The strange carnivorous fish known as the goby was said to have interfered with Antony's flagship at Actium, and likewise with Caligula's vessel on a voyage from Astura to Antium.[20]

Caligula is credited by Pliny with the establishment of a fifth *decuria*, or panel of ten men, for the sake of expanding the number of men who could enjoy the curious privilege of being allowed to wear rings of gold.[21] Pliny associates this innovation of Caligula with the spectacle of having freedmen vying with freeborn citizens for membership in the honoured ranks. At one time rings of iron were the distinguishing marks of equestrians and judges, but now there were former slaves privileged to wear gold.

On one occasion, Caligula is said to have brought some 124,000lb of silver on a mobile scaffold into the theatre.[22] Pliny cites this fact as evidence of how one day men will look back on the Romans as having perpetrated legendary deeds associated with precious metals. The occasion or reason for the contraption and its argentine burden are not specified.

The obsession of Caligula with gold is also recorded among the encyclopedist's treatment of metallurgy.[23] He notes that there is a method for making it from orpiment; the orpiment is mined in Syria for the sake of painting supplies.[24] Caligula ordered a massive amount of orpiment to be melted down for gold, and while the result was not entirely unsuccessful, the investment ultimately failed because of the relatively low yield of gold. Pliny notes that no one else ever tried the same process; Caligula's madness for gold had engendered the experiment, and he received the more or less just merits for his avarice.

Pliny also affords us a glimpse of Caligula, the art thief.[25] After giving a brief synopsis of the history of painting, Pliny notes that there are paintings in the Temple of Ardea that pre-date the foundation of Rome, and that at Lanuvium there were portraits of the mythical huntress Atalanta (depicted as a virgin) and of Helen of Troy; both were nudes that were painted by the same hand. Caligula tried to have them removed, but the nature of the plaster was such that they could not easily be pilfered.[26]

The aqueducts that Caligula started, which were finished only after the accession of Claudius, are also cited by Pliny.[27] The projects are noted for their high cost, far surpassing previous such ventures. Pliny, we should note, is careful to praise the whole enterprise as being one of the great achievements of ancient engineering. There is no question that he considers the initiative to be among the positive aspects of the reigns of Caligula and Claudius alike.

Caligula's slippers are said to have been sewn with pearls.[28] Pliny mentions this detail concerning the emperor's footwear in his descriptions of the fascination the Romans had with pearls in the wake of the victory of Pompey the Great over Mithridates. Caligula is cited alongside Nero as an example of a Roman with a noteworthy appreciation for pearl decorations. Pliny is more critical of Pompey than of either of the Julio-Claudians, noting that after

Pompey's indulgence in pearls, no one could justly criticize either Caligula or Nero for their gemstone foibles.

The nature of Pliny's work does not permit anything approaching a definitive assessment of the author's appraisal of Caligula. The anecdotes told of him in the *Historia Naturalis* run the gamut from examples of the emperor's madness, to at least neutral treatment of such initiatives as the aqueducts. Caligula had already earned a largely negative reputation in the literary tradition by Pliny's time. The lack of the sort of venom we find in Seneca's appraisal of the *princeps* may reflect both Seneca's personal peril at the hands of Caligula, and his own experience of Nero. Pliny wrote from the comparatively pleasant vantage point of Vespasian and Titus, and his work is imbued with a more dispassionate reaction than that of his Stoic predecessor.[29] Still, there are clear enough signs of the same historiographical tradition that informs the work of other first-century sources. If there were any 'neutral' ancient writers on Caligula, they have not survived – and we have little reason to imagine that they ever existed.

Chapter Ten

The Evidence of the Fragmentary Roman Historians and Additional Sources

Whe are fortunate to have significant remains of many otherwise lost works of Roman historiography. From these scattered citations and quotes, some additional material on Caligula may be assembled, though perhaps what could fairly be called a disappointing array.[1] One of the main points of interest in the 'lost' Roman historians is the question of what influence these authors had on writers such as Suetonius, Tacitus and Dio Cassius. No fragments remain that provide a clearer picture of any particular facet of the emperor's life or reign than that to be obtained from the major sources of Suetonius, Tacitus, Dio Cassius and Josephus. Much of the material that falls under the heading of 'fragmentary' has been sometimes difficult for the general reader to access; our point in the present chapter will be to review some of what survives that is of potential interest to a study of the Caligulan principate, with an invitation to further study and consultation of the standard collections (Cornell for the Roman historians, Smallwood for documents).

Two members of Caligula's immediate family wrote historical works, and the loss of their texts is undoubtedly a blow to Caligulan studies.[2] The emperor's uncle Claudius was an antiquarian with extensive historical, political and rhetorical interests.[3] Claudius is said to have composed a work on Etruscan history in twenty books and a work on Carthaginian history in eight, and is also credited with an Etruscan dictionary, a defence of Cicero as an orator and a volume on dice-playing. The influence of his childhood tutor Livy is clear.[4]

But of perhaps greater interest for the study of Caligula is the report that Agrippina the Younger – Caligula's own sister – also composed memoirs. Agrippina's work is mentioned by Pliny the Elder as a source for the seventh book of his *Historia Naturalis*; Tacitus mentions the *commentarii*, or 'memoirs', of Agrippina at *Annales* 4.53.2.[5] These are the only extant surviving references to her work, and the date of composition is quite uncertain. There has been reasonable argument (not to say speculation) that the work dates to the Claudian period; it would certainly have made mention of Agrippina's imperial brother, though we would give much to know exactly how Caligula's sister depicted him. As for Claudius, Balsdon notes that historians may have taken their 'cue' from Caligula's uncle; once he had declared in public that his nephew was mad, they would have felt free to concur and to assert the same conclusion in their histories.[6] The new emperor of AD 41 was a writer of history. He would certainly be a natural model for historians interested in analysis of recent and contemporary events. To have his work side by side with that of his niece and wife Agrippina would no doubt offer a remarkable insight into the period and its players.

Pliny the Elder composed a work on the German wars – the *Bella Germaniae* as it is called by his nephew Pliny the Younger. It is certainly plausible that Pliny's work included mention of Caligula's (mis?)adventures in the region, though we cannot be sure of the chronological scope of the work. Pliny's natural history has scattered references to Caligula, as we have seen. We would much welcome the historical narrative the polymath also composed – especially given that the Caligulan activities in Germany are among the foreign policy initiatives of the principate that we would most like to see elucidated.[7]

Cluvius Rufus is perhaps the most famous fragmentary historian, however, of relevance for the study of Caligula.[8] It is possible that this Cluvius is the consular Cluvius mentioned by Josephus as being present on the day of the assassination of Caligula.[9] Cluvius was the man who urged silence after the remark of the senator Balthybius about how tyrant-slaying was on the spectacle programme for the day – silence lest any of the Achaeans might hear the report.[10] Scholars debate the question of whether or not Cluvius' historical writings were a source for Josephus' extensive account of the emperor's assassination. Once again, we are quite uncertain as to date, with some thinking that Cluvius wrote under Nero, while others date him to the end of Vespasian's reign (the Flavian emperor of 69-79). There is also doubt as to the contents of Cluvius' work (e.g. did he compose a history of the Julio-Claudian principate, as some speculate, or did he give an edition of the so-called Long Year of 69, when Galba, Otho and Vitellius all quickly rose to the purple and then fell in the aftermath of Nero's suicide?).[11]

Cluvius Rufus, in short, is a figure who undoubtedly had something of interest to do with at least the end of Caligula's reign, though almost every detail of his life is in dispute – even his *praenomen* is quite uncertain. But it is reasonably clear that he was a major source of information for Tacitus, at least in that historian's consideration of the reign of Nero, and also for Plutarch. We cannot prove definitively that Dio Cassius and Josephus used him, let alone Suetonius – though some have argued for just that influence on all three. The fact that Cluvius is mentioned in Josephus in connection with a quote from Homer has led some scholars to consider that such passages of Greek quotation may be taken as hallmarks of 'Cluvian' style.[12]

In truth, we have but four 'fragments' and one anecdote that survive to tell us about Cluvius' histories. Two of the 'fragments' are from Plutarch and two from Tacitus.[13] One of the Tacitean passages cites Cluvius as evidence for the incestuous relationship between Agrippina the Younger and her son Nero, and for Seneca's use of the freedwoman Acte to keep Nero from the tawdry influence of his mother.

Wiseman is of the view that Cluvius Rufus – a master orator and rhetorician as well as noted historian – was likely a key source for Josephus on Caligula.[14] Wiseman considers Cluvius to have been an artist of some note in his composition of history: 'Equally brilliant [that is, to the death scene of Nero in Suetonius that Cluvius may have inspired] is the passage transmitted by Josephus (127-52) of the scene Cluvius himself witnessed in the theatre in 41. The man who wrote those things was a literary artist of some stature.'[15] While one must be cautious in asserting too much in the face of a dearth of hard evidence, Wiseman's conclusion is sound: Cluvius Rufus was not only a major source for Josephus' work on the death of Caligula, but he was a skilled writer and vivid storyteller. We have no clear sense, we might note, of whether or not Cluvius addressed the much discussed question of the insanity of Caligula. Wiseman does well to note that Josephus' obituary of Caligula makes no mention of the madness, despite his earlier discussion of it in connection with his striving for divine honours and desire to have a statue erected in his honour in the Jerusalem Temple.[16]

Fabius Rusticus may have also addressed the reign of Caligula. He was a friend of Seneca the Younger, a fellow compatriot from Spain. Tacitus praises him lavishly in the *Agricola*, where he calls Livy the most eloquent writer of earlier ages, and Rusticus of more recent.[17] Rusticus was said to have praised Seneca;[18] he apparently wrote about the death of his dear friend.[19] We have no idea if Rusticus wrote of Caligula, let alone what he said about the emperor – but this has not prevented scholars from indulging in speculation (even if reasonable enough).[20]

Fragments and so-called *testimonia* present something of a siren song to ancient historians. It can seem at times that quite minor passages are subjected to undue analysis and more criticism than they merit. Certainly there is a tremendous risk of reaching hasty conclusions on the basis of scanty, slender remains. We are certainly able to appreciate how the surviving works of such luminaries as Tacitus and Josephus benefited from the research and writing of predecessors – but it is impossible to do more than speculate more or less securely on how the general portrait of Caligula that emerged from his reign was not terribly much altered in subsequent decades.

Under the heading of 'fragmentary' historians and related sources we may also conveniently include those scattered records that survive inscriptionally, records such as the *Acta Fratrum Arvalium*, or Acts of the Arval Brethren; also numismatic evidence or evidence from surviving coinage.[21] The *Acta* are of immense use in determining details of Roman prosopography, besides providing details of Roman religious traditions. We have already encountered the evidence of these Arval records in the matter of the consular lists for the reign of Caligula. Poor Tiberius Gemellus was a member of the Arval Brotherhood; the *Acta* record that he was replaced on 24 May AD 38, by Publius Memmius Regulus. The Arval Brethren appointment that Gemellus enjoyed may not have been a particularly prestigious appointment, but his replacement offers clear enough evidence to assist in dating his downfall.

The *Acta*, then, are invaluable for providing information and/or confirmation of key dates in Roman history. The *Acta* are generally considered a reliable source, so that, for example, when the Arval record says that Tiberius died in 16 March and Dio reports that the death occurred ten days later, the *Acta* are usually favoured.[22]

We do have a record of Gemellus' tomb inscription, which refers simply to Tiberius Caesar, the son of Drusus Caesar.[23] Some have taken the brief epitaph as evidence that Gemellus was indeed deprived of particular honour, though this may simply be an over-reading based on the ample proof available from other sources of how Gemellus was viewed according to official state propaganda.[24]

A *sestertius* coin from Rome, AD 37-38, shows a head of Gaius with laurel crown on the obverse, and representations of his three sisters as the goddesses Securitas, Concordia and Fortuna on the reverse.[25] A *dupondius* of the same period has Caligula's two brothers Nero and Drusus on the reverse, on horseback.[26] Fragments of a reign, then – but tantalizingly scanty remains. There is little to attest to historical events of the Caligulan era;[27] some remains of oaths of allegiance survive, such as one from Lusitania (modern Portugal) and another from the Troad. Caligula is saluted as 'Germanicus' below a statue of a fighting equestrian from Lydia, where a female statue is labelled as Germania – but we have of course no way of knowing exactly why the statues were erected.[28] Coinage confirms that Caligula did associate himself with Tiberius, at least at first; one *aureus* from Lugdunum shows the two men on opposite sides of a coin, with Tiberius' head radiate and starred.[29] Another coin from Rome shows Pietas seated, with her arm resting on a small standing figure – apparently Caligula.[30] A bronze coin from Alexandria dated to AD 37-38 shows a bust of Caligula on the obverse, and a half-moon on the reverse; we may recall the emperor's fascination with the moon goddess Selene. Another bronze coin from Smyrna depicts a laureate Caligula on one side and his sister Drusilla as Persephone.[31] A *sestertius* from Rome has another image of a laureate Caligula, with the emperor on the reverse mounted on a platform addressing five soldiers, four of whom carry standards.[32] A letter of Caligula is preserved inscriptionally, dated 19 August AD 37, addressed to local leaders in Greece.[33] Barrett notes that in Caligula's first year of power (37-38), he appears sometimes bare-headed, sometimes laureate (one wonders if he preferred the laurel to conceal his baldness); the three sisters are one motif for the reverse, the address to the army another.[34] Pietas provides another motif, the so-called *corona civica*, or 'civic crown', yet another. There is also the inscriptional reference to Caligula having pledged his support for the Turkish city of Assos in AD 18.[35]

A numismatic mystery is the appearance in later 39 of coins depicting the *pileus*, or cap of liberty.[36] The occasion for this motif is quite uncertain, but it may have something to do with the suppression of the supposed Lepidus conspiracy. Barrett notes that the different motifs did continue to be used throughout the emperor's short reign, with the exception of the 'sister' coin type, which was of course inappropriate after the surviving sisters were sent into exile.

All of these remains are precious artifacts of a brief and memorable reign. If the scattered remnants of inscriptions and coins do not add much to our understanding of the Caligulan enigma, they at least provide another window of insight into one of the more poorly documented periods in imperial Roman history.[37]

The fragmentary historians are easy to label 'minor' since we lack their complete works. In a very different category is Paulus Orosius, the student of the celebrated bishop and ecclesiastical doctor Augustine of Hippo. Orosius composed a massive work, the *Historiarum Adversum Paganos Libri VII*, or 'History against the Pagans', in seven books, which probably dates to the early fifth century.[38]

Orosius' history has a decidedly Christian flavor, and by the time his work reaches the Julio-Claudian period, the treatment of events is somewhat cursory. The author is a dramatic verbal stylist, as may be evidenced by the commencement of his treatment of Caligula's reign: *Anno DCCXC tertius ab Augusto Gaius Caligula regnare coepit mansitque in imperio annis non plenis quattuor, homo omnium ante se flagitiossimus et qui vere dignus Romanis blasmphemantibus et Iudaeis persecutoribus punitor adhibitis videretur.*[39] The bald facts: Gaius Caligula came to power as the third in the Julio–Claudian line, in the 790th year of the city. He remained in power for not more than four years; he was the most criminal of all men, truly a worthy punisher of both the Romans for their pagan blasphemy, and the Jews for their persecution of the Christians.

Orosius cites the oft-repeated line about how Caligula wished that the Romans had but one neck, offering it as the best summary of all the wickedness of the emperor.[40] The comment that Caligula complained that his era was deprived of any disasters is also mentioned.

For the Christian Orosius, however, there is a certain revel and joy in the fact that the Caligulan era lacked major disasters. Indeed, Orosius even quotes the Virgilian lines from the *Aeneid* about the chaining of Madness (*Furor impius*), which for the historian is now a reality thanks to the coming of Christ.[41]

Orosius does record that Caligula sought an enemy in Germany and Gaul. The historian connects the venture with the lack of disasters that the emperor complained about in Rome. He stopped in sight of Britain. One 'Minocynobelinus', the son of a king of the Britons who had been expelled by his father, surrendered to Caligula with a few men.[42] Orosius is generally thought to have rendered the name of the prince incorrectly.[43]

Deficiente belli materia: with no materiel for war, Caligula returned to Rome.[44] A frustratingly brief account, then, of the emperor's military affairs in Gaul, Germany and at least within view of Britain.

The Jews, Orosius moves on to declare, were justly suffering persecution everywhere because of their involvement in the passion of Christ.[45] Orosius notes the rise of a sedition in Alexandria, and the slaughter and expulsion of the Jews from the city. Philo was sent as an emissary to Rome. Caligula was especially hostile in those days to the Jews (Orosius notes that the emperor's anti-Semitism was shared by all men, *cum omnibus hominibus*); the embassy of Philo was rejected firmly, and the Jews were obliged to accept pagan sacrifices in their temples (even in Jerusalem), and for statues and images to be introduced that would mean desecration and abomination. The Jews were in short ordered that they should revere Caligula as if he were a god.[46]

To this period Orosius also ascribes the suicide of Pontius Pilate.[47] Eusebius says the same thing in his ecclesiastical history,[48] where he notes that Pilate fell into such disfavour in the reign of Caligula, that he was compelled to commit suicide, thus making expiation for his role in the death of Christ. Eusebius says that those who record the Greek Olympiads relate this event, though no independent confirmation has been found. Like Orosius, Eusebius blames the Jews for their own troubles in the first century AD, noting that it was all part of the atonement for the crucifixion of Christ.

The traditions about Pontius Pilate, we may note in passing, are many and varied. The Ethiopian Christians even considered him a saint and martyr, with a feast day in the liturgical calendar for 25 June.[49]

Orosius continues his historical summary of the reign with another notorious story. Caligula was also so debauched that he committed incest with his sisters, and then drove them into exile.[50] He then ordered them to be slain, but he was first slain, and by his protectors (*ipse autem a suis protectoribus occisus est*).

Orosius also repeats the information about how two journals were found in Caligula's possession after his death, the one titled 'Sword' and the other 'Dagger'; senatorial and equestrian names were found in both that had been marked down for death. Poisons were also found in a chest, deadly potions that Claudius ordered to be poured into the sea, such that immense quantities of fish were killed.[51] For Orosius, the number of fish that were killed is testament enough to how much worse the times of Caligula might have been. Orosius takes the position (novel in the works we have thus far considered) that divine providence saw to it that Caligula's reign was really not quite as bad as it might have been without the kindly hand of God.[52]

We have already mentioned Eusebius of Caesarea. In his ecclesiastical history, he notes that Caligula inherited the sovereignty from Tiberius, and at once made Agrippa the king of the Jews.[53] Agrippa was also given the tetrarchies of Philip and Lysanias, and eventually that of Herod, who was sentenced to banishment; Eusebius notes that this was the Herod famous at the time of Christ's passion (with the implication again that Caligula's action was actually the just desserts merited by the participant in the trial and death of Christ). Eusebius explicitly cites Josephus as his source for this information.

Eusebius gives words of praise for Philo of Alexandria, noting that he was devoted in particular to the study of Plato and Pythagoras. Eusebius cites the five books that Philo devoted to the question of what happened to the Jews in the time of Caligula, noting that Philo combined in his work the question of the insanity of Caligula, the proclamation of his divinity and the countless acts of arrogance and insolence from his reign. The famous embassy to Gaius is mentioned, complete with the mockery and ridicule Philo received, and how he was fortunate to have left Rome with his life.

Eusebius again cites the testimony of Josephus, as well as the main points from Philo's own account *de legatione*; like Orosius, he blames the Jews for the predicament in which they found themselves under Caligula.

Were it not for the dealings of Caligula with the Jews of Alexandria in particular, we should be lacking in the fairly extensive mention of and references to the emperor in the writings, then, of these Christian and Jewish authors. We see a clear strain of the argument that Caligula was actually an instrument of the just wrath of God; also alleged evidence for the kindly disposition of the divine for humanity in that Caligula was not able to do even more damage to the world than he managed to accomplish in his short reign. Orosius on the Latin side and Eusebius on the Greek do not offer much in the way of evidence to solve outstanding mysteries of the Caligulan principate, but they do help to supplement a picture of those four years – indeed, four years that left ample mark on both the historical and the rhetorical tradition.

We may also give some attention to the enigmatic collection of biographies known under the heading of the so-called *Augustan History*.[54] The lives of the emperors in this collection stretch from Hadrian in 117 to Numerianus in 184. The work's authorship and provenance are the subject of fairly intensive scholarly debate and argument, but the likeliest date of composition for the lives is late third or early fourth century. The lives are clearly modelled on those of Suetonius.

Caligula is mentioned several times in the lives of the later emperors: he offers a stereotypical example of the worst of emperors. In the life of Marcus Aurelius, we learn – not surprisingly – that the emperor was worried that his son Commodus would turn into another Nero, Caligula or Domitian – the 'big three' of first-century AD imperial monsters.[55]

Lucius Verus is said to have acquired the habit of dice-playing in Syria, and to have spent the whole night at the game – indeed, he is reported to have rivaled the vices of Caligula, Nero, and Vitellius to such an extent that he wandered about through the night haunting the brothels and engaging in other deplorable conduct.[56]

Commodus is said to have commented that no emperor who was good was ever conquered or defeated by a pretender, and that the rulers who had been slain had all deserved it: Nero and Caligula for example (while as for Otho and Vitellius, they had not really wanted to rule).[57]

Commodus ordered the death of one man (he was thrown to wild beasts), merely on the grounds that he had read Suetonius' life of Caligula – because he shared Caligula's birthday.[58] This anecdote is referenced by Barrett at the start of his history of Caligula. It provides a grim sequel to the accounts of earlier imperial attempts to suppress histories and the works of unpopular authors. In this case, Caligula could be derided for allegedly taking yet another victim – even from beyond the grave, the horror of his reign remained deadly.

The opening of the biography of the notorious emperor Elagabalus contains the 'apology' of the author that he would never have committed the biography to the page, were it not that there had also been a Caligula, a Nero and a Vitellius.[59] Elagabalus is said to have been well-versed in the debaucheries of Tiberius, Caligula and Nero.[60] The author of the same life apologizes for the seemingly strange fact that Elagabalus was able to stay alive in power for some three years, noting that there was no one then in the state who could act like those who rebelled against Nero, Vitellius and Caligula.[61] Lastly, the author of the life of Aurelian lists Vitellius, Caligula and Nero as examples of the worst emperors of a past age.[62]

The lives of the *Historia Augusta* are known for indulgence in salacious, scandalous details of their subjects. And so it no surprise that the mentions of Caligula are all as examples of one of the worst of the emperors; alongside Nero and Vitellius, he becomes the classic example of the worst of the *principes*. If there is a constant from the time of Suetonius to the age of the writers of the *Historia Augusta* to the present day, it is the strange fascination and curious appeal of the lurid. Caligula's life offered material in abundance for such pursuits.

We may also mention here the brief information on Caligula offered by Sextus Aurelius Victor in his *De Caesaribus*.[63] This fourth-century abridgement of Roman history commences (like Tacitus' *Annales*) with the death of Augustus. He notes that Gaius Caesar, *cognomento Caligula*, assumed power to the delight of all (*aventibus cunctis*). Aurelius Victor mentions the sympathy that was generated by Tiberius' persecution of Caligula's mother and brothers. Caligula had been born as the darling of the army, and Rome was sympathetic, wishing to treat well and soothe the scion of so much undeserved suffering from the Tiberian menace. Aurelius Victor muses that often great beginnings yield worse endings – sometimes the best of parents have the worst of children, so that it is sometimes said that wise men do well not to have them. Aurelius Victor's Caligula knows how to conceal his worst traits, and so at the beginning of his reign he continued the pattern that he had mastered before assuming the principate. After a conspiracy was uncovered, the mask came off; soon there was slaughter aplenty, such that the world was stained and made foul by the killings of the senators and leading men of the state.[64] The incest with his sisters is mentioned, and also his mockery of noble marriages (i.e. his affairs and wife-stealing); so also the assumption of the dress and manner of the gods, notably Jupiter on account of his own sororial incest.

The hope of crossing into Germany is also cited, with the detail that the legions were all brought together into one (*contractis ad unum legionibus* – not at all true) and the ordering of the soldiers to pick up shells (*conchas*) and what are perhaps supposed to be 'pebbles' (Latin *umbilicos*).

And so soon enough there was a conspiracy, led by Cassius Chaerea. In the historian's estimation, those who participated were those who were possessed of Roman virtue (*quibus Romana virtus inerat*). It was all reminiscent of Brutus' action in removing the Tarquins from power. Claudius was advanced to power not long after.

We should also note the *Epitome de Caesaribus* that is falsely attributed to the same author. This late fourth-century work briefly covers the emperors from Augustus to Theodosius the Great.[65] The passage on Caligula adds the detail about the alleged brothel for noble women on the Palatine, and also the bridge of boats.

These late Roman historical sources do not add much to our knowledge about Caligula. Aurelius Victor is of interest for his acceptance of the thesis that Caligula was a master of dissimulation, at least, that is, until he came to power. It is perhaps of interest with the briefer ancient sources to note what details from the tradition they consider worthy of inclusion. But certainly our fourth-century references to Caligula do not diverge from what some would call the hostile tradition. Caligula had been exposed for the monster he was, and the conspirators acted nobly.

Chapter Eleven

Towards a Reconstruction of the Caligulan Reign

T he main division between scholars of the principate of Gaius is the question of whether or not the emperor qualifies for such labels as 'insane' or 'mad'. In other words, do the hostile traditions of much of our ancient historiographical evidence accord with the historical reality, or has Caligula been the more or less unfair recipient of a biased appraisal that has won acceptance in the popular conception?

J.P.V.D. Balsdon's 1934 Oxford monograph *The Emperor Gaius (Caligula)* was for years the standard scholarly treatment of our emperor (at least for anglophone audiences). Balsdon's work may be seen as something of an exercise in revisionism. He attempted to show that Caligula was not quite as crazy as rumour and report would have it, and that in fact he was quite competent in a number of his initiatives, and certainly in his political administration of foreign affairs. Anthony Barrett's 1989 Yale work *Caligula: The Corruption of Power* is not quite as quick to defend Caligula; it has more or less supplanted Balsdon as the 'standard' work of reference on the reign, and throughout it succeeds in maintaining a balanced view of a difficult period.

Arther Ferrill's 1991 work *Caligula: Emperor of Rome* (Thames and Hudson) offered a different appraisal from Balsdon and Barrett. For Ferrill, the ancient sources are quite correct: Caligula was a monster and a lunatic, and no attempt at whitewash can triumph over the prevailing evidence.

Aloys Winterling's 2003 Munich monograph (translated into English for a 2011 California edition) focuses on a different but related question about Caligula. Taking it more or less for granted that the Balsdon-Barrett line is correct and that Caligula was the object of something akin to character assassination, Winterling attempts to disentangle exactly why Caligula's contemporaries would want to do him harm. In short, why was Caligula's reputation assailed both in life and shortly after death? Winterling notes that one infamous story – the account of how Caligula forced people to fulfill their deadly vows in the wake of his survival from illness in AD 37 – could be interpreted as evidence of a policy of frank and brutally honest communication with his subjects.[1]

We have noted that the common view of Caligula in the early twenty-first century is that Suetonius was right (in other words, the Ferrill argument). Of the notorious 1979 Italian-American pornographic film *Caligula*, nothing ought be said – but its sentiments are perhaps all too reflective of the general perception and reputation of our emperor.[2] More nuanced and complicated is the view of Caligula presented in Albert Camus' theatrical masterpiece, *Caligula*, itself a work unquestionably influenced by the political and military realities of the age of its composition.[3] Camus' Caligula is even seen as deliberately orchestrating his own suicide as part of his (pseudo-?)philosophical attempts to resolve his perplexities with humanity.

The portrayal of Caligula by the actor John Hurt in the 1976 British Broadcasting Company production of Robert Graves' *I, Claudius* is universally acclaimed as a masterpiece of the dramatic and darkly comedic arts. Hurt's Caligula exactly captures the spirit (and, often, the letter) of the Suetonian depiction of the madman. For those who have seen it, it remains an indelible image of the emperor.[4]

Historical inquiry aims at discovering the truth about events and famous people, about memorable deeds and extraordinary individuals. We may now attempt to examine the life of Caligula in light of the ancient evidence that we have detailed.

We may note first that the Augustan system of the principate was still fairly young and relatively untested in AD 37. Tiberius had been the first successor, and had also had an unusually long reign of over two decades. Caligula was significantly younger on his accession than either of his predecessors, and came of age in a fraught political and family situation, not least because of the inherent tensions between the Julian and Claudian factions of his domestic background.

On the home front, Caligula's main challenge – beyond the usual difficulties that are attendant on the rise to power of the unusually young in a competitive environment – was the foreign arena. As would be the case for almost every other emperor in the first century, Rome's foreign affairs were always seemingly on the verge of bursting forth into a paroxysm of chaos and trouble. There was the vast German frontier, the distant East and the threat of the organized state of Parthia – as well as the immense territory of North Africa, the southern desert frontier of the empire. Caligula had potential problems on three borders – and in the space of only four years, he managed to deal with affairs in all three realms. If nothing else can be said of Caligula, he did focus on a wide range of problems and issues in a relatively short scope of years. His were four busy years – however we choose to appraise the results: lazy, Caligula was not.

Caligula may have been seen as destined for foreign life almost from birth. Born in 12, in the waning years of the Augustan principate, Caligula was sent by Augustus to join his father Germanicus in the spring of 14. Augustus would be dead some three months later. Some of the early dates are known: 31 August for the birthday, 18 May for the departure for Gaul and Germany, when the boy was not even 2 years of age.

Caligula returned to Rome with his parents in the spring of 17. At some point in the same year, Germanicus' family travelled to the East –so Caligula would have seen the second major frontier of the empire by the time he was but 5. Again, an interesting circumstance: by a young age, Caligula had actually seen more of Rome's territories than either of his predecessors had when they were 4 or 5. There is an interesting inscriptional reference to Caligula's visit to Assos (near the site of Troy) in modern Turkey when he was but 6; apparently he addressed the people there and promised his defence of the locale – a vow that was remembered years later.[5]

By the age of 6, Caligula was a true golden child. He had already made a public address, participated in his father's triumph and seen Gaul, Germany and the East. Life certainly changed for him after October of AD 19, when Germanicus mysteriously died, leaving his son fatherless at 7. Caligula returned with Agrippina to Rome early in 20. The next several years could not have been easy, and are marked by obscurity. We simply have too little evidence for what Caligula was doing in his childhood years.

Caligula entered the house of Livia late in 27, when he was already 15. Livia would live to see the year 29; after her death, Caligula would move to the house of Antonia. It has been noted that the future emperor was fortunate in having the protection of these powerful women in difficult years, but given the historical reality, one could say it was remarkable that Caligula survived his teenage years.

When the future Augustus was 19, he was busy in the aftermath of the assassination of his adopted father Julius Caesar. When Caligula was the same age, he was invited by the aging emperor Tiberius to come to Capri. The year was AD 31; Sejanus would be dead before the end of October in the same year. The survivor managed to navigate the most difficult years of his young adulthood. He did not fall victim either to Sejanus or to the bloodletting that followed the fall of the powerful praetorian prefect. He also never ran seriously afoul of Tiberius, and thus he escaped the fate of his brothers Nero (who died in 31) and Drusus (who died in 33) – let alone the destiny of his ill-fated mother Agrippina (who also died in 33). His uncle Claudius allegedly survived by relying on the perception that he was dull-witted and no threat to anyone but himself, but how Caligula managed to survive is not entirely clear. Was he truly seen by Tiberius as a kindred spirit, a fellow purveyor of pornography?[6] Was Sejanus merely constrained by time, taking on too many enemies and facing his own (inevitable?) fall before he could manage to eliminate Caligula?

Luck may have been what saved the young Gaius more than anything – and the same may well be said of his uncle Claudius. Just as it may be unfair to condemn those who did not survive these years - that is, those who fell victim say to a sadist like Sejanus – so it may be unreasonable to praise those who survived. Simply put, had Sejanus lived, Caligula would likely have been eliminated sooner rather than later.

The year 35 was the decisive one in terms of setting the course for the post-Tiberian principate. That was the year in which Tiberius named Caligula and Tiberius Gemellus as joint heirs. By the age of 23, Caligula was in a position to aspire to the purple – the only real question was what would become of Tiberius' grandson Gemellus. Again, the years between the fall of Sejanus and the settlement of Tiberius' inheritance are murky as to detail; clearly Tiberius was caught between whatever desire he may have had to promote his grandson, and the obvious enough popularity of the house of Germanicus and the young scion of the family, Gaius.

And so by the time we come to 16 March 37 – the day of Tiberius' death and the *de facto* commencement of Caligula's reign (he was 24) - we may be struck by the very different youth and young manhood of Rome's third emperor in comparison to Augustus and Tiberius. Whatever personality traits he had, Caligula's youth had been spent in a very different milieu and social setting than either of his two predecessors. With Tiberius he shared the uncertainty of seeing multiple possible contenders for the principate all arrayed as if to be targets for elimination, one after the other.

Part of the luck that was attendant on the young Caligula was just how arrogant and conceited the praetorian prefect Sejanus seems to have been. No equestrian had ever risen to his station; no one had emerged in the early principate with so much power and authority outside of the imperial family. Certainly he did conspire against Caligula – why ever not, given his conspiracies against the other members of the house of Germanicus – and he aimed at something even higher than his station as Tiberius' *socius laborum*, or 'partner of his labours'.

Again, we have many question marks about the early years of Caligula, questions that our ancient sources simply do not address. For example, we have no clear understanding of why Caligula was sent to the households of Livia and then Antonia. The decisions to squirrel him away with those two powerful women may well have been the decisive factors in his survival; certainly Antonia was instrumental in seeing to the downfall of Sejanus. If she had any reservations about Caligula, her main concern in the autumn of 31 was the upstart prefect, not the young son of Germanicus. Claudius was acclaimed as being of a scholarly bent, and noted for having spent much time in research and academic pursuits – and there is every reason to believe that Caligula was devoted to his studies, or at least a quick learner. Scholars inevitably note that he apparently knew his Homer reasonably well (or at least well enough to quote this or that Homeric tag line); his oratorical skills have already been noted.[7]

This is the period, of Caligula's alleged incest with his sisters. Scholars have sometimes been tempted to discount the ancient evidence, but for Arther Ferrill, in contrast, there can be little doubt that when Caligula was between 17 and 20, he was engaged in incestuous relations with his sister Drusilla, who was then 14 to 17. Are we to imagine that in the difficult years of Sejanus and his terror, Caligula was alternately reading the *Iliad* and indulging in illicit unions with Drusilla? This is what the ancient evidence would seem to indicate, and certainly life at Tiberius' retreat at Capri was marked by less than noble pursuits.

But even if we may ignore the stories of Caligula's adolescent and young adult perversions, it is impossible to discount the intense pressures under which the future emperor would have been living on Capri. Tiberius clearly hated Agrippina, and Caligula was forced to engage in a more or less delicate dance of seeking the approval of an emperor who despised his mother. One need not engage in perhaps fruitless psychological or pseudo-psychological analyses to appreciate the difficulties of these years for the young Caligula.[8] None of this is to excuse the actions of the emperor (or the emperor-in-waiting) – but simply to acknowledge that if Caligula was crazy, so too was the environment in which he was reared. Ferrill is certainly correct to sum up the point with, 'His family life was an unmitigated catastrophe.'[9] In short, it would have been miraculous had Caligula emerged from this period without some blot on his record. And if Caligula was, for example, complicit in the death of Tiberius – notorious pillow story with Macro and all – there would probably have been quite few in Rome who would have mourned the passing of the hated tyrant. We may believe the evidence that Caligula's accession was greeted as the dawn of a potential new Golden Age, and we may trust that the general reaction to the coming to power of the son of Germanicus was heartfelt and warm.

More mysterious and problematic is the question of why Tiberius was willing to name Caligula his heir, even in partnership with Gemellus. Some would argue that Tiberius saw something of merit in the young man, but others might take the opposite view and argue that Tiberius realized that Caligula was so bad that he himself would look better in a *deterior* comparison. The truth may be a mix of the two, or simply the not mutually exclusive idea that there were exceedingly few candidates for the job left alive by the year 35. If the principate was to remain a family affair, Caligula was certainly the leading contender for the job – qualifications or personality flaws quite aside.

Tiberius could not reasonably exclude his own grandson from the succession plan – Gemellus had to be accorded some place in the system. But there is equally no question that Gemellus was an inconvenience. Tiberius had had no partner in his accession in 14, and certainly nobody viewed Caligula and Gemellus as a neo-Augustus and Agrippa. And as with Tiberius, there was probably little in the way of public mourning or outcry when Gemellus died – his death significantly simplified the imperial equation.

Certainly Caligula had an easier accession in the spring of 37 than Tiberius had enjoyed in the late summer of 14. There would be no mutiny, no serious question of disloyalty to the new regime. Caligula was acclaimed as *Imperator* by the Senate on 18 March, a mere two days after Tiberius had departed this mortal coil. By the end of the month, Caligula would be in his capital of Rome, and in possession of the powers of his office by senatorial decree.[10] Power needed to be taken quickly, especially given that the new emperor was untested and unproven at his young age – though he had, of course, proven that he could survive in difficult straits. There is no reason to disbelieve the report that the early days of the reign were generally received with favour and rejoicing by all constituencies.[11]

One can well imagine that the young Caligula did all that he could to curry favour with all classes of people in the early stages of his reign – however could he not? Suetonius credits this seeking of popular favour with the decision to have Claudius finally enter public life.[12] Soon enough, Caligula was sensitive even to the issue of having his uncle – the noted imbecile – be in charge of him in any way. He was allegedly furious with the Senate for sending Claudius as part of the delegation that was dispatched to Germany to congratulate Caligula on the discovery of the conspiracy of Lentulus Gaetulicus.[13]

The notorious illness of the emperor occurred in the autumn of 37, sometime after 21 September. He would be sick until late October – perhaps a month, then, of perilous health. The illness has occasioned a large bibliography (especially in conjunction with the question of the state of his mental health).[14] While theories have been advanced, they are necessarily speculative, and the only general agreement is that whatever happened to Caligula that autumn was quite significant – but there is no consensus as to whether the problems were more physical than psychological.

We may wonder if there was any connection between the emperor's illness and the Senate's award to him of the Augustan title of *Pater Patriae* on 21 September. Was Caligula simply overwhelmed by the sheer speed of it all, by the dizzying heights to which he had at last been propelled by a series of strange circumstances and more than a little dose of luck? Was the 'illness' really what we might vaguely identity as a nervous breakdown? Certainly those scholars who argue that definitive answers are impossible in the face of extant evidence are correct. Caligula did dedicate a temple to Augustus before the end of the year 37; it is impossible to know for certain whether he intended this in some way as a special tribute of thanksgiving for his recovery. In short, it is interesting that 'Augustan' references seem to frame the timeline of Caligula's illness – but certainty is definitively elusive without new discoveries. There is good reason to suspect that Caligula was exhausted by the autumn of 37; he had lived a longer life than most by the age of 25. Dizzying power was now his – and perils both close at hand and afar.[15]

The year 37, then, had certainly started auspiciously for Caligula with the bright spring of new promise, but the autumn was darker and fraught with medical peril, physical and/or mental. Those who wanted to see signs of instability and even madness could no doubt have found them; certainly there was evidence of ruthlessness and even bloodthirstiness, but nothing that seemed worthy of concern in the wake of the long Tiberian tenure.

Macro and his wife were certainly dead early in 38, while Gemellus was also dead either by the end of 37 or fairly early in 38. Silanus was dead in November or December 37. Whatever happened to Caligula in terms of his health, he quickly moved to eliminate perceived threats and problems from his inner circle. There would be no rival for power in Gemellus; there would be no powerful praetorian prefect to conjure up memories of Sejanus. Again, the reactions of the senators and equestrians would have varied here. Realism in politics would have demanded understanding for some sort of purge by the young and perhaps rightly nervous emperor, at least among the cynical.

The death of Drusilla on 10 June 38, however, was a death of a very different sort. If the autumn of 37 had imperiled Caligula because of illness, the summer of 38 was marked by the mourning for his sister and quite possibly lover. She was consecrated as a goddess on 23 September (the birthday of Augustus, we might note – perhaps a coincidence). Those who were in search of evidence of mental instability would have had a field day with the apotheosis of the emperor's sister, while those who knew about any incest would have had even darker thoughts.[16] And at some point – likely by early 39 – the old charge of *maiestas* that had been so grimly exercised under Tiberius had been restored to the annals of Roman jurisprudence.[17]

If Caligula had decided that he needed to move against Gemellus, Macro and his wife, and Silanus, it is perhaps not surprising that he broadened the scope of his targets and began to persecute the senate early in AD 39. Indeed, for someone who was afraid of threats to his power, this course was all too predictable (though no less deplorable, and ultimately to no avail in forestalling his eventual assassination). The signs of cruelty became more difficult to miss or to ignore, and there is no question that Caligula was harsher and more savage in his temperament – and in his sadism – than Augustus certainly, and also Tiberius for that matter.[18] There is no evidence that the emperor's marriage to Caesonia 39 brought him any particular lessening of his anxieties or improvement of his temperament, nor the birth of his daughter Drusilla in record time.[19] The celebrated episode of the building of the bridge at Baiae can be dated to 39 as well (summer); of that notorious affair one can at least note that it was less problematic in some aspects at least than the apotheosis of Drusilla.

But what of foreign and military affairs? The year 39 was certainly the commencement of Caligula's serious attention to events and problems outside Rome. At some point before 27 October in 39, Caligula had departed Rome for Mevania in northern Italy, and thence to the north. What exactly Caligula intended to do on his quite large expedition is uncertain. The year 39 would also be that in which Caligula would banish his surviving sisters Livilla and Agrippina the Younger; Gaetulicus and Lepidus were charged with conspiracy, and both men probably died in 39. Gaetulicus had been governor of Upper Germany or Germania Superior; the borders of the Roman province included portions of modern Germany, France and Switzerland. Caligula has been praised by some for his replacement of Gaetulicus with the competent commander Servius Sulpicius Galba, who would become emperor himself in the frenzied events of the Long Year, AD 69.[20]

As with so much in the Caligulan reign, the nature of the conspiracy of 39 is uncertain. While there is good reason to believe that there really was a conspiracy to eliminate Caligula, there is no report of why exactly the emperor's sisters and selected leading men of the state were involved (if indeed they all were). Arther Ferrill concludes that the 'most obvious' answer is that Caligula's sisters, and Lepidus, had come to the conclusion that Caligula simply needed to go – that he was unacceptable as a leader because of his instability. Gaetulicus was an obvious choice to aid in the matter, given his powerful position and armed forces.[21]

What we may be certain of is that Germany was an obvious place for Caligula to commence his foreign policy. His father had made a name for himself in those northern lands, and Caligula's own formative experiences had included time in Germany. Germany more than anywhere in the empire was the place most associated with Caligula and his immediate family.

If there was a genuine conspiracy, it shows that movement against Caligula dates from a fairly early stage of his principate. It was likely also a family affair, aided and abetted if not orchestrated by the emperor's closest living relatives. We have no sure sense if Caligula's marriage to Caesonia played into the equation, while still less do we know how the emperor came to learn of the conspiracy.[22]

Caligula was only in power for less than four years, and he spent more than one of those years across the Alps, from the autumn of 39 until the summer of 40. We should perhaps pay attention to the fact that neither Augustus nor Tiberius was in the habit of visiting the provinces once they assumed the purple. Both had travelled extensively before their principates of course – but Caligula was an emperor who would proceed in person to the front, as it were.[23] Caligula had made numerous journeys abroad before he became emperor, but only as the child of Germanicus; he had no record of foreign service in politics or the military. In this he was the opposite of his two predecessors.[24] The fifth-century historian Eutropius briefly mentions the German expedition of Caligula in his short outline of the reign.[25] He notes that Caligula undertook an expedition against the Germans (*Bellum contra Germanos suscepit*), and that he entered Suevia and did nothing with vigour (*nihil strenue fecit*).[26]

Ancient claims for the expedition to Germany range from replenishment of Batavian bodyguards to a plain search for money and treasure. There is no reason to discount the idea that the young Caligula was eager to prove that he could do what his predecessors had left unfinished and untried: the complete conquest of Germany and Britain. Caligula would certainly have viewed this initiative as his birthright, as the son of Germanicus and descendant of Julius Caesar.

How to fit the conspiracy into the narrative of the German/British expedition is difficult. Some would argue that the 'plan' was for Gaetulicus to see to the death of Caligula when he arrived in Germany (with Lepidus then taking control of the government, backed by Gaetulicus' forces).[27] Whatever the case, Caligula arrived in Germany, and both his sisters and his governor – not to mention Lepidus – were soon all condemned.

There followed whatever happened on the so-called German expedition. Balsdon argues that many German warriors fled as soon as it was clear that the emperor was arriving with a large force.[28] The autumn and winter of 39-40 was spent in training. For Balsdon, some of the seemingly bizarre details in the ancient sources make sense only if they are taken not from actual military events, but from mock battles in training of the troops.[29] Thanks to the records of the Arval Brethren, we have the fixed date of 27 October AD 39 for the offerings that were made in thanksgiving for the discovery of the conspiracy of Gaetulicus. Caligula decided at some point that he would spend the winter in Lugdunum, meeting the first envoys from the Senate while in residence there.[30] To this period may be dated the infamous episode where the senatorial emissary Claudius was thrown into the river, and would have been slain had he not been such a fool.[31] There was certainly a purge in Rome of anyone who was suspected of complicity in the conspiracy. According to Suetonius, one of those who was apparently quite happy to be involved in settling accounts for Caligula was the praetor Vespasian, himself eventual emperor.[32] Vespasian proposed that those who were killed for their involvement in the plot against the emperor should be denied burial rites. He also saw to celebrations in honour of the German victory – whatever that victory might have been.[33] Some have speculated that foreign achievements were exaggerated to cover up any uncomfortable mention of conspiracies – though the Arval Brethren apparently had no problem recording the latter.[34]

At some point, it seems that Caligula shifted his focus from Germany to Britain. The impetus for this may well have been the surrender of Adminius, the son of Cunobelinus.[35] Balsdon notes that the retreat of the Germans into heavily forested areas may have also have been a factor in the decision.[36] As for what happened at the Channel shore – that is, not very much of military note – Balsdon cites the evidence of Dio Cassius, who has the rebel queen Boudicca note in the reign of Nero that the Britons will benefit from the same fear on the part of the Romans that aided them in the days of Julius Caesar and of Gaius Caligula.[37] For Balsdon, it was likely enough that Caligula suffered a mutiny of sorts, a refusal of his men to embark on an expedition into Britain (especially if they had been training and planning for a German action).[38] The celebrated command to 'pick up shells' may well have been Caligula's attempt to insult the very troops who had insulted him by their refusal to sail for Britannia.[39]

We may well be tempted to sigh and inquire what really happened, and what was Caligula's intention in heading to Germany, Gaul and – if he had had his way – Britain?[40] It would appear likeliest that Caligula was caught between the problems of domestic, civil conspiracy and his grand plans for northern conquest. In theory his idea was sound (if not novel): Rome should expand to the River Elbe in Germany, and effect a settlement of the British question. Conquest of Germany to the Elbe would relieve pressure on currently occupied Roman areas, and expand Roman prestige and military power, while the conquest of Britain would ensure security on the Gallic front and lucrative trade with the island.[41]

While Caligula was in the north, however, there is some reason to believe that disturbances had already broken out in Alexandria regarding the relationship between Jews and Greeks. Ptolemy of Mauretania was summoned to Rome sometime early in AD 40 – we cannot be sure of exactly what was afoot in North Africa, but it seems at least possible that Ptolemy was indeed implicated in the Gaetulicus conspiracy.[42] Whatever the exact cause of Ptolemy's summons and his eventual execution in perhaps the summer of 40, what is certain is that Caligula incorporated Mauretania into the Roman Empire: from client kingdom, Mauretania was transformed into provincial territory.[43] This certainly provided an air of greater stability on the African front, and it should be noted that Caligula – extraordinarily enough – was involved in major foreign policy issues on multiple fronts at the same time. Any *princeps* would have found the whole business difficult to manage – and Caligula was but in his twenties.

Part of the foreign policy mess, of course, was occasioned by Caligula's decision to insist that his image be placed in the Temple of Jerusalem. That decision may have come in the spring of 40; certainly the Philo delegation from Alexandria was en route to Rome in the winter of 39-40, in response to the disturbances in that city that had commenced as early as the summer of 38. By the end of May 40, it appears that Caligula was somewhere near Rome, having abandoned his escapades and expeditions in the north; at the end of the month he seems to have had his first meeting with the Jews and Greeks from Egypt.[44]

Was it simply a case, then, that too much was going on at once, and that Caligula did not think he could spend more than one winter away from his capital? Was a nervous and inexperienced emperor worried that his domains were in danger of fragmenting, and that conspiracy was afoot in Rome and elsewhere? Was the decision to insist on his image in Jerusalem a sound measure to take when there were nascent and more longstanding problems on several different fronts simultaneously? The decision to insist on the image in Jerusalem was eventually rescinded, to be sure, but there is no question that significant damage had been done.

Caligula returned to Italy in the spring of 40, then, though plans were soon undertaken for a journey to Alexandria – the next major foreign policy problem he may have wanted to tackle was in the East. Some would note that the emperor was no doubt in fear for his life; in the end, he did remain in Rome once he arrived in the city on his birthday (31 August AD 40), and he remained in the city until his assassination in January 41.[45]

Balsdon argues that the conspirators of the winter of 40-41 – that is, the men who finally succeeded in ridding Rome of Caligula – were motivated more by personal hatred of Caligula than by any passion for the abstract concept of liberty.[46] There may be some truth to this, though Caligula's temperament and actions may have done more than a little to inspire a resurrection of republican sentiments – and personal enmity for the emperor and devotion to *libertas* are certainly not mutually exclusive positions. We know more about the death of Caligula than about any other aspect of his reign (for this we may thank Josephus in particular). There are puzzles here and there with respect to some aspects of the details, but the general course of the conspiracy and the actual assassination are fairly well and consistently documented in our sources. Whatever conspiracies or conspirators were uncovered late in 40, we have no way of knowing. The memorable death of the chess-playing Julius Canus, for example, may perhaps be dated to this last full year of Caligula's life – but we have no means of certainty.[47] But whatever the status of conspiracies against Caligula in the winter of 40-41, the end result of the emperor's assassination definitively resolved all question of the truth or fiction of plots against Caligula. In some sense, a tyrant's death by conspiracy and assassination is always the ultimate proof of the validity of the paranoia that infected his reign.

Chapter Twelve

Assessing the Foreign Policy of the *Princeps*[1]

M ost of the scholarly consideration of what Caligula did in Britain and Germany – or, some would prefer to say, what he did not do – focuses on explaining away this or that seemingly bizarre aspect of the historical record (most notoriously, the seashell story). Scholars have spent much ink trying to disentangle and dissect exactly what Caligula did and did not do, and how this or that imperial act was either willfully misinterpreted, or retold in ignorance or exaggeration of what had actually happened.

It is reasonable to conclude that if Caligula did plan for a conquest of Germany to the Elbe, and an invasion and occupation of at least part of Britain, his initiatives were strategically sound. There is clear evidence that the logistical plans for the northern campaigns were huge; this was certainly no haphazard attempt at major military operations. And yet it came to naught. Caligula at best accepted the surrender of a minor British prince, while he did little in Germany, it would seem, beyond temporarily cowing the population with fear of invasion.[2] Of course he assumed the title 'Britannicus', and saw to the construction of a memorial lighthouse to commemorate his triumph over the Ocean – elements of seemingly outrageous propaganda that are not entirely out of line with the visions of the Augustan poets of an earlier age for the submission of Parthia and even fabled India.[3]

The reasons for Caligula's failure to achieve an appreciable victory in the north, however – if failure is the right word – are many. Certainly the conspiracy of Gaeticulus and Lepidus – not to mention the sororial involvement – would have spelled delay and hazard for the German/British plans. Soldiers would not have needed to mutiny or threaten to revolt; the emperor would have had enough to worry about in the face of existential threats to his reign. Any movement of the legions toward refusal to embark for Britain would have added to a situation already fraught with peril.

Another emperor – another Julius Caesar – might well have been able to do more with the situation that faced Caligula in the north. We may indict Caligula for a long list of offences, including aspects of his behaviour in the north, but the actual foreign policy position that he seems to have embraced was eminently sound. We should also note that Caligula lacked strong backing and support in Rome during this time away in the north. His youth and inexperience worked against him, and he did not have a solid network of clients and friends in the capital to safeguard his interests. He simply could not stay away from Rome indefinitely, even if Rome was ultimately a quite perilous place for him. There was no Mark Antony to see to Caesar's affairs in the absence of the great man from Rome and the daily drama of the Senate.

In Africa, the Mauretania problem may have been occasioned by the same Gaetulicus conspiracy. We simply do not know whether or not Ptolemy was involved. But again, the Caligulan plan passes muster for reasonableness: Mauretania would be provincial, not a client kingdom. The settlement of affairs in North Africa that Caligula pursued was a wise decision in light of the military and political history of Africa Proconsularis, and the dangers that province faced from the west. Ptolemy was no master of competent rule during his tenure in office; Mauretania was a weak spot in the frontier defences of the empire. Caligula may have been especially motivated to remove him from power because of conspiracies and plots – but again, the foreign policy position was not at all reckless or inappropriate given the circumstances. Caligula was not opposed to client kingdoms – his settlements in the East amply attest to this – but North Africa was a different situation, the reasons for which are not clear. But even if Ptolemy was innocent of complicity in the Gaetulicus plot, an argument could be made that his administration of his kingdom had not been entirely competent.

We must note, however, that the removal of Ptolemy came at a high price: rebellion broke out almost at once in Mauretania. We cannot be sure of how Caligula would have seen the whole matter through, as assassination intervened. Ptolemy's freedman Aedemon was a leading figure in the affair, and there was clearly some destruction at Volubilis in modern Morocco.[4] It is not fair – at least in the face of the extant evidence – to say that Caligula made the Mauretanian question worse by his removal of Ptolemy. There were problems afoot before Gaius came to power, and the problems would continue into Claudius' reign.

If Ptolemy was indeed in cahoots with Gaetulicus, his cousin Caligula had little choice but to remove him from power. On the whole, we may award an above average grade to Caligula for North Africa, without risk of being overly generous.

Less successful an appraisal can be given to Caligula's foreign affairs record in the East, at least insofar as the Jewish question is concerned. As Barrett notes, 'It was during Caligula's reign that the relations between Rome and the Jews reached their first serious crisis.'[5] Caligula may not be to blame for the genesis of whatever tensions existed in such cities as Alexandria and Jerusalem, but his actions worsened the situation and exacerbated tensions. Claudius may have invaded Britain, but he also notified the Jews of Alexandria that he considered his predecessor's policies with respect to Jewish affairs to have been an exercise in madness. The problems were not entirely of Caligula's making, and the solution would not come with his death and removal from power.[6]

Barbara Levick blames Caligula's pursuit of divine honours for his troubles with the Jews,[7] citing his financial exactions from wealthy Gauls as further evidence for his problematic foreign policy. But nothing involving Gallic landowners came anywhere close to the seriousness of the Jewish problem.

Much of Caligula's policy toward the East was influenced, no doubt, by his dealings with Julius Agrippa – and some scholars have commended Caligula for his settlement of affairs with individual Jewish leaders. On the whole, the emperor did not achieve any lasting success in the East, though we must keep in mind that he had a rather full foreign policy docket for his relatively brief principate. The riots that broke out in Jamneia – probably in the winter of 39-40 – came just as Caligula was quite preoccupied in the north. If indeed Caligula's reaction to the news was to insist on the setting up of his image in the Temple of Jerusalem, and the attendant conversion of that sacred site into a shrine for the honour of Caligula and the Caesars, then certainly the vengeful expedient did not succeed in resolving the problems in Judaea – far from it. If Caligula did intend to visit Alexandria (and elsewhere in the East?) in the spring of 41, it stands to reason that he may have intended finally to settle the problems in that sphere of the empire, just as he endeavoured to do the same in the north in 39-40. He may have felt that his domestic position was stronger in the aftermath of the suppression of the conspiracies of Gaetulicus and others. But throughout, we are left with an abiding sense that there was simply too much for him to handle. Claudius would unquestionably prove more competent, certainly more so than he had been given credit for, both inside the imperial family and out.

Caligula's eastern associations were the direct inheritance of his connection to the Antonians. Mark Antony had been the master of the East in the days leading up to the break with Octavian and the celebrated civil war that would culminate in the defeat of the Antonians at Actium in 31 BC and Alexandria in 30 BC. To appreciate Caligula's dealings in the East, one must therefore understand that the young emperor was torn between his Julian/Augustan and Antonian origins. Mark Antony was a model for the creation of a new, Hellenized Rome in the East – divine honours and all, we might think. Rome, after all, had been Eastern in origin: the Trojan spell was no doubt potent for the scion of the line of Iulus and Aeneas. Literary interests (not to say pretensions) would have been part of this approach to dealing with the East.[8]

Despite all this, we do well to remember, too, that our principal sources for Caligula's dealings with the Jews are Philo and Josephus, authors whose prejudices have been cited by some as evidence of an allegedly biased tradition against Caligula.[9] There seems little reason to doubt that Caligula did press the issue of his divinity and the images of his godhead. Less clear is whether he planned some war against the Jews – though again, this is exactly what did take place some decades later. Just as Claudius would invade Britain, and Rome maintain a hold on Britain to the fall of the western empire, so Rome would respond with military force to Jews, and the Temple that was threatened with the desecration attendant on the erection of Caligula's image would be destroyed under the armies of the Flavians. Barrett and others argue that the blame for the deterioration of relationships between Romans and Jews in the East was a mutual affair; Caligula may have been provocative, but so were certain of the Jewish leaders (especially in Alexandria). Yet it is difficult to escape the conclusion that Tiberius and Augustus were far wiser in how they handled the question of Jewish religious sensitivities.[10]

Was Caligula really more preoccupied with inspecting a villa when Philo and the Jewish delegation were in his presence to discuss the Alexandrian crisis? The story is easily enough believed – and it could be taken as evidence of a decadent madman, or of a crafty negotiator who wanted to appear quite disinterested in the whole affair. Whatever the case, assassination cut short any plans Caligula had for the settlement of the Eastern question. Julius Caesar had been assassinated on the eve of a planned departure for Parthia to do exactly the sort of thing one imagines was on Caligula's mind – fixing the persistent, seemingly intractable problems of the Roman East – and he would be slain just as his storied ancestor was – at home in Rome, not abroad. The killers of Caligula had diverse motives for wanting to see him dead – in some sense what united them all was solely the desire for his end – but foreign affairs do not seem to have much entered the equation of their decision.[11]

The appointments of Agrippa and Antiochus IV Epiphanes as client kings in Judaea and Commagene have been seen as essentially rational, stabilizing acts of Caligulan foreign policy. As we have seen, the other territorial dispositions inaugurated by Caligula in the East were also not without merit. Winterling is fair in his appraisal that in the span of less than two years – a time period also marked by his notorious illness – Caligula had managed to travel to Sicily, settle Rome's complex system of borders in the East and plan for a massive military action against Germany.[12] Much that was contemplated was cut short by events and circumstances that were not entirely Caligula's to control or manage. Claudius would be in Britain a mere two years after his nephew was assassinated. Britain would at last be a Roman province, and the dream of the two Gaiuses fulfilled by the alleged imbecile of the Julio-Claudian family.[13] Claudius would take the name 'Britannicus' for himself and his son by Messalina; his sixteen days on the island would be followed by a triumph that few could have thought undeserved.

We do well to ask if Caligula was possessed of a grand vision for the Roman Empire. Certainly his involvement – often on the scene – in different parts of the Roman world bespeaks an active interest in foreign affairs. Martin Millett has argued, 'We should not seek any grand strategy behind Rome's expansion, as the motivation for each successive conquest lay in the primarily personal nature of power at Rome and with the particular political circumstances of the times.'[14] Different scholars will react in diverse ways to this assertion and argument. It is within the realm of possibility that Caligula had a grand scheme for the empire, one that certainly would redound to his own glory once completed. It was a scheme that was very much in the tradition of the Julians, of his ancestor Caesar who had contemplated the invasion of Britain, and who like Caligula was rumoured to have wanted to transfer the capital of the empire to the East.[15]

Richard Alston concludes, 'Gaius' military policy may have been underestimated. Claudius' accession was marked by a spate of military activity in Germany and Africa ... and it seems very likely that Gaius commenced these campaigns. Claudius also launched the invasion of Britain very early in the reign, leaving open the possibility that he benefited from Gaius' preparations ... a show of force on the beaches of Gaul without committing his forces to a lengthy and costly campaign may have been a sensible policy.'[16]

Is the truth, then, somewhere between the extremes of a Balsdon and those of a Ferrill? Was Caligula depraved on so many levels, and yet more or less possessed of a correct appraisal of what should happen in Roman foreign policy? Again, if we judge the organizational decisions in both North Africa and the East, the answer must be that Caligula was rational. Claudius' successful invasion of Britain amply justifies the wisdom – or at least the reasonableness – of that undertaking. The continuing failure to settle the perennial German question did not bode well for Roman security in the north. And the destruction of Jerusalem in AD 70 afforded ample proof that Rome's problems in Judaea could not all be blamed on Caligula's actions in 39-40 – not even remotely.

Rational decisions, then, were married with a daunting array of problems and an inherently weak imperial position – simply because of the emperor's youth. In the positive estimation, Caligula had the powerful name of Germanicus. But that could only carry him so far, and the hatred of so many for Tiberius was both a potential blessing and a bane for Caligula – the successor could be viewed as the bringer of a new period of blessings, but there was also a profound animosity toward the Julio-Claudian line that certainly prevailed in certain senatorial factions.

Caligula was certainly a literate man, possessed of fine rhetorical skills and knowledge of classical literature and ancient history. He was also undoubtedly possessed of personal qualities that would have made an Augustus shudder, and that left a poor impression on both his family and his inner circle. Critics of his reign and temperament/behaviour are correct in noting that even if only half of the Suetonian and other stories are true, the picture is still damning. Those afflicted with serious personality traits are still capable, to be sure, of rational behaviour in their public affairs – and it may be that Caligula's talent was more for foreign affairs than domestic. We should be careful, however, at coming to any hasty conclusions in this regard; Caligula did have a notable building programme, including projects that Claudius thought important and worthwhile enough to complete, and certain measures were taken in domestic affairs that were not entirely unreasonable, indeed in some cases even admirable.

For Winterling, the essential characteristic of Caligula's dealings with the Senate, for example, was his determination to remove the veil or mask of hypocrisy that he saw as a defining characteristic of the principate. According to this thesis, Caligula saw clearly that the Augustan system offered a sham of republicanism; the truth was that power was really concentrated in the hands of one man.[17] Caligula in a sense challenged the Senate to take responsibility for their part in the mechanism by which this fraud continued to be perpetrated. In Winterling's estimation, the rumoured plan to move the imperial residence to Alexandria was actually a true initiative – Caligula felt that divine honours would be easier to affect in that eastern city. His ancestor Mark Antony would have understood his reasoning.

The question, then, becomes one of whether Willrich and others after him are right. Was Caligula actually a wise and judicious thinker, aware that the Augustan system of masquerade was doomed to failure, and that the only answer was a monarchy without apology or question? As a political thinker, was Caligula correct in assessing that republics are doomed to failure, while monarchies have a chance of survival? Caligula was a sharp wit and a determined critic. For Winterling, the infamous suggestion that the horse Incitatus should become a senator was not a serious intention on the part of the *princeps*, but rather an attempt to mock the senators for their behaviour and attitude. If Winterling is correct in his assessment of Caligula's relationship with and attitude toward the Senate, one wonders how much of his thinking was influenced by his formative experiences with Tiberius on Capri.[18]

Barrett sums up his verdict on Caligula: 'Caligula was clearly capable of acting right to the end in a rational manner ... What emerges from the sources is that while he was not clinically mad he was so obsessed with a sense of his own importance as to be practically devoid of any sense of moral responsibility. This attitude might well have resulted from the experience of his early youth ... what is clear is that once in power he manifested a totally self-centred view of the world.'[19]

Barrett goes on to compare Caligula to Joseph Stalin, citing the Soviet dictator as an example of a man who was capable of quite rational and reasonable behaviour, though also of extreme cruelty and savagery.[20] His judgement may be considered fair and indeed eminently reasonable. The eccentricities and bizarre, indeed sadistic behaviour of Caligula can be paralleled across time and space in the *résumes* of other despots; in reading of the behaviour and sardonic wit of the *princeps*, one is sometimes reminded of other historical monsters. Suetonius has faced criticism from some modern scholars for his simple, binary juxtaposition of the *princeps* and the monster – with the monster, as we have seen, receiving far more of the biographer's attention than the *princeps* – but on the whole, there would seem to be more of truth than fiction in the ancient narratives. If Seneca and others engaged in character assassination, it is quite possible that the assassination was amply merited.

Barrett notably provides an appendix devoted to the 'named victims' of Caligula. Some scholars have noted that the list is not especially long (it is of course a grim business to compare imperial conduct in terms of the number of dead). Philip Matyszak notes that, 'even if we double the number of Gaius Caligula's named victims, we still fall short by dozens of the number of Roman nobles slain by Octavian the triumvir or by Caesar in the civil wars.'[21] As for the charge of killing relatives like Gemellus (or, for that matter, his cousin Ptolemy), Matyszak notes that while Caligula was guilty in this regard, Octavian had slain his 'half-brother' Caesarion, and Agrippa Postumus had been slain at the commencement of Tiberius' reign. Again, different scholars will have different views here; nobody would likely have seriously considered Cleopatra's son to be a kinsman of Octavian, for example.

At some level, one is left with an abiding sense that Caligula's problem was that he came to power at too young an age, and devoid of the careful mentoring of anyone who might actually have directed his unquestionable talents into productive areas. We cannot be sure of the influence of Livia or Antonia over him – but a Sutorius Macro or a Silanus cannot have been particularly effective or even desirable tutors for the young prince.[22] And of course Seneca's tutelage of Nero did little to save either Rome or the Stoic from the monster of a later age. Caligula may or may not have had some clinical diagnosis of physical and/or mental ailment, but the circumstances of his upbringing and young adulthood certainly did little to help to soothe whatever afflictions he suffered.

We are left with a vast canvas for speculation, and a deep sense of not being able to come fully to terms with the Caligulan enigma. It is perhaps his greatest legacy that so much of what he planned and considered right for the foreign policy of the empire is exactly what happened during subsequent reigns.[23] *In fine*, however, we cannot blame allegedly hostile and unfair contemporary sources for the development of some Caligula myth that has no sound basis in reality. Once he had commenced his principate, no one did Caligula more harm than Caligula. This was often and even almost always the case with tyrants.

Conclusions

Time and again in this study, we have highlighted how there has been relatively little new evidence discovered on Caligula since the days of Balsdon. The available evidence – from writers who in some cases may well be judged as mediocre, and who may reflect their own prejudices and literary agendas more than any accurate rendition of 'what happened' – tantalizingly invites the work of scholars and amateur sleuths of ancient history alike to try to find answers to the enigma of Caligula.

He was not some misunerstood genius, compelled to commit violent acts on occasion that were no worse or better than the excesses of other autocrats of the Roman imperial line. Neither was he merely the victim of enemies in the Roman aristocracy who were able to achieve the final victory over him by manipulation of the historiographical record.

My undergraduate students are regularly keen to comment on how very much certain personages of Roman history had experienced by the age when they find themselves sitting in a classrom, mulling over the Julio-Claudians and their legacy. Caligula was 24 when he succeeded Tiberius, and just shy of 29 when he was assassinated. His youth may be the most significant factor that divides him from his immediate predecessors; the contrast with his uncle Claudius at the time of his accession in that momentous January of 41 must have been just as stark as that with Tiberius in March of 37 – though for different reasons. By the autumn of 54, Rome would again face the prospect of having a bright young man of promise ready to don the purple, and there would be another potential young man in the way of the *princeps* who would need to be dead sooner rather than later.[1]

Some scholars are ready to blame the Senate for so young and inexperienced a man, and there may well be some validity to that charge. In the face of Macro's securing of the Praetorian Guard, it is not clear that they had any more real freedom of action – at least not without deadly hazard to themselves – than they may have felt they had in the wake of Caligula's assassination. Rome was already well on the way to seeing the praetorians as kingmakers – a legacy, in no small way, of the era of Sejanus.

Caligula was young, and his formative years had been unquestionably difficult – and not in the manner of the young adulthood of an Augustus or a Tiberius. There is every reason to believe that he was bright, though here it it difficult to conclude that he was any more gifted than his predecessors (Tiberius, we do well to note, was acknowledged as a highly literary man, sexual perversions and indiscretions aplenty notwithstanding – there is no immunity from perversion accorded to those who are skilled in Greek).

Caligula hated his nickname, and he also, it seems, hated the name Gaius – a name that may have been all too potent an onomastic reminder of his glorious predecessor, the problematic Julius Caesar. Caesar had, after all, been the founder of the Julian political and military dynasty, but he also represented the tension between autocracy and republicanism, and unlike Augustus and Tiberius – who seemed better able than either of the Gaiuses to balance the tension – he would be murdered in a conspiracy.

Caligula was the inheritor of this Julian legacy, and lived under the shadow of the name and glory of his own unforgettable father Germanicus, but he was also the descendant of Mark Antony, himself the legendary descendant of the hero Anton, the son of Hercules – and Mark Antony represented the temptations and perils of the East, the dream of Alexander the Great and the world of Hellenistic monarchies and oriental ruler cults. He represented the allure of godhood and the siren song of adventure and untold wealth in the fabled lands of Egypt and beyond. And every step eastward was a step away from traditional Roman republicanism and old Roman virtue and morality. The Trojan progenitors of Rome had headed west, away from the smoke of the dying city of Priam – Julius Caesar had died on the eve of a planned expedition east, to Parthia, and Mark Antony had been entangled in more or less disastrous misadventures in the East – and Caligula now stood as *princeps* of a Mediterranean empire that could not neglect the East and the political and military realities of Parthia, Armenia, Egypt Judaea and the rest.

I am prepared to conclude that Caligula's 'illness' of the second half of the year 37 was what today would be conveniently labelled a nervous breakdown. He would not, perhaps, be labelled 'insane' in the clinical sense – though it is unquestionably problematic to try to diagnose subjects from the first century AD, either physically or mentally.

Did he recognize a certain hypocrisy in the way the Senate behaved, and the impossibly contradictory nature of the Republic in which he was 'first citizen'? No doubt. If he did, his method of education and maintenance perhaps left much to be desired. He certainly felt that autocratic monarchy was the best solution to the problems of government of so vast an empire. In his family relationships, concern for the maintenance of the imperial succession as a family affair may well have led to incest – unlike some modern historians, I am willing to believe that the ancient sources are correct that he had incestuous relations with Drusilla, Livilla and Agrippina. Certainly the literate young man would have noted the example of Jupiter, and, for that matter, the practice of Ptolemaic Egypt. Virgil had cautioned against such unions in the fourth book of his *Aeneid*, where Aeneas and Dido are presented as a new Apollo and Diana, brother and sister in a manner that evokes the Ptolemaic tradition of sibling incest.[2] Caligula was young, and if there was anything that had been demonstrated by the imperial practice of the last two reigns, it was that the succession was the key and abiding problem that confronted each new *princeps*. Even at his age, Caligula would need to be worried about the future – and at the time of his death, he had but one child, an infant daughter. The dynastic succession was in no way assured, and Agrippina's son Nero was already in the wings as a potential heir. Caligula needed sons, and he needed them quickly.

Politically, then, it would seem reasonable to conclude that Caligula wanted a monarchy without pretence, a monarchy that would accord absolute powers – or at least something more readily defined as absolute than the sham that he saw in the rule of Tiberius and Augustus. Such a monarchy demanded an obvious familial line of succession. It might well have done better to be housed at Alexandria, the storied city that held the body of Alexander the Great, than in Rome with its tradition of slaying would-be tyrants and the home of the hypocritical Senate that one day fawned on its darling *princeps*, only the next day to complain and to conspire. For all we know, Caligula may have reasoned that his ancestor Antony was more intelligent than his ancestor Augustus in the matter of how to manage a Roman Republic that was now stretched from one side of the Mediterranean to the other, a burgeoning empire that could not be run like some central Italian, Latin republic.

But none of this changes the essential intelligence and competence that marks what we know of Caligula's foreign policy and military intentions. He was correct in his general assessment of what needed to be done in Britain and Germany, and later history would confirm the soundness of his reasoning. He was also right-minded in his judgements and plans for North Africa and the client kingdoms of the East. We cannot be sure what would have happened, of course, had he continued to rule, but the foreign policy record such as we have it does not permit us to dismiss Caligula as a madman who had no sense of how to manage the foreign affairs of Rome. If anything, he shows an above average intelligence for one so young, and displays a certain acumen and gift for knowing how to make appointments of governors and client kings. Whether or not he wanted to be a monarch in the style of an oriental potentate, his analysis of what needed to be done to safeguard Rome's borders and to expand the empire was correct.

Throughout, however, we do well to consider that scholars are sometimes prone to scrutinize and analyze the evidence from the Caligulan reign more intensely than that of other periods in Roman history, precisely because there is a relative dearth of information, and such an unquestionable fascination with coming to terms with Caligula. While the available evidence does not allow us simply to dismiss him as some incompetent lunatic, it also has very real limits in terms of our ability to judge the man fairly and accurately.

The title of this volume describes Caligula as an 'unexpected general'. His mother Agrippina the Elder may have entertained grand dreams for him in those dramatic days of Germanicus' conducting of operations on the Rhine frontier, and in the East – but she was also fertile and had older sons. No one could have reasonably expected that Caligula would be in power less than a quarter century after the death of Augustus in that fateful late summer of 14. And on the day of his accession in March of 37, no one could have expected that the young Caligula would move so quickly to try to settle Roman affairs on at least three major frontiers.

The 'unexpected general' would not succeed in his initiatives. He would never set foot in Britain, nor manage to arrive in Alexandria for his planned sojourn in 41. On the day he was given the fatal lesson that he was most certainly not, after all, a god, he had, however, charted the course that in large part his older, more experienced uncle would pursue as *princeps*. Claudius was in his own way an unexpected emperor – and he would do much to erase the bad memory of Caligula and the legacy of what his nephew had done in his relations with the Senate and the leading equestrians. But in the arena of foreign affairs, he would largely follow the path that his ambitious young nephew had delineated.

In short, it may be said that perhaps only a young man could have dreamed the grandiose visions that haunted Caligula's insomniac nights. And perhaps only an older man could actually conquer Britain, and follow through rather more deftly on trying to resolve the enduring problem of how to reconcile the principate with republicanism. By the time Claudius would learn that mushrooms were, after all, the food of the gods,[3] another young man – the notorious Nero – would arrive on the scene, soon enough to resurrect the dreams of Troy, the East, Dido's gold and all the rest. And with him, in due (perhaps inevitable?) course, the Julio-Claudian line would die at last.[4]

Endnotes

Preface and Acknowledgments

1. The citations of Barrett in this book are mostly from the first edition, not the second. This is a deliberate choice (cf. Denise Reitzenstein's remarks in her *Bryn Mawr* review of the second). The first edition is widely available, including in a very inexpensive paperback edition; the second is far costlier (and only available in hardback). The second edition, as we have noted, does not present much that is new regarding the author's appraisal of Caligula. The material is organized in a somewhat more logical way in the second edition, and the material on numismatics and portraiture is given greater prominence – but on the whole, if there was rather little new evidence about Caligula from Balsdon to Barrett 1.0, there was even less between 1989 and 2015.

2. Here and there as appropriate there are recommended translations and editions of primary sources in the footnotes. The Loeb Classical Library provides access to the major sources (Suetonius; Tacitus; Dio Cassius; Philo; Josephus); there are good editions in the Oxford World's Classics series of Suetonius and Tacitus. Smallwood's valuable collection of 'documents illustrating' the reign of Caligula is available in a paperback reprint edition from Cambridge University Press.

Chapter One: The Life of Caligula by Suetonius,
Part I (Caligula the *Princeps*)

1. There are a number of editions of the lives of Suetonius. The Loeb Classical Library provides a two-volume set of the surviving work of Suetonius, with Latin text and English translation by J.C. Rolfe (the revised edition of 1998 has significant updates). There is an Oxford Classical Texts edition of the extant Suetonius edited by Robert A. Kaster (*C. Suetoni Tranquilli De Vita Caesarum Libros VIII et De Grammaticis et Rhetoribus Librum*, Oxford, 2016); Kaster has also published a companion

to his Oxford text on the textual problems of the lives of the Caesars, *Studies on the Text of Suetonius' De vita Caesarum* (Oxford, 2016). Among recommended English translations of the lives are those of Catharine Edwards for the Oxford World's Classics series (*Suetonius: Lives of the Caesars*, Oxford, 2000) and Robert Graves for Penguin Classics (*Gaius Suetonius Tranquillus: The Twelve Caesars*, London: Penguin Books Ltd, 1957). The Penguin was significantly revised in 1979 and again in 2003. Donna Hurley has produced a translation with introduction and notes for Hackett Publishing Company (*Suetonius: The Caesars*, 2011); Hurley argues in her preface that Suetonius' lives might well be the one book permitted the shipwrecked survivor on a desert island.

2. For a convenient introduction to Suetonius, note especially Andrew Wallace-Hadrill, *Suetonius* (London: Gerald Duckworth & Co. Ltd, 1983; second edition 1995, with corrections).

3. Donna W. Hurley is the author of *An Historical and Historiographical Commentary on Suetonius' Life of C. Caligula* (Atlanta, Georgia: Scholars Press, 1993) (American Classical Studies 32). Note also David Wardle's *Suetonius' Life of Caligula* (Bruxelles: Éditions Latomus, 1994, for the Collection Latomus). There is also a Bristol Classical Press edition by Hugh Lindsay from 1993. Not surprisingly given his popularity, Suetonius has been the subject of a healthy number of commentaries on the individual lives, and Caligula has been especially richly served in this regard.

4. The major loss for Caligulan studies is that of the relevant portions of Tacitus' *Annales*.

5. Balsdon notes (p.226) that the life of Caligula is shorter than the Suetonian lives of Julius, Augustus and Tiberius – but longer than any other (despite the emperor's relatively brief tenure). Similarly, we may note the appreciably high level of scholarly commentary that has been afforded to the short principate. Caligula's four years in power are among the most studied months in Roman imperial history.

6. Suetonius surprises the reader at the start of his twenty-second chapter, where he announces the thematic transition.

7. There is a biography by Lindsay Powell, *Germanicus: The Magnificent Life and Mysterious Death of Rome's Most Popular General* (South Yorkshire: Pen & Sword Military, 2013).

8. For Drusus, see especially Lindsay Powell's *Eager for Glory: The Untold Story of Drusus the Elder, Conqueror of Germania* (South Yorkshire: Pen & Sword Military, 2013).

9. Venus was the patron goddess of the Julian *gens*.

10. Nero was certainly born there; he was also there during the Great Fire of AD 64.

11. As we shall see, for Suetonius, Caligula's 'real' name Gaius was associated with the destiny of violent death; the biographer will close his treatment of Caligula on an onomastic note, observing that the members of the Caesarian house who were named 'Gaius' were destined to die violently (cf. Gaius Julius Caesar).

12. Suetonius speaks of *taedium urbis*, or 'tedium with the city' – a trait that Caligula shared with Tiberius.

13. Suetonius notes that the mourning occasioned by the death of Germanicus was so great, that even barbarian peoples consented to a truce out of a shared grief for the loss of the great man. The King of Parthia is said to have suspended his customary hunting activities, and to have given up banquets with his court for a period of mourning.

14. Our principal extant source for Piso is Tacitus (*Annales*, Books 2-3); we are fortunate to have the so-called *Senatus consultum de Cn. Pisone patre* of 10 December, AD 20, the senatorial decree that records the punishments imposed on Piso and his associates. The text was inscribed on bronze that came to light near Seville in the Roman province of Baetica in the late 1980s; the inscription is of inestimable value for determining just what Piso was accused of, and for the relationship of the senatorial decree with the trial narrative found in chapters 1-19 of Tacitus' *Annales* 3. There are two 1996 editions of the work we may note, the result of a collaborative effort in Spain and Germany. The Spanish version is edited by A. Caballos, F. Fernández and W. Eck under the title *El Senadoconsulto de Gneo Pisón Padre* (Sevilla: Europa artes graficas); the German under the title *Das senatus consultum de Gn, Pisone patre* (München: C.H. Beck, Vestigia 48). The reconstructed text of the decree is found in both editions; the Spanish volume has colour illustrations and a comprehensive guide to where in Spain the discoveries were made.

15. Or 'Baby Boot', in the memorable appellation of J.P.V.D. Balsdon in his *The Emperor Gaius (Caligula)* (Oxford, 1934), p.5.

16. For the attempted ingratiation with the common soldiers by Agrippina and Germanicus, see F.R.D. Goodyear, *The Annals of Tacitus, Volume I (Annals 1.1-54)* (Cambridge, 1970), p.287. Goodyear's work offers a comprehensive commentary on Tacitus' work; there are translations of the *Annales* in both the Penguin Classics and Oxford World's Classics series, the latter with extensive annotations.

17. On this episode and its place in the lore of the family of Germanicus, see Donna W. Hurley, 'Gaius Caligula in the Germanicus Tradition', in *The American Journal of Philology*, Vol.110, No.2 (Summer 1989), pp.316-38.

18. Book I, chapters 40 and following.

19. Suetonius, *Caligula* 8.1. The verses are found in Willy Morel's edition of the fragments of the Latin poets under the title *Populares Versus in Caligulam*: *In castris natus patriis, nutritus in armis / iam designati principis omen erat* ('He was born in his father's camp, nourished in arms / this was an omen of the one already destined to be *princeps*').

20. For Livia, recommended reading is Anthony A. Barrett, *Livia: First Lady of Imperial Rome* (New Haven, Connecticut/London: Yale University Press, 2002).

21. For the chronological question, see Hurley's commentary notes on Suetonius, *Caligula* 10.1.

22. Suetonius gives here a hint of the transvestite practices for which Caligula would later be infamous.

23. The Tiberius presented by both Suetonius and Tacitus has his own deplorable qualities; it is a mark of Caligula's unseemliness that even Tiberius seeks to improve his character.

24. The myth was the subject of a play by Euripides that survives in a fragmentary state; the most famous extant account is by Ovid in his epic *Metamorphoses* (1.747-2.400). The story of Phaëthon (which straddles two books of Ovid's masterpiece and is the longest single narrative in his poem of transformation and change) may well be a verse commentary of the problem of the imperial succession and the transition from the stability of the Augustan Age to an uncertain future; there may be political significance in Tiberius' alleged remarks about his eventual successor. The Phaëthon image was an especially apt mythological *comparandum* for the problem of the imperial succession.

25. Another daughter of Marcus Vipsanius Agrippa, by his first wife, Pomponia Caecilia Attica.

26. Book 4 of Tacitus' *Annales* is concerned with the events of AD 23-28; Tacitus marks the start of this period with the commencement of a marked change in Tiberius, as the emperor came increasingly under the influence of the wicked Sejanus. Most of Book 5 of Tacitus' work is lost, though Book 6 survives integrally and provides an invaluable account of the final stages of Tiberius' reign. The Cambridge 'green and yellow' series of Greek and Latin classics has an edition of Book 4 by R.H. Martin and A.J. Woodman (Cambridge, 1989); there is a larger edition of what remains of Books 5-6 in the Cambridge 'orange' series (A. J. Woodman, *The Annales of Tacitus, Books 5 and 6*, Cambridge, 2017); in the Aris & Phillips set of editions of classical texts, there is a Book 4 by D.C.A. Shotter (1989; reprinted with corrections 1999), and of Books 5-6 by R.H. Martin (2001). All are replete with extensive notes and commentary on historical matters.

27. Sejanus was from Volsinii, the modern Bolsena; his greatest power came after the death of Tiberius' son Drusus in AD 23. Interestingly, Tiberius did not permit him to marry Drusus' widow, Livilla, with whom he had been having an affair; it is clear enough that for all his confidence and trust in Sejanus, the emperor was not willing to bring an equestrian into the imperial family. Still, after Tiberius left Rome in 26, there was little doubt who would be in *de facto* charge in Rome. He was in some sense the first casualty of Caligula; his downfall came in part for alleged plotting against the young Gaius. It is rather uncertain what his ultimate aim was; he was certainly corrupted by blind ambition and intoxicated with his own increasing power.

28. Regarding the end of Sejanus, Arther Ferrill comments, 'When the Emperor was finally ready to act, he did so with a sudden, deadly rapier thrust.' (*Caligula: Emperor of Rome*, London: Thames and Hudson, 1991, p.77).

29. It was Antonia who had exposed the Sejanus and Livilla plot to Tiberius.

30. For Antonia, note Nikos Kokkinos, *Antonia Augusta: Portrait of a Great Roman Lady* (London/New York: Routledge, 1992).

31. For a good example of the argument that Suetonius is simply wrong about Caligula's relationship with Tiberius, see Aloys Wisterling, *Caligula: A Biography* (Berkeley/Los Angeles/London: The University of California Press, 2011), pp.47-48 (a translation from the original German work *Caligula: eine Biographie* (München: C.H. Beck, 2003).

32. Fortune is cited by Suetonius with respect to the accession of Claudius in the wake of his nephew's killing; cf. *Claudius* 10.

33. Cf. the threats of military rebellion in the wake of the death of Augustus.

34. The history of Caligula's nuptial unions and disunions is complicated; see further David Wardle's comprehensive study, 'Caligula and His Wives', in *Latomus* 57 (1998), pp.109-26.

35. The praetorians played a major role in the history of early imperial Rome; for a convenient introduction to a vast topic, see Sandra Bingham, *The Praetorian Guard: A History of Rome's Elite Special Forces* (Waco, Texas: Baylor University Press, 2013); also Guy de la Bédoyère's *Praetorian: The Rise and Fall of Rome's Imperial Bodyguard* (New Haven/London: Yale University Press, 2017). Ennia was possibly the granddaughter of Thrasyllus, the astrologer to Tiberius. We shall revisit the question of the exact nature of the liaison between Ennia and Caligula (in particular, the problem of who initiated the relationship) in our consideration of the surviving evidence of Tacitus and Dio Cassius; Suetonius casts Caligula in a negative light, to be sure, by putting the blame for the whole business squarely on him (as opposed to arguing that Macro was a willing conniver, or even instigator, in the prostitution of his wife).

36. At *Tiberius* 73, Suetonius notes that some sources think that Caligula administered a slow, wasting poison to Tiberius, while others say that Tiberius was denied food while in convalescence from a fever. The pillow story is also mentioned. For commentary on this and other passages of the Tiberian life, see especially H. Lindsay, *Suetonius: Tiberius* (London: Gerald Duckworth & Co. Ltd, 1995) (a commentary on the Latin text of the life, with extensive historical notes).

37. We may recall how Augustus had ensured that the assassins of his adoptive father Julius Caesar would all be eliminated – *pietas* on full display.

38. Suetonius, *Caligula* 3.

39. That is, the victims of the loss of the three legions in the Teutoburg forest. On the infamous catastrophe, note especially Jason R. Abdale, *Four Days in September: The Battle of Teutoburg* (South Yorkshire: Pen & Sword Military, 2016) (revised second edition of the Bloomington, Indiana: Trafford Publishing, 2011, original). For the fascinating archaeological story of the hunt for the site of the battle (near the modern German city of Osnabrück), see Tony Clunn, *The Quest for the Lost Roman Legions: Discovering the Varus Battlefield* (El Dorado Hills, California: Savas Beatie LLC, 2005).

40. Generally on the life of Tiberius, note the extensive treatment in the 'Aspects of Greek and Roman Life' series by Barbara Levick, *Tiberius the Politician* (London: Thames and Hudson Ltd, 1976, revised edition from Routledge, 1999). Levick's book is the standard English study of Tiberius.

41. *Caligula* 13.

42. Cf. the names/titles mentioned in *Caligula* 22, at the commencement of the 'monster' section of Suetonius' life.

43. *Gemellus* is the Latin word for 'twin'. The boy Tiberius Julius Caesar Nero Gemellus was born on 10 October, AD 19; his twin brother Tiberius Claudius Germanicus II Gemellus died in 23 of unspecified causes.

44. For the urns with inscriptional testimony to the simple *pietas* of the emperor, see Balsdon, p.30; the memorial for Agrippina records that she was the daughter of Agrippa, the granddaughter of Augustus, the wife of Germanicus and the mother of the *princeps* Gaius Caesar Augustus Germanicus. That of Caligula's brother Nero notes that he was a priest of Augustus and quaestor.

45. Of all the Roman imperial attempts to rename months, the only ones that succeeded in enjoying longevity were July and August. Commodus would be infamous for deciding that the entire year's worth of months needed to be renamed in his honour. The honour shown to Germanicus would conveniently put his month of September in line after the months dedicated to Julius Caesar and to Augustus. There is no record of the rescinding of the September decree – but then again, in the aftermath of Caligula's assassination it is quite possible that many decrees of the dead *princeps* were more or less quietly forgotten.

46. Livia had been granted the name of 'Augusta' after the death of her husband; Antonia would now be honoured with the same title.

47. Balsdon (p.32) notes well: 'Thus was emphasized and advertised the unity of the surviving children of Germanicus, the inner ring of the imperial family, on the outer fringes of which stood the Emperor's adopted son, Tiberius Gemellus, and his uncle, Claudius.'

48. Suetonius, *Caligula* 14.

49. Suetonius, *Caligula* 10.

50. *ut nec immerito sit dictum nec servum meliorem ullum nec deteriorem dominum fuisse.*

51. As we shall see, this may not actually have been done; cf. *Caligula* 30.

52. Gossip that he was the son of Sejanus would not have endeared the young man to the Senate or the people.

53. 'A type of male prostitute', in the vague yet dignified language of the *Oxford Latin Dictionary*.

54. Cf. Suetonius, *Tiberius* 43.1.

55. His savagery may be seen here – or, perhaps, a desire to be seen as exceptionally upright. To Tacitus we may ascribe any cynical tendency to see disingenuousness in the emperor's actions.

56. On these figures, note the magisterial three-volume edition of T.J. Cornell, *The Fragments of the Roman Historians* (Oxford, 2013), with introduction, texts, translations and copious commentary. Aulus Cremutius Cordus was memorably accused of having praised Brutus and Cassius as the 'last of the Romans'; see further the work of Mary R. McHugh, 'Historiography and Free Speech: The Case of Cremutius Cordus', in Ineke Sluiter and Ralph M. Rosen (eds), *Free Speech in Classical Antiquity* (Leiden: Brill, 2004), pp.391-408. Needless to say, very few fragments survive of Cordus' fatal histories.

57. There were also comparatively minor legacies, to the Vestals, the soldiers and commoners, and the masters of the city wards (*magistri vicorum*).

58. Hurley notes in her commentary that this is the only place in Suetonius where the author uses this title of Livia.

59. Hurley mentions the general distaste for 'personality cults' that marked Tiberius' policies.

60. A lavish, indeed extraordinary honour. The Parilia was a spring festival that was connected with agriculture; it later acquired a connection with the founding of Rome by Romulus. The meaning of the gesture was clear: Rome was experiencing rebirth in the springtime commencement of the reign of Caligula (the date of Tiberius' death and Caligula's assumption of power may have played into the decision). Regarding the distaste for Tiberius among the populace, one need only recall the slogan *Tiberium in Tiberim* that was popular (Suetonius, *Tiberius* 75) – the call for the body of the emperor to be cast in the river. Prayers were offered to the immortals of the lower world that Tiberius be granted an abode only among the impious. Suetonius notes that hatred for the emperor only increased when some prisoners were killed even after his death, since Caligula was not in Rome and there was no one who could be approached on questions of appeal or reprieve – the *saevitia*, or savagery, of Tiberius endured even beyond the grave.

61. Wilhelm Henzen, the German philologist and epigrapher, was editor of the *Acta Fratrum Arvalium quae supersunt* (Berlin: Reimer, 1874). Later discoveries of additional *acta* may be found in A. Pasoli's 1950 Bologna edition (*Acta Fratrum Arvalium, quae post annum MDCCCLXXIV reperta sunt*). For Caligula's accession, see p.xliii of Henzen's edition. E. Mary Smallwood has conveniently gathered the relevant texts in her *Documents Illustrating the Principates of Gaius Claudius and Nero* (Cambridge, 1967). The *Fratres Arvales*, or 'Brothers of the Fields', were a college of priests in Rome that had connection to harvest festivals and rituals.

62. The Saturnalia was traditionally observed from 17-19 December; Caligula added 20 December to the festival. Cf. Dio 59.6.4; also 60.25.8 (Claudius restores the fifth day that had been designated by Caligula but then abolished).

63. Suetonius, *Caligula* 6. The lament may have been especially intense given that the biographer records that an early report had indicated that Germanicus had recovered from his illness; Tiberius is said to have been awakened from sleep by the singing of the verse *Salva Roma, salva patria, salvus est Germanicus* – 'secure is Rome, secure is the fatherland, secure is Germanicus' – another unforgettable image, as the dour emperor is roused from sleep by cries redolent with the spirit of love and longing for Germanicus.

64. The bibliography on the world of the Roman games is formidable. For a start, one may profitably consult Richard C. Beacham, *Spectacle Entertainments of Early Imperial Rome* (New Haven, Connecticut/London: Yale University Press, 1999); cf. also Christopher Epplett, *Gladiators & Beast Hunts: Arena Sports of Ancient Rome* (South Yorkshire: Pen & Sword Military, 2016). Still useful is the classic work of George Jennison, *Animals for Show and Pleasure in Ancient Rome*, originally published in 1937 by Manchester University Press, and reprinted in 2005 by the University of Pennsylvania Press. Jennison is especially useful for his marginal citations of classical passages referencing the use of animals in the games.

65. Virgil memorably presents the *lusus Troiae* in his epic *Aeneid* (5.545-603).

66. Balsdon notes (p.52) that Suetonius includes the enterprise under the accomplishments of the *princeps*, not the monster.

67. The famous astrologer in question is Tiberius Claudius Thrasyllus, who had met Tiberius in Rhodes and had been granted Roman citizenship by Tiberius

(hence his name). He died in AD 36, not long before Tiberius – and not late enough to see the accession of Caligula. Suetonius notes in his life of Tiberius (69) that the emperor was somewhat neglectful of the gods and religious cult, but addicted to astrology – besides being notably afraid of thunder.

68. Suetonius, *Caligula* 3.

69. The aqueduct, Suetonius notes, was finished by Claudius, but the amphitheatre is said to have been abandoned. Calgula's aqueduct initiatives are mentioned by Frontinus, who notes that he started two aqueducts in the second year of his reign (*De Aquaeductu* 1.13). For commentary on the aqueducts, see R.H. Rodgers, *Frontinus: De Aquaeductu Urbis Romae* (Cambridge, 2004), *ad loc*.

70. Polycrates was a sixth-century tyrant. For the isthmus project, a *primipilaris*, or 'chief centurion', is said to have been sent to survey the necessary labour.

71. For the criticisms that could be raised in the matter of excessive projects, see Catherine Edwards, *The Politics of Immorality in Ancient Rome* (Cambridge, 1993), pp. 146 ff. (with reference to Caligula's initiatives).

72. 'Arguably Suetonius' best-known sentence,' as Donna Hurley notes in her commentary.

73. Suetonius, *Caligula* 22.

74. As Wardle notes in his commentary (p.65), 'Suetonius' rubrics generally entail the abandonment of chronology, so that the dating of many incidents is impossible without a chronological framework from another author.'

75. Suetonius, *Caligula* 6.

76. Caligula may also have been seen as attempting to emulate Alexander the Great, the greatest 'westerner' to have invaded the East.

77. We also do well to remember that Caligula was also a descendant of Mark Antony. There was certainly room for speculation both during and after his life that some of his behaviour resembled that of the defeated triumvir – namely the ready indulgence in lower-class entertainments, and also the spendthrift generosity and taste for grand gestures of ingratiation.

Chapter Two: The Life of Caligula by Suetonius, Part II (Caligula the *Monstrum*)

1. *Pater exercituum* may have been Caligula's version of the Augustan title *pater patriae*.

2. *Iliad* 2.704, where Odysseus advised devotion to Agamemnon in the wake of Achilles' withdrawal from the war over the question of Briseis.

3. For a good introduction to a vast subject, see Adrian Goldsworthy, *Caesar: Life of a Colossus* (New Haven, Connecticut/London: Yale University Press, 2006), pp.493 ff.

4. The statue would literally get the 'last laugh'; cf. the prodigies that attended the assassination of the emperor that Suetonius describes at *Caligula* 57.

5. Castor and Pollux were the brothers of Helen of Sparta/Troy, the children of Leda. The former was the son of the mortal Tyndareus, while the latter was the divine son of Zeus. They were also known as the Dioscouri or Gemini; after the death of Castor, Pollux asked Zeus to allow him to share his divinity with his brother.

6. For the adjective cf. Ovid, *Metamorphoses* 15.481.

7. See further here Hurley's commentary notes on *Caligula* 22.2.

8. On the place of the moon in Caligula's imperial ideology, note the work of F. Gury, 'L'idéologie impériale et la lune: Caligula', in *Latomus* 59 (2000), pp.564-95.

9. *Iliad* 23.724. As for the flamingo feasts, the bird would figure in the prodigies that accompanied the emperor's assassination (cf. *Caligula* 57).

10. The most extensive study of Agrippa is Lindsay Powell's *Marcus Agrippa: Right-Hand Man of Caesar Augustus* (South Yorkshire: Pen & Sword Military, 2015).

11. Some have questioned the truth of this assertion on the grounds that the aforementioned inscription on Agrippina's urn mentions Agrippa. It is difficult to imagine that Caligula could have omitted her father's name, even if he did feel deep resentment at the place of his ancestor in his lineage. And certainly slurs about alleged incest could not find a place on an epitaph.

12. For the details and citations, see especially Hurley's commentary on *Caligula* 23.2. She concludes that 'Gaius was correct ... but Suetonius, with his penchant for research on families and places ... was anxious to prove him wrong.'

13. An example of the so-called 'weighted alternative' that is familiar to students of Tacitus.

14. It is possible that the later matricide of Nero may have coloured accounts of Caligula's behaviour toward his grandmother.

15. Robert Graves has a 'colonel' sent to Gemellus to decapitate him in his rendition of the event in the 1934 novel *I, Claudius*.

16. Balsdon is less sympathetic about the death of Silanus, noting, 'He owed his death to his own indiscretion.' (p.38).

17. The identification of the Silanus referenced in the *Agricola* is uncertain. Caligula's father-in-law Silanus was suffect consul in AD 15, but there was another consular Silanus who was an enemy of Caligula. See further the commentary notes of A.J. Woodman and C.S. Kraus, *Tacitus: Agricola* (Cambridge, 2014), *ad loc*. The 'other' Silanus (consul in 19) is cited at Tacitus, *Historiae* 4.48, where we see the lengthy note of G.E.F. Chilver, *A Historical Commentary on Tacitus' Histories, Books IV and V* (Oxford, 1985). 'It is uncertain what relation he was to … Gaius' father-in-law, who was forced to suicide in Gaius' first year as *princeps*.'

18. *Caligula* 24. On the charge of sororial incest, Balsdon comments, 'Such devotion [that is, non-sexual attachment] within the family was as exceptional in early imperial Rome as was the desire for seclusion which took Tiberius to Capreae. And so, as the contemptible imagination of despicable men explained the latter in terms of revolting obscenities, the other was interpreted as incest.'

19. For Agrippina, see especially Anthony A. Barrett, *Agrippina: Sex, Power, and Politics in the Early Empire* (New Haven, Connecticut/London: Yale University Press, 1996).

20. The story of Antonia having caught Caligula with Drusilla is usually linked with her death so soon after his accession, as a suitably salacious story to prove how the daughter of Mark Antony recognized early on Gaius' debauched perversions.

21. Hurley speculates in her commentary notes *ad Caligula* 24.2 that the emperor's sudden trip to Syracuse may have been designed deliberately to provide time to arrange for his sister's promotion to the ranks of the goddesses.

22. *Caligula* 12.

23. This is the same Piso who would later be the head of the great conspiracy against the emperor Nero in AD 65. Cf. Dio 58.8.7.

24. See here Hurley's commentary on *Caligula* 25.1, with reference to Suetonius, *Augustus* 69.1.

25. Barrett's first edition places this marriage shortly after 23 September in the year 38; his second edition opts for 'soon after October'. Other than this date,

the only significant changes in Barrett's timeline of Caligula's reign between his two editions are that he fixes Flaccus' arrest on 21 October 38 (the same day as a fire in the Aemilian district); he believes now that Petronius was ordered to place the emperor's statue in the Temple of Jerusalem in summer and not possibly spring of 40; and he thinks that Caligula visited the English Channel in the spring of 40, though he is not certain.

26. Scholars have determined that the consul's *praenomen*, or first name, was actually Publius.

27. The goddess would not prove to be a good patroness or protector for the unfortunate child.

28. He was a cousin to Caligula; the admittedly somewhat distant family relationship apparently did not trouble the emperor.

29. Balsdon (p.212) excuses Caligula for this with the note that he need not be condemned for introducing a 'comic turn' to the games.

30. The commentators dispute the exact meaning of Caligula's alleged comment that the victims would be chosen *a calvo ad calvum*, that is, from bald head to bald head. The point of the Suetonian story is that Caligula did not bother to read the charges against the men (so as to condemn to such a cruel fate only those who were particularly culpable); he may have chosen arbitrarily those unlucky enough to be standing between two bald men, or perhaps he chose everyone (the phrase being taking proverbially as a reference to life from cradle to deathbed). Cf. Dio 59.22.3.

31. Cf. *Caligula* 14.2.

32. 'It was something that any tyrant might do' (Hurley on *Caligula* 27.3).

33. *Per genium suum.* The *Genius* was properly the male spirit of a *gens*, who inhabited whoever was currently the head of the clan or family.

34. A perversion of the great sense of wrongness and tragedy associated with death *ante ora parentum*.

35. Gangrene, as Hurley notes on *Caligula* 27.4.

36. Atellan farces were vulgar comedies; Atella was a town in Campania, where it seems the buffoonish shows originated (they were originally composed in Oscan, an ancient Italic language of southern Italy).

37. The punishment of the styluses is similar to that recorded for the Christian martyr Cassian of Imola (date unknown), a schoolmaster who was handed over to his own charges for stabbing with their writing implements.

38. Suetonius, *Caligula* 11.

39. *Caligula* 29.

40. 'None of the other single Greek words in Suetonius is glossed' (Wardle's commentary note).

41. Cf. the *summa confidentia* referenced at *Caligula* 51 in Suetonius' appraisal of the emperor's conflicting personality.

42. *Omnia mihi et in omnis licere* (*Caligula* 29).

43. The vile comment is actually a fairly learned witticism, which the commentators duly explicate. It references the notorious burying alive of a Gallic and a Greek couple in the third century BC (to fulfill a prophecy that the Gauls and Greeks would one day possess Rome), and plays on the name of Galatia in Asia Minor, said to have been founded by Celts/Gauls. It also alludes to Julius Caesar's subjugation of Gaul, and, in the original Latin, to sexual conquest (*subegisse*).

44. *Caligula* 30.

45. The line is from the second-century BC Roman tragedian Lucius Accius' work the *Atreus*. The line is also referenced in Seneca's work *De Ira* (1.20.4), where a reference to the days of Sulla is noted (Accius, we should note, apparently lived to a great age). The fragment of Accius may be found conveniently in the second volume of the Loeb Classical Library editions of the *Remains of Old Latin*, p.383.

46. Cf. *Caligula* 15.

47. Cf. Dio 59.16, where the historian marks the start of the time when Caligula became intolerant of criticisms of his predecessor.

48. Hurley argues that it could also have been 'assigned to him by those who thought him impatient to inflict capital punishment' (commentary on *Caligula* 30.2) – but it seems more likely that this 'witticism' was Caligula's alone. Dio records the same quote at 59.13.6.

49. The incident is recorded by Suetonius at *Tiberius* 40, and by Tacitus at *Annales* 4.63.1; anywhere from 20,000 to 50,000 were killed in the catastrophe – likely far worse than the disaster of Varus in terms of casualty figures.

50. Cf. Suetonius, *Caligula* 54.

51. The Apelles story is one of the anecdotes that Balsdon passes over *sans commentaire* (p. 161).

52. The passage in question is *Respublica* 377-393.

53. The great length of Livy's *Ab Urbe Condita* no doubt provided ready excuse for Caligula to condemn the great Augustan writer and tutor of his uncle Claudius.

54. Some have seen in the attack on Virgil and Livy a repudiation of the Augustan past. Whatever Caligula thought of the two writers, he did not follow through on whatever intention of censorship he had. 'In literature as in all else he was a fearless critic and his views are interesting and heterodox' (Balsdon, p.205). For the subject of Caligula's views and influence on literature, note F.R.D. Goodyear, 'Tiberius and Gaius: Their Influence and Views on Literature', in *ANRW* 2.32.1 (1984), pp.603–10.

55. Cf. *Caligula* 26.

56. There are insinuations in Suetonius' story that Aesius Proculus was chosen for his humiliation and untimely end for sexually suggestive reasons.

57. Balsdon assures us (p.149) that the old priest may have fled before he had the chance to face his younger successor. Caligula may have been interested in reviving certain lapsed elements of Roman religion, but the sadistic import of the story cannot be ignored.

58. The gladiator Porius was an *essedarius*, a British chariot driver; his fate is not recorded.

59. 'Sexual license was another characteristic of the typical tyrant. Stories of incest and homosexuality have to be understood as representing Caligula's tight political control over his family, and over others who might threaten him' (T.E.J. Wiedemann, 'Tiberius to Nero', in Alan K. Bowman et al. (eds), *The Cambridge Ancient History, Second Edition Volume X: The Augustan Empire, 43 B.C. – A.D. 69*, Cambridge, 1996, p.226).

60. Cf. Tacitus, *Annales* 11.36.1, with the commentary notes of S.J.V. Malloch (Cambridge, 2013). Mnester is mentioned again at *Caligula* 55.

61. The story is famously told of Cleopatra with Caligula's ancestor Antony in Pliny the Elder, *Historia Naturalis* 9.119-21; Caligula follows in the traditions of his storied relative and his paramour. Wardle's commentary considers the antacid properties of the concoction, and modern chemical experiments to recreate the ancient anecdote.

62. Suetonius, *Caligula* 37 ... *aut frugi hominem esse oportere dictitans aut Caesarem.* The saying conceals a pun; Cassius Frugi was the father of Julius Caesar's great rival Pompey; cf. Latin *frugi* and English 'frugal'. See further Hurley's commentary *ad loc.*

63. *Nihil tam efficere concupiscebat quam quod posse effici negaretur.*

64. A classic joke from the world of auctions.

65. Aloys Winterling (pp.139 ff.) argues that this infamous brothel story was really a case of the emperor inviting prominent wives and children to live in the imperial complex as hostages for the good, cooperative behaviour of their husbands. Less salacious a case of bad behaviour, perhaps – but hardly commendable either. As for the taxes, those accustomed to a thoroughly debauched, licentious Caligula are sometimes surprised to learn of his taxation of prostitutes; on this, the best study is the work of Thomas A.J. McGinn, *Prostitution, Sexuality, and the Law in Ancient Rome* (Oxford, 2003).

66. Augustus was said to have been quite fond of playing dice. See further David Wardles's commentary notes on Suetonius, *Augustus* 70.2 (Oxford, 2014). Dice were associated with sexual license and general excess – the world of the symposium with its wine and women. Technically it was illegal to participate in the game.

67. *Caligula* 42.

68. The reference is to the so-called *strenae*, or good luck tokens, that were traditional New Year's presents.

69. 'The final image in this rubric of greed is Gaius rolling in money' (Hurley *ad Caligula* 42). Note also here Guey, Julien, 'Les bains d'oer de Caligula *immensi aureorum acervi* (Suétone, *Cal.*, 42.3)', in *Mélanges de l'école française de Rome* 89 (1977), pp.443-46, who connects the 'bathing in gold' with Egyptian lore about being impregnated by the gold (on the notion that gold belonged to kings alone).

70. Wardle's commentary analyzes in detail the possible reasons why the streets were swept and watered in such a fashion – speed and ease of journey being prominent among them.

71. Suetonius, *Caligula* 44.

72. The first part of the name means 'hound', while the second references the Celtic solar deity Belenus. For this expansionist monarch of the house of Tasciovanus, see Peter Salway, *The Oxford Illustrated History of Roman Britain* (Oxford, 1993), pp.41 ff.

73. We may compare the Nazi trickery before the invasion of Poland on 1 September 1939. Hurley argues in her commentary that the point of the lunch detail was that Gaius' meals were more important than his military

concerns – but the point may have been to time the theatrical display for when the soldiery would be preoccupied with their midday break. On these prisoners, note D. Woods, 'Caligula's Gallic Captives (Suet., *Calig.* 47)', in *Latomus* 66 (2007), pp.900-04.

74. 'Bear up and preserve themselves for favourable circumstances' (*Aeneid* 1.207). In context, the Trojan hero Aeneas was shoring up the flagging spirits of his men in the wake of their shipwreck in Carthage. The actual Virgilian verse is an imperative, *durate, et vosmet rebus servate secundis*, which either Caligula or Suetonius rendered in indirect command (the latter is likelier).

75. See here M.B. Flory, 'Pearls for Venus', in *Historia* 37 (1988), pp.498-504, for the theory that Caligula was being sarcastic: the soldiers could collect seashells and not pearls.

76. Cf. here e.g. Balsdon, pp.91-93. Balsdon notes that Suetonius is the first extant source to tell the story of the shells.

77. See here the useful overview of opposing viewpoints by David Woods, 'Caligula's Seashells', in *Greece & Rome* 47.1 (2000), pp.80-87.

78. Unforgettable is the performance of John Hurt as Caligula in the British Broadcasting Company production of *I, Claudius*, where he describes the 'loot' from Neptune as he orders the seashells to be displayed to the Senate on return from his German campaigns. Arther Ferrill (pp.1,127-128) dismisses the idea that an error of interpretation would have been made and left uncorrected between the time of Suetonius and that of Dio Cassius.

79. David Wardle cites the mysterious passage of Juvenal, s. 6.419-420, as being of possible relevance, where a matron orders the picking up of *conchae* (i.e. vessels for use in bathing), and where the language reflects a military metaphor. On the Juvenal text, see Lindsay Watson and Patricia Watson, *Juvenal: Satire 6* (Cambridge, 2014), *ad loc.*

80. Balsdon (pp.92-93) considers the whole story 'too absurd to be entertained for one moment'.

81. 'The mention of the other orders shows him looking for other bases of support, but nothing could replace the senate' (Hurley *ad Caligula* 49.1).

82. An error, given that he died on 24 January AD 41. The commentators variously try to explain the discrepancy by identifying some other date than 31 August as the intended start of Suetonius' death clock for Caligula.

83. Whatever favour he had shown to the *equites* on his return from Germany did not, it would seem, last very long.

84. The sword for executions; the dagger for enforced suicides and also assassinations.

85. Suetonius, *Caligula* 49.

86. Julius Caesar was also balding; cf. Suetonius, *Iulius* 45.

87. *Caligula* 50.

88. Cf. the similar stories told of the poet Lucretius and the statesman and military commander Lucullus. The unattractive, older Caesonia was apparently afraid that Caligula would cease to love her; the potion, however, rendered the emperor insane.

89. The Latin is *species pelagi*. Once again Caligula is depicted as having an adversarial relationship with the ocean.

90. Cf. the *I, Claudius* depiction of Caligula's insane Aurora dance, inspired by reports in *Caligula* 54.

91. The angry soldiers would be either praetorians or, perhaps, his Batavian bodyguards.

92. Virgil had indicated in the last book of his epic that the Trojan element in the future Rome would be suppressed in favour of the Latin in terms of customs and language; did Caligula find this offensive given his Julian ancestry and pride therein, and is the explanation for his apparent disdain for Virgil to be found in his opinion of Virgil's commentary on the place of Troy in the Roman imagination?

93. *Caligula* 52.

94. *Caligula* 53.

95. 'Flashy theatrical displays' – Balsdon (p.206).

96. All disreputable activities and pastimes for the participation of an emperor or *princeps*.

97. Cf. *Caligula* 32, of the *murmillo* who was killed by the Thracian Caligula.

98. Cf. the story told that when Nero was drawing near to his end, he uttered the words *qualis artifex pereo* – 'what an artist is dying' (Suetonius, *Nero* 49). Caligula would not live to make his debut; cf. *Caligula* 57.

99. Once again we are reminded of the emperor's problems with the ocean and the sea.

100. Cf. *Caligula* 36.

101. *Caligula* 55; the Latin is *equiti Romano tumultanti*, which does not clearly indicate what exactly the *eques* did.

102. The *murmillo* was the usual opponent of the Thracian; Caligula was seeking to help his favorite type of gladiator. The *murmillo* was usually armed with a heavy shield and sword, a helmet and arm guard; such a gladiator would need to be impressive muscularly to manage so much weighted gear, and would normally be paired against a more agile opponent.

103. The name is connected to the Latin *columba*, meaning a 'dove'.

104. The names of the driver and of Caligula's favourite horse are appropriate; Eutychus = 'Lucky' and Incitatus = 'Swift'.

105. The story is among the most notorious associated with Caligula. Suetonius, to be fair, does not say outright that Caligula intended to do this – only that the report was current that such was the emperor's intention – but it seemed believable, at least to many, because of the extreme favour shown to the animal.

106. The two men, we shall learn, were Cassius Chaerea and Cornelius Sabinus.

107. *Caligula* 56.

108. These had been instituted by Livia in honour of the Divus Augustus.

109. One wonders if Cassius – like the Brutus of the spring of 44 BC – was aware of the significance of his name.

110. Lindsay notes in his commentary that the prodigies in Suetonius always serve a purpose – in the case of Caligula's impending death, to highlight his hubristic nature.

111. Caligula had ordered that the statue be decapitated and brought to Rome so that it could be re-crowned with his own head; cf. *Caligula* 22.

112. These prodigies would have occurred many months before the assassination; they connect the one Gaius Julius Caesar with the other.

113. The more famous Sulla, we might note, had sought the ruin of Caesar in a previous age.

114. In Latin, *Fortunae*, twin goddesses of Luck.

115. He would be spared only by the timely intervention of Caligula's own death.

116. *Caligula* 22.

117. The incest connection may reflect the stories about Caligula and his sisters. Philip, like Caligula, was killed by a member of his armed retinue.

118. Laureolus is also mentioned at Juvenal, s. 8.186; on this celebrated highwayman, see Edward Courtney, *A Commentary on the Satires of Juvenal* (London: The Athlone Press, 1980).

119. *Caligula* 54.

120. For the problems of dating the death precisely, see Hurley's commentary on *Caligula* 58.1. Part of the issue is the length of the Palatine games and whether or not Caligula extended them to allow for his stage premiere.

121. There is no question that the Suetonian narrative has maximum suspense: Caligula had a stomach ache; the *princeps gregis*, or leader of the youth performers, was feeling chilly. See further Hurley's commentary for the role of fortune in the account.

122. For the sacrifice imagery in Suetonius' narrative, see Hurley's note on *Caligula* 58.2.

123. Cf. the English 'ratified'. We may recall the prominent role of Jupiter in the prodigies surrounding the assassination; Caligula was essentially being struck by Jovian lightning.

124. With deep irony, we might think, given his alleged pretensions to divinity.

125. The exact location of the final resting place is not specified by Suetonius.

126. The early psychoanalyst Hanns Sachs (translated by Hedvig Simger) memorably writes (*Caligula*, London: Elkin Mathews & Marrot, Ltd, 1931): 'Thus the Age of Caligula was brought to an end … The eternal and ineradicable pre-human, the bestial, whose subjugation is civilisation's pre-eminent aim, had always lurked in ambush, had even ventured now and again to creep forth from its hiding-place; but with Caligula it had stepped boldly into the glaring light of day, impudently usurping the highest place and perching upon the throne of World-Empire, before which the peoples prostrated themselves in adoration. Thenceforth the Sign of the Beast dominated the antique world.'

127. That is, of Julius Caesar, Augustus, Livia, Caligula and his sister Drusilla. On the senatorial actions in the aftermath of the assassination, Balsdon notes: 'Beyond arranging for the murder of Caesonia and her child the members of the Senate accomplished nothing' (p.105).

Chapter Three: The Evidence of Dio Cassius for the Life and Reign of Caligula

1. The most convenient edition of Dio Cassius' history for English speakers is the Loeb Classical Library set in nine volumes, with Greek text, English translation and brief annotations; the relevant volume for the study of Caligula is Volume VII, *Dio's Roman History* (translation by Earnest Cary,

'on the basis of the version' by Herbert Baldwin Foster). There is a British Columbia dissertation from 1976 by Humphrey that provides a commentary from the historical point of view on Dio's Book 59. Humphrey comes to the conclusion that 'Such topics as his [i.e. Caligula's] administration of the provinces, his campaigns in Germany and Gaul, his fiscal policy, and his behaviour in private and public life are shown to be not immoderate but rather balanced and sensible, if subject to a certain rashness.' For Humphrey, as for others, what doomed Caligula in the eyes of the Senate and the historical tradition was his open contempt for republican institutions. There is a certain cynical honesty in all this. Caligula is acquitted from some of the charges of his accusers for being honest enough to call the principate what it was: 'his disregard of the senate, however justified it may have been, was to prompt our aristocratic sources to consider him in the same light as Nero, Domitian, and Commodus.' There is also a volume by Jonathan Edmondson, *Dio: The Julio-Claudians: Selections from Books 58-63 of the Roman History of Cassius Dio* (LACTOR 15) (London: London Association of Classical Teachers, 1992). Edmonson provides a translation and annotation of several passages from Dio that help to fill in what is missing from the lost portions of Tacitus' *Annales*.

2. Invaluable as a general introduction to the historian and his excerptors is the work of Fergus Millar, *A Study of Cassius Dio* (Oxford, 1964).

3. Dio notes too that Caligula could have just ignored the will entirely, but given that others were no doubt aware of the contents, he opted for the expedient of simply disregarding what was said about Gemellus, and honouring everything else to the letter.

4. Dio 57.5.6-7.

5. Dio 58.7.4; cf. Suetonius, *Caligula* 12.1.

6. Dio 58.23.1 ff.

7. Caligula was, after all, one of the three sons of Germanicus, all of whom had been named Caesars in Augustus' will (Dio 57.18.11 = Zonaras 11.2). Caligula, as we have seen, was the survivor (Dio 57.22.5).

8. Cf. Suetonius, *Nero* 38. The verse is found in Nauck's edition of the Greek tragic fragments (*Adespota* 513). Nero changed the verse to indicate a wish that the world might be mingled with fire while he still lived (in the context of the incendiary madness of AD 64).

9. Dio 58.27.4. Tacitus deals with the charges levelled against Arruntius in Book 6 of his *Annales*.
10. Dio 58.28.2.
11. Dio 58.28.4.
12. The point being that at first he loved (or at least was in lust) with these women, only later to come to despise them.
13. The implication is that whatever Antonia complained about was quite minor.
14. Dio 59.4.1.
15. One wonders if Dio's commentary on the Caligulan response to the memory of Tiberius was occasioned by his own experience of Commodus in the wake of the reign of Marcus Aurelius.
16. Dio 59.4.4.
17. The annals of tyrants across time and space are replete with the same impossible circumstance of arbitrariness.
18. Dio 59.5.2.
19. Cf. Suetonius, *Caligula* 54.
20. Dio 59.6.1.
21. Dio records that Claudius had been of the equestrian order, and had been the representative of Caligula to the *equites* after the death of Tiberius; his nephew made him a senator and a consul in one day, despite his relatively advanced age of 46. The incumbent consuls were Gnaeus Acerronius Proculus and Gaius Petronius Pontius Nigrinus. Caligula and Claudius took over on 1 July, yielding on 1 September to Aulus Caecina Paetus and Gaius Caninius Rebilus (Smallwood, p. 2).
22. Again, there seems to have been no significant outcry or protest; certainly others were done away with at the same time, and a climate of fear may already have settled over Rome.
23. Cf. Suetonius, *Caligula* 17.
24. Since Gemellus was both co-heir with and adopted son of Caligula.
25. Cf. Suetonius, *Caligula* 16.
26. Cf. Suetonius, *Caligula* 14; 27.
27. Cf. Suetonius, *Caligula* 23.
28. Dio records that one of the jibes was to call Silanus a 'golden sheep' (58.8.5); the exact point of the taunt is unclear, but it may refer to the subservience

of one who also seemed to have put on airs. For the 'golden sheep' taunt, cf. Tacitus, *Annales* 13.1.

29. Cf. Suetonius, *Caligula* 25.
30. There was obvious enough concern over how much money was being squandered, and over the prerogatives of the nobles with respect to voting.
31. Dio 59.10.1–2.
32. Cf. Suetonius, *Caligula* 27.
33. Cf. Suetonius, *Caligula* 27.
34. Cf. Suetonius, *Caligula* 24.
35. For a detailed study of the iconographical evidence of the honours accorded to Caligula's sister, see Susan Wood, 'Diva Drusilla Panthea and the Sisters of Caligula', in *The American Journal of Archaeology* 99.3 (1995), pp.457–82. Wood argues that the sisters of Caligula were seen as having the potential to give birth to Julian children. The view of Wiedemann in the *Cambridge Ancient History* (p.225) is that 'there was nothing un-Roman about her cult', given the associations of the Julian family with Venus and the evocation of the Trojan mother goddess Cybele in the title 'Panthea'. Indeed there may have been something of an attempt on the part of Caligula to emphasize certain divine elements of both the Julian and Trojan heritage of Rome. That said, the deification of Drusilla was certainly unprecedented, and this fact cannot be ignored or escaped.
36. The official in question was Livius Geminus.
37. The water was to be mingled with wine.
38. Cf. Suetonius, *Caligula* 25.
39. *Antiquitates* 19.8.
40. 'The arrangements that Caligula made in the East in fact reflect the one talent that he clearly did seem to possess as an administrator, the ability to choose competent subordinates' (Barrett, p.223).
41. *Annales* 12.23.
42. See further on this Barbara Levick, *Vespasian* (London: Routledge, 1999), pp.10–11.
43. Dio 59.1–2.
44. Again, for Dio the hallmark of the reign is arbitrary judgment or lack thereof.
45. Cf. Suetonius, *Caligula* 30.

46. For the place of pachyderms in Rome, see H.H. Scullard, *The Elephant in the Greek and Roman World* (London: Thames and Hudson, 1974), pp.178 ff.

47. Cf. Suetonius, *Caligula* 38.

48. Dio 59.14.5.

49. Claudius would pay it back once he was emperor; cf. Dio 60.17.2.

50. See here especially J.W. Humphrey and P.M. Swan, 'Cassius Dio on the Suffect Consuls of AD 39', in *Phoenix* 37 (1983), pp.324–27; cf. Barrett, pp.96 ff. Humphrey and Swan succeed in eliminating several candidates for the office of the ill-fated suffect consul colleague of Corbulo; they are able, however, to settle on no definitive or even likely candidate for the office.

51. We should also note that the identity of this Corbulo is uncertain; was he the father of the famous Corbulo who was a general under Nero, or was he his grandfather? See here Barrett, pp.96–97. For Afer, see below on 59.19 ff.

52. Dio 59.16.1.

53. Cf. Dio 59.4.

54. The people were also confused; cf. 59.16.8.

55. Dio 59.16.8.

56. Cf. Suetonius, *Caligula* 19.

57. On the whole episode, note especially Marc Kleijwegt, 'Caligula's "Triumph" at Baiae', in *Mnemosyne* 47.5 (1994), pp.652–71. For when exactly the whole business took place, see David Wardle, 'Caligula's Bridge of Boats: AD 39 or 40?', in *Historia: Zeitschrift für alte Geschichte* 56.1 (2007), pp.118–20.

58. Darius and Xerxes.

59. Dio 59.18.1.

60. For the relative dearth of names of Caligulan victims, see Barrett, p.99.

61. Cf. Barrett, pp.100–01.

62. Cf. Tacitus, *Historiae* 1.48.2–3, with the commentary of Cynthia Damon, *Tacitus: Histories Book I* (Cambridge, 2003), *ad loc.*; also Plutarch, *Galba* 12.1.

63. Dio notes that the beloved freedman Callistus was instrumental in the release of Afer; Domitius had sought to ingratiate himself with the *libertus*, so as all the better to shore up his position with Caligula. When Callistus later challenged Caligula for having assailed Afer at all, the emperor noted that it would have been wrong to keep such an excellent speech to himself.

64. Dio 59.19.8–8.

65. Cf. Suetonius, *Caligula* 23.

66. Again, the recurring theme in Dio's account of the arbitrary nature of Caligula's rule.

67. We know that Afer's colleague in office was one Aulus Didius Gallus, thanks to *tabulae cereatae* discovered at Pompeii; see further Barrett, p.97.

68. Dio 59.20.6.

69. His carelessness in an age that permitted few mistakes is noteworthy.

70. The exact nature of Caligula's change in the government of Africa Proconsularis has been the subject of scholarly debate, in particular given the evidence of Tacitus, *Historiae* 4.48–50, where the historian notes that Caligula – who is said to have been *turbidus animi*, or troubled in mind – was afraid of the ill-fated Marcus Silanus, then governor of Africa, and removed the province from proconsular control and assigned it to an imperial legate. See further Barrett, pp.119 ff., who concludes that Silanus may have served in 38–39, and then a change was effected before Piso assumed his office for 39–40.

71. Dio 59.21.

72. Dio notes that Caligula also handled the sale of the confiscated goods of his victims himself, for the express purpose of securing a higher price, given that people would pay more for that which the emperor himself was placing on auction.

73. *Caligula* 28.

74. Dio 59.22.5.

75. See, e.g., Balsdon, pp.66 ff.

76. Balsdon – who in general is always ready to try to defend Caligula – notes (p.74): 'He had committed treason already under Tiberius … and it may well be that now he deserved his death.'

77. *Caligula* 24.

78. Another example of Caligula's perverse logic.

79. Cf. Suetonius, *Caligula* 25.

80. Cf. Suetonius, *Caligula* 26.

81. He would be most famous to history as the evil prefect of the Praetorian Guard under Nero.

82. Cf. Suetonius, *Caligula* 17.

83. They were Gaius Laecanius Bassus and Quintus Terentius Culleo; the latter apparently did not assume his office until 29 May (cf. Smallwood, p.2).

84. Tiberius was now rehabilitated, at least to a degree, after a fashion and for a time.

85. Dio 59.25.
86. A recurring feature in the Caligula narratives is that even 'positive' developments were stained by death and mayhem.
87. See further on this Barrett, pp.156–57.
88. Cf. Suetonius, *Caligula* 16.
89. Cf. Suetonius, *Caligula* 49.
90. Cf. Suetonius, *Caligula* 28.
91. Cf. Suetonius, *Caligula* 16.
92. Cf. Suetonius, *Caligula* 22.
93. For the Bacchic imitation cf. Philostratus, *Vita Apoll.* 5.32.
94. The story is another indicator of the capriciousness of Caligula's behaviour.
95. Cf. Suetonius, *Caligula* 21.
96. Cf. Suetonius, *Caligula* 22; 57.
97. Cf. Suetonius, *Caligula* 22.
98. Cf. Suetonius, *Caligula* 41.
99. Again, we may recall Caligula's devotion to his Julian lineage.
100. Cf. Suetonius, *Caligula* 57.
101. It would appear that this was Apollonius of Tyana, the subject of the long 'biography' written by the Greek sophist Philostratus in the early third century AD.
102. Cf. Smallwood, p.2.
103. Dio's epitomic tradition disagrees.
104. The narrative in Dio emphasizes the theatrical element of the assassination, as if the conduct of the Palatine festival was what finally pushed Cassius and the rest over the edge.
105. A ghastly, gruesome detail not found in Suetonius.
106. Humour that is also not found in the emperor's Latin biographer.
107. They risked, after all, being suddenly unemployed in the absence of an emperor.
108. Dio 60.3.4, from the resumed text of the historian.

Chapter Four: Tacitus on Caligula

1. Book 5 survives only in fragment; Book 6 is substantially entire (this fact is obscured in the introduction to my student edition of the incomplete Book 16); all of Books 7–10 are missing, as well as part of Book 11. It is generally

held that Caligula's reign would have occupied two books. The *Annales* follow a hexadic structure. Books 1-6 are devoted to Tiberius, and Books 13-18 to Nero (the surviving text breaks off in 16), while 7-8 are generally held to have been Caligulan, with 8-12 devoted to Claudius. The loss of the Caligula section is more keenly felt, given that it appears that two books covered the material of but four years.

2. For English translations, there are Oxford World's Classics and Penguin Classics editions of the *Annales*, the former edited by John Yardley and Anthony Barrett, with detailed notes. The most extensive English commentaries are those of the Cambridge 'orange' series, with volumes covering Books 1-3 and what remains of 5-6, and also 11; other volumes are in progress as of this writing. The 'green and yellow' Cambridge set has a Book 4; at the time of composition of this book, a Cambridge 'orange' by Woodman is announced as forthcoming (to finish the series' coverage of the first hexad). Various school editions exist of individual books. The older Oxford commentary of Furneaux on the entire work remains valuable. The Church & Brodribb translation of the complete Tacitus in the Modern Library commends itself both by its accurate, lucid rendering of the Latin and by the convenience of having the complete Tacitus in one volume. The Latin text is available in the Loeb Classical Library and the Oxford Classical Texts series. Among secondary works on the historian, Syme's two-volume Oxford monograph *Tacitus* stands apart. Rhiannon Ash's 2006 *Tacitus* for the Bloomsbury *Ancients in Action* series offers a lucid, sober introduction on a briefer scale.

3. Cf. *Annales* 1.32.

4. Caligula's assassination is also referenced at *Annales* 11.1, where Valerius Asiaticus is accused of having been the principal party responsible for the emperor's murder (*praecipuum auctorem*). Asiaticus is famous in Dio for having said that he would have wished to have been involved in the killing; we shall return to his role in the downfall of Caligula. Asiaticus killed himself, noting that it would have been better to die under Tiberius or Caligula than because of the machinations of Claudius' notorious wife Messalina (11.3). The freedman Callistus is mentioned at 11.29, where Tacitus notes that he had already discussed him when he dealt with Caligula's death (i.e. in a lost section of the *Annales*). See further S.J.V. Malloch, *The Annals of Tacitus: Book 11* (Cambridge, 2013), *ad loc.*

5. For commentary on the passage, see especially F.R.D. Goodyear, *The Annals of Tacitus, Volume I (Annals 1.1-54)* (Cambridge, 1970).

6. Classic rhetorical flourishes. For the whole question of the place of Caligula in the narrative of what happened on the Rhine, see Donna W. Hurley, 'Gaius Caligula in the Germanicus Tradition', in *The American Journal of Philology* 110.2 (1989), pp.316-38.

7. Tacitus, *Annales* 1.42.

8. *Annales* 1.44.

9. The identity of the child Agrippina was expecting is mysterious; the generally accepted conclusion is that this was a stillbirth.

10. *Annales* 1.69. Here the nickname of the soldiers is explicitly associated with the will of Agrippina – at least in Tacitus' description of what Tiberius is alleged to have said. Tacitus' Tiberius would of course impute questionable decisions and duplicitous intentions to Agrippina; what some might call charming and harmless was for the emperor evidence of *de facto* conspiracy.

11. See here the commentary notes of F.R.D. Goodyear, *The Annals of Tacitus, Volume II (Annals 1.55-81 and Annals 2)* (Cambridge, 1981).

12. For commentary, see here A.J. Woodman, *The Annals of Tacitus, Books 5 and 6* (Cambridge, 2017), *ad loc*.

13. See here Woodman's note on *Annales* 5.3.1 *adlatas*.

14. There is a brief reference to Caligula at *Annales* 4.71, of little historical value; Tacitus notes amid his chronicle of the events of AD 28 that he wanted to jump ahead and record the fates of some individuals who died later, including under Caligula's rule. See further the notes of D.C.A. Shotter, *Tacitus: Annals IV* (Warminster: Aris & Phillips Ltd, 1989), *ad loc*.

15. *Annales* 6.3. See Woodman's commentary on the name, which was almost certainly Lucius Sextilius Pasconianus; the textual tradition is vexed here.

16. *Annales* 6.5. The text here has occasioned disputes as to reading and punctuation (one interpretation of the passage is that Cotta referred to Caligula as 'Gaia' on account of his alleged lack of virility). Cotta was the great-uncle of Caligula's *quondam* wife Lollia; cf. Tacitus, *Annales* 12.22.

17. *Annales* 6.20.

18. Woodman argues that problems of chronology and Latinity require that the text actually be emended to say that Caligula was accompanying Tiberius on his *return* from Capreae (the departure thither having been described

in the lost portion of Book 5). The date of the marriage of Caligula and Claudia is uncertain: Suetonius is little help thanks to his frustrating lack of detailed chronological markers; Dio (58.25) puts it in AD 35. Some scholars (Hurley; Martin on *Annales* 6.20) think that it came shortly after the year 30-31.

19. The Latin is *immanem animum subdola modestia tegens*.

20. *neque meliorem umquam servum neque deteriorem dominum fuisse*. Cf. Suetonius, *Caligula* 10.2; also Sextus Aurelius Caesar, *De Caesaribus* 6.

21. *Annales* 6.45.3 *nimia iam potentia Macronis*.

22. The Latin here is *dum dominationis apisceretur*. Woodman notes in his commentary that Caligula might have rejected Ennia because she was not of noble birth.

23. *nam etsi commotus ingenio simulationum tamen falsa in sinu avi perdidicerat*. Caligula may have been troubled in his mind, but he had learned at least one lesson well – the arts of deception. And he had mastered this useful skill in the very lap of Tiberius.

24. *Annales* 6.46.

25. The language Tacitus uses connects the favour that Caligula enjoyed with the throng (*vulgi studia*) with exactly the sort of thing Agrippina and Germanicus tried to foster with the army in Germany.

26. It would be Commodus – the blood son of Marcus Aurelius – who would prove the main undoing of that system.

27. The Latin is *quippe illi non perinde curae gratia praesentium quam in posteros ambitio*.

28. 'Sulla, a classic example of a man whose career was divided between good and bad' (Woodman on *Annales* 6.46.4).

29. The Latin is *imminentis iuventam*, a vivid phrase very much in the Tacitean style. Arruntius' sentiments offer something of a twist on the observations of Tiberius about Macro's watching the rising and not the setting sun.

30. Cf. *Annales* 6.50.

31. Lucullus was notoriously given to luxury and indulgence – charges that were perhaps exaggerated by his enemies. His one-time home is a fitting final resting place for the decadent Tiberius. For the gardens of Lucullus, cf. *Annales* 11.1.

32. *Annales* 6.50.5.

33. *Annales* 13.3.

34. All the same, Claudius noted that she should be prevented from doing any harm to the state, and she did suffer a heavy indemnity and exile.

35. Cf. Dio 58.8.5.

36. Plutarch alludes to the same scandalous lore in his life of Galba (9.1 ff.), where it is noted that Nymphidius let it be known that he was the son of Caligula. Plutarch relates that Caligula had been on intimate terms with Nymphidius' attractive mother, whom he identifies as the daughter of the freedman Callistus. The sexual union, however, of Caligula and this woman was too late, Plutarch says, for Nymphidius to have been the result. He was believed rather to be the son of the gladiator Martianus.

37. Cf. Dio 59.25.5b.

38. See here Malloch's commentary *ad loc.* for detailed notes.

39. Cf. Barrett, pp.63-64.

40. There is another brief reference to the arrest in Seneca, *De Tranq. An.* 11.12: *Armeniae Mithridatem inter Gaianas custodias vidimus.* The king's life was spared: Claudius would restore him to his throne (cf. Dio 60.8.1).

41. The Oxford World's Classics series offers a translation (with detailed explanatory notes) by W.H. Fyfe (revised and edited by D.S. Levene), *Tacitus: The Histories* (Oxford, 1997). The Loeb edition offers the Latin text with a translation, while there is an Oxford Classical Texts edition and a Penguin. Cambridge 'green and yellow' commentaries exist for the first two books; there is a complete Oxford historical commentary in two volumes, minus Book 3 (the subject of a 1972 Sydney volume by Kenneth Wellesley, *Cornelius Tacitus: The Histories Book III*).

42. The Latin is *pacis adversa*.

43. Note also *Historiae* 2.76, where Vespasian recalls the imperial family of Gaius, Claudius and Nero; also the mention of Caligula in the blistering address of Curtius Montanus at 4.42, where it is noted that some of those who outlived the days of Tiberius and Caligula thought that they had escaped tyranny and domination, only to find that there were others tyrants waiting in the wings.

44. See further Barrett, pp.100-01. Cf. Plutarch, *Galba* 12.1.

45. See further Balsdon, p.76.

46. Cf. Barrett, pp.119, 121-23; Tacitus, *Agricola* 4.1.

47. Cf. Suetonius, *Titus* 4.

48. Suetonius, *Domitian* 11.

49. Cf. Barrett, pp.161 ff.

50. The notorious wish of the emperor is even cited by Polydore Vergil in his *De inventoribus rerum* (2.23.1).

51. The *Agricola*, *Germania* and *Dialogus de oratoribus* are conveniently found in both the Loeb and Oxford Classical Texts series; also the Oxford World's Classics and Penguin series. Cambridge 'yellow and green' editions exist for the *Agricola* and the *Dialogus*. There is a Clarendon Ancient History series edition of the *Germania* by J.B. Rives, with extensive annotation; note also the briefer volume of Herbert Benario for the Aris & Philipps series, with good commentary.

52. Latin *satis constat*.

53. See further on all this the commentary notes of R.M. Ogilvie and Ian Richmond, *Cornelii Taciti: De Vita Agricolae* (Oxford, 1967), *ad loc*. 'The great army collected by Gaius in Gaul is stated to have been marched to the coast as if to embark, and then to have been led back, after being told to pick up shells as spoils of the ocean.' Ogilvie and Richmond do not bother to enter into the controversy over the shells.

54. *Germania* 37.5.

55. See further here the commentary of J.G.C. Anderson, *Tacitus: Germania* (Oxford, 1938); also J.B. Rives, *Tacitus: Germania* (Oxford, 1999), *ad loc*. 'Since the sources are scanty and hostile, there is much uncertainty … it [i.e. Caligula's expedition] seems to have been directed first towards Germania and then towards Britain.' Anderson could not have been more non-committal in his exegesis.

56. *Dialogus* 17.

Chapter Five: Josephus on Caligula

1. Josephus, *Life* 5.5.

2. The most convenient edition is the nine-volume Loeb Classical Library set with Greek text and English translation. The relevant volume is eighteen, translated by Louis H. Feldman (1965).

3. *Antiquitates* 18.124.

4. *Antiquitates* 18.166-68.

5. Cf. Josephus, *Bellum Iudaicum* 2.179.

6. Josephus offers a long digression on Tiberius' penchant for procrastination that almost works as a literary enactment of the emperor's propensity for delay.

7. And so it would happen, once Caligula became emperor.

8. *Antiquitates* 18.211 ff.

9. *Antiquitates* 18.223.

10. Josephus does not relate the drama of the pillow and the like; even under the best and most innocuous of circumstances, there would certainly be conflicting initial reports.

11. He was still under guard.

12. Was this the last occasion on which Caligula listened to any advice of Antonia?

13. *Antiquitates* 18.255. This Herodias, we might note, was the infamous Herodias of the story of John the Baptist, the prophet who upbraided Herod for the impropriety of his adulterous union with his brother Philip's wife – the criticism that would lead to the notorious accounts of Salome's dance and the decapitation of John.

14. *Antiquitates* 18.257 ff.

15. See further here Barrett, p.100.

16. An interesting hedging of the issue.

17. *Antiquitates* 18.305.

18. Invaluable here is the work of T.P. Wiseman, *The Death of Caligula* (Liverpool University Press, 2013) (2nd edition; the volume is dedicated *dis manibus Cornelii Sabini*). Wiseman provides a translation of and commentary on Josephus' account of the emperor's end. The Loeb edition of Louis Feldman also provides significantly more extensive annotations than usual for volumes in that series. Note also L.H. Feldman's 'The Sources of Josephus' "Antiquities", Book 19', in *Latomus* 21 (1962), pp.320–33.

19. *Antiquitates* 19.1.

20. This is a constant refrain in the surviving sources.

21. Seneca also includes the episode among the later indications of Caligula's madness; we shall discuss the evidence of *De Brevitate Vitae* 18.5-6 when we examine Seneca's references to Caligula in detail.

22. Publius Memmius Regulus was governor in Achaea.

23. Wiseman notes on Memmius Regulus (p.45): 'i.e. P. Memmius Regulus, suffect consul in 31 and imperial legate of Moesia (with responsibility also for Macedonia and Achaea) from 35 to 44; in 38 he had been summoned to Rome to give his wife Lollia Paulina in marriage to Gaius (Suet. *Cal.* 25.2L

Gaius soon divorced her, but Memmius did not get her back).' At one point Claudius contemplated a marriage with her (cf. Suetonius, *Claudius* 26).

24. Josephus' account is thus more grandiose than Suetonius', who merely mentions the placing of the child on the statue.

25. Frustratingly, Josephus does not divulge the details of the charges against Claudius, or the means by which the future emperor escaped death.

26. The common lot and fear of all tyrants.

27. This figure would seem to be otherwise unknown; Josephus does not follow up with any details about what this Regulus did or did not do *in fine*.

28. The name would seem to be confused in Josephus' extant work; the historian elsewhere also mentions a Minucianus, a name he seems to use to designate both Vinicianus and Marcus Vinicius. Onomastic confusion, to be sure, and perhaps understandably so, given the similar sounds.

29. The implication being that Caligula was giving him a reputation for effeminacy.

30. Once again, the financial struggles of the empire under Caligula are highlighted.

31. Josephus thus provides a reason for Caligula's mockery of Cassius Chaerea: the man was too slow in collecting money, and too charitable and merciful toward the people who were in financial hardship.

32. This is likely the 'Pomponius' of Dio's account at 59.26.4.

33. *Antiquitates* 19.42 ff.

34. Cf. Josephus' preoccupation with divine providence.

35. Clemens, after all, had not proven to be terribly eager to be involved.

36. Every day, of course, was another opportunity for the emperor to kill any of them on the slenderest of pretexts.

37. *Antiquitates* 19.64.

38. Josephus gives his personal view that the story was fabricated; he notes that Caligula would never have tolerated the delays, were he determined to see Claudius dead – and that Callistus was hardly likely to disobey Caligula in this matter. Once again the historian credits divine providence with the salvation of Claudius (and in some sense, it is miraculous that Germanicus' brother had survived this long).

39. *Antiquitates* 19.75.

40. The implication in Josephus' account is that the others simply lost their nerve again and again.

41. *Antiquitates* 19.87.
42. *Antiquitates* 19.90.
43. Cf. Homer, *Iliad* 14.90–91.
44. The *Laureolus*.
45. The Myrrha story of incest.
46. Josephus places the assassination at a later hour than Suetonius, where the time is closer to one (*Caligula* 58).
47. Josephus notes that in reality the assassins wanted to remove any chance of having someone try to defend Caligula.
48. An interesting comment, at least in the case of Claudius.
49. He is otherwise another figure quite unknown to history.
50. Originally militaristic war dances; eventually the name came to be applied to more graceful performances on mythological themes.
51. The point seems to be that either the wound dazed him severely, or else that given his mental state, he had no idea what was happening – the difference between the two alternatives not being particularly great.
52. *Antiquitates* 19.110.
53. *Antiquitates* 19.115 ff.
54. There was a Lucius Norbanus Balbus who was consul in AD 19; this may be the same man.
55. He is unknown outside Josephus.
56. *Antiquitates* 19.127.
57. Josephus is careful to note that the emperor was motivated not only by a desire to captivate and appease the crowd with 'bread and circuses', but also by his own sadistic nature.
58. We may recall the tradition that the emperor was a competent orator.
59. *Antiquitates* 19.137.
60. In fact they would continue to have a career and secure employment under Claudius and Nero.
61. Apparently Alcyon had been drafted by the soldiers of the Guard into providing medical assistance to some of their number who had been wounded in the chaos.
62. Cf. Dio 59.30.
63. *Antiquitates* 19.162.
64. He would share the consulate with Claudius in AD 41, taking office from 25 June.

65. *Antiquitates* 19.184.
66. The dating being from the first accession to the consulship of Julius Caesar (59 BC). Again, this was very much a reaction against the Julian line.
67. *Antiquitates* 19.190.
68. *Antiquitates* 19.201 ff.
69. Josephus is somewhat inconsistent in his appraisal of Caligula's popularity. No doubt the commoners were as fickle in their praise of the emperor as he was in his behaviour.
70. The historian makes clear that the project was never finished because Caligula wasted so much money on so many useless things.
71. *Antiquitates* 19.212.
72. *Antiquitates* 19.236 ff.
73. Agrippa's action with the body may be associated with the general rumours and confusion in the wake of Caligula's death. Presumably he was buying time with the bodyguards before seeing whither the winds were blowing.
74. It would seem that Chaerea's opinion was that the entire imperial family needed to be eradicated from Rome.
75. Though one who had perhaps feigned it all, we should remember; cf. Suetonius, *Claudius* 38.
76. He had not, after all, come this far in the conspiracy to see a partial victory.
77. The point really was that Claudius was not safe so long as Chaerea lived.
78. *Antiquitates* 19.271.
79. *Antiquitates* 19.278.
80. *Antiquitates* 19.284.
81. The work was originally composed in Aramaic and then translated by Josephus into Greek.
82. *Antiquitates* 18.252.
83. Again a discrepancy: in the *Antiquitates* (18.262) there were only two legions.
84. The same town referenced in the *Antiquitates*.
85. The eulogistic treatment of Petronius in Josephus does not account for the fact that Caligula could probably be expected simply to send another, less enlightened or compassionate governor to Judaea, someone willing to slaughter everyone who questioned the emperor's edicts.
86. *Bellum Iudaicum* 2.202.

87. Scholars note that the actual term was three years and ten months; Josephus says eight months in both the *Bellum Iudaicum* and the *Antiquitates* (19.201).

88. *Bellum Iudaicum* 2.205. Another inconsistency here in Josephus' works: the *BI* says that the Senate assigned three cohorts to protect Rome; the *Ant.* says the number was four.

Chapter Six: The Evidence of Philo's *De Legatione ad Gaium*

1. As with Josephus, so with Philo the most convenient edition of the extant works is to be found in the Loeb Classical Library. Volume 10 provides the Greek text of the *De Legatione*, or 'Embassy to Gaius', together with an English translation by F.H. Colson (1962).

2. The so-called *De Legatione* is arguably of greater significance for an appreciation of Caligula than the author's *In Flaccum*, which we shall consider in the following chapter. The difficult (not to say intractable) problem of the relationship between the two works will be discussed there.

3. *De Legatione* 8 ff.

4. *De Legatione* 13.

5. *De Legatione* 21.

6. The motif of dissimulation.

7. *De Legatione* 23.

8. Or perhaps afraid and quite unwilling; the point of the ignorance of the boy may well be to excite the pathos of the reader for the sad scene.

9. *De Legatione* 32 ff.

10. *De Legatione* 34.

11. Another weak argument, but Macro did not have many cards to play, as it were.

12. *De Legatione* 42.

13. *De Legatione* 52 ff.

14. I.e. Macro delivered the army to Caligula and guaranteed their loyalty.

15. *De Legatione* 59 ff.

16. *De Legatione* 64.

17. *De Legatione* 66.

18. The whole thing is a wonderfully subtle, indeed richly psychological portrait of a nation in fear: essentially the populace was trying to assuage their feelings of apprehension that Caligula was an unpredictable monster, by justifying

whatever he had done as being for the good of the state and not evidence of a disordered or irrational mind.

19. *De Legatione* 69.

20. In all of this there is a hint that the people rationalized the doings of Caligula as being the natural enough responses of a young man who was justly afraid of not being taken seriously by his elders. According to this argument, Caligula had to work overtime to secure his position by asserting his authority and supremacy over all.

21. This would also have been the natural course of wishful thinking in the wake of the Tiberian reign.

22. The occasion for the legation that Philo would undertake to Caligula.

23. *De Legatione* 78-79.

24. *De Legatione* 81. Philo proceeds to detail the blessings that Heracles, Dionysus and the Dioscouri brought to men – in implicit contrast with Caligula, who did nothing of the sort for humanity. In a powerful apostrophic address, Philo attacks Caligula for all that he failed to do – a powerful indictment in which one can sense the anger and rage of the one-time emissary to the monster.

25. Of course the gods were also guilty of heinous acts of immorality and libidinous conduct, all of which Caligula practiced in faithful obeisance to his divine models (cf. his claim of Jovian justification for the practice of sororial incest).

26. And so with Apollo and the other gods; Apollo was the god of the sun and light, but Caligula preferred the darkness and the night (*De Legatione* 103).

27. For a convenient treatment of Caligula's attitude toward and relationship with the Jews, see Barrett, pp.182 ff.

28. A custom associated by the Romans with the decadent East; we may compare the elements of Augustan propaganda with respect to Cleopatra's Egypt.

29. *De Legatione* 119.

30. Philo's account of the treatment of the Jews in Alexandria reads hauntingly like a page from the history of Nazi Germany.

31. *De Legatione* 132.

32. *De Legatione* 134.

33. Interestingly, Philo notes that since the Alexandrians were in a hurry and did not want to waste time casting a new bronze chariot, they borrowed one that had been dedicated, rumour had it, to Cleopatra.

34. *De Legatione* 138 ff.
35. *De Legatione* 143 ff.
36. We should note that Philo makes clear that he is sympathetic to monarchy (*De Legatione* 149); he expresses understanding that the system of having one man rule has undeniable advantages.
37. The whole business was too Eastern, too Cleopatran for him.
38. *De Legatione* 159 ff.
39. Philo is savage in his indictment of the Egyptians of Alexandria; cf. *De Legatione* 166, where he notes that the Egyptians have dispositions that are just like the asps and crocodiles they worship.
40. For the ethnicity of Helicon cf. Barrett, p.84. Philo describes the Alexandrians as 'Egyptians'; we would probably do better to call them Greeks – best of all, 'Alexandrian Greeks'.
41. *De Legatione* 171.
42. *De Legatione* 178.
43. There are possible textual problems with the *De Legatione* here; there may be some text missing, since rather abruptly Philo proceeds to the actual legation to Caligula in which he took a prominent part.
44. *De Legatione* 186 ff.
45. *De Legatione* 198.
46. *De Legatione* 199.
47. I.e. Jabneh on the north-western border of Judaea.
48. Like Josephus, Philo is careful to note that the maleficent received the merit of their deeds: Helicon was killed under Claudius, and Apelles subjected to extreme torments under Caligula (*De Legatione* 206).
49. *De Legatione* 212.
50. Philo considers it to have been granted by the dispositions of divine providence (*De Legatione* 220).
51. *De Legatione* 226 ff.
52. Philo even records that the Jewish appeal mentioned the story of Perseus' monster, the Gorgon Medusa who could petrify those who gazed on her; he notes that while the Jews dismissed the fabulous story, they did note that if Caligula's image were forcibly erected in their Temple, they would be turned into stone if they gazed on it (*De Legatione* 237 ff.).
53. *De Legatione* 247 ff.

54. *De Legatione* 261 ff.

55. *De Legatione* 275 ff. On this missive note Solomon Zeitlin, 'Did Agrippa Write a Letter to Gaius Caligula?', in *The Jewish Quarterly Review* 56.1 (1965), pp.22-31. Zeitlin concludes (p.31), 'The letter of Agrippa to Gaius, as recorded by Philo, was composed by Philo in accordance with his theology. The speech of Agrippa to Gaius, as recorded by Josephus, was composed by Josephus in the spirit of the historiography of the Greeks.'

56. *De Legatione* 291. Apparently there was no fear that Caligula would resent the mention of his less than noble ancestor.

57. *De Legatione* 299 ff.

58. Cf. the modern Caesarea Maritima National Park on the Israeli Sharon plain.

59. *De Legatione* 319-20.

60. *De Legatione* 331 ff.

61. And thus the tyrant could have some faith and trust in him, though the end result of acquiescence with what Agrippa was enjoining was difficult to stomach.

62. *De Legatione* 334.

63. *De Legatione* 336.

64. I.e. the Alexander legend.

65. We may recall the story of how the exile who had indicated that he had spent his banishment praying for the death of Tiberius and the accession of Caligula, unwittingly succeeded in securing the deaths of every exiled person who had been banished under the new regime.

66. *De Legatione* 346.

67. *De Legatione* 346.

68. *De Legatione* 349 ff.

69. *De Legatione* 180 ff.

70. *De Legatione* 353.

71. The detail is of particular interest in the difficult pursuit of a chronology for the drama of Caligula and the Jews.

72. *De Legatione* 364 ff.

Chapter Seven: The Evidence of Philo's *In Flaccum*

1. The Greek text, with English translation by F.H. Colson, may be found conveniently in Volume IX of the Loeb Classical Library edition of Philo's works (1941).

2. Cf. Barrett, pp.187–88, who notes that while 39–40 is likely the correct date, 38–39 cannot be excluded as impossible.

3. *Historia Ecclesiastica* 2.18. The work is found in the Loeb Library, with translation by Kirsopp Lake.

4. Cf. the so-called *Hypothetica* and *De Providentia*.

5. A so-called work 'Concerning Virtues'.

6. A successor volume (cf. Philo's 'palinode') may have been planned if not executed.

7. *In Flaccum* 8 ff.

8. *In Flaccum* 9.

9. Unless he simply wished to remain 'under the imperial radar', as one might say.

10. *In Flaccum* 10 ff.

11. If true, Tiberius was of course correct in his assessment – though it would not have been difficult to make these predictions and judgments.

12. Philo thus races through details of the story that he tells at greater length in the *De Legatione*.

13. *In Flaccum* 16 ff.

14. Philo notes that the 'Egyptian' (i.e. Greek) inhabitants of Alexandria were especially prone to all manner of unrest and uprising, for the slightest of provocations.

15. Philo employs a dramatic theatre and stage metaphor to describe the treatment of Flaccus; the prefect is reduced to the role of stage prop. Philo names the three principal culprits in the manipulation as Dionysius, Lampo and Isidorus.

16. *In Flaccum* 24.

17. *In Flaccum* 32 ff.

18. Philo quite skips over the question of whether or not Caligula had a reason for sending Agrippa to Alexandria that had nothing to do with any pretext about safe sailing, etesian winds or a more appealing travel itinerary. The emperor no doubt wanted to see exactly what Flaccus was doing, aware as he no doubt was that Flaccus was a partisan of Gemellus and a close friend of the fallen Macro.

19. *In Flaccum* 36 ff.

20. *In Flaccum* 53 ff.

21. *In Flaccum* 56.
22. *In Flaccum* 62.
23. As with the description of the same horrors in the *De Legatione*, one is reminded of the miseries of twentieth-century Europe under the Nazi occupation.
24. *In Flaccum* 73.
25. Philo gives a somewhat macabre digression on the different types of whips used in the punishment of criminals real and alleged.
26. *In Flaccum* 86.
27. *In Flaccum* 96. One is reminded of the horrors described in the books of the Macchabees.
28. *In Flaccum* 97.
29. The impression one gleans from Philo's account is that Flaccus was carefully poised at all times between outright persecution of the Jews and independence from the actions of the Alexandrians – hedging his bets in a sense, but also practicing the dissimulation for which his patron Tiberius was so notorious.
30. *In Flaccum* 103 ff.
31. Once again Philo is a master of suspenseful narration.
32. *In Flaccum* 114.
33. Caligula, for once, ordered an act that met with Philo's approval.
34. *In Flaccum* 116 ff.
35. I.e. the feast of Sukkot or Booths, an agricultural celebration of thanksgiving for the harvest. The whole story is also reminiscent of the story behind the Jewish festival of Purim, with the deliverance of the Jews in Persia from the wicked Haman at the behest of Queen Esther.
36. Philo notes that the Jews have compassion enough not to gloat or rejoice in the matter of the misfortune of another (in this case, Flaccus; cf. *In Flaccum* 121).
37. *In Flaccum* 128 ff.
38. *In Flaccum* 125 ff.
39. *In Flaccum* 145.
40. Indeed, this no doubt was the real reason why Caligula was inclined to condemn him on whatever pretext.
41. *In Flaccum* 155 ff.
42. Colson notes in his Loeb that this provides unique surviving testimony to Flaccus' age; he was probably between 50 and 58 at the time of his banishment.

43. *In Flaccum* 163 ff.

44. *In Flaccum* 179.

45. *In Flaccum* 183.

46. *In Flaccum* 185.

47. Classical literature is replete with references to the hazards of the sea.

48. *In Flaccum* 188 ff.

49. *In Flaccum* 191. Philo is generally taken to be referring here to Sejanus, whose death would have been described in another part of his tracts against those Romans who persecuted the Jews; like the *De Legatione*, the *In Flaccum* closes with something of a mystery.

50. Balsdon (p.137) notes well: 'Philo was a contemporary, but he was in Italy at the time [that is, of the troubles regarding the question of the proposed statue of Caligula in Jerusalem] and must have found it hard to get good (and impossible, had he tried, to get unbiased) accounts from Judaea.'

51. *Inscriptiones Latinae Selectae* 8899.

Chapter Eight: The Evidence of Seneca the Younger

1. Seneca was a voluminous writer, and much of his work survives. Once again the Loeb Classical Library provides Latin texts with English translation of the complete surviving corpus. There are Oxford Classical Texts for the so-called *Dialogi* and *Epistulae ad Lucilium*, as well as for the tragedies. Penguin Classics and Oxford World's Classics editions exist for selected works. There is a useful Cambridge 'green and gold' edition of Gordon D. Williams on the *De Otio* and the *De Brevitate Vitae* (Cambridge, 2003). C.D.N. Costa has an Aris & Phillips edition of the *De Vita Beata*, the *De Tranquillitate Animi*, the *De Constantia Sapientis* and the *Ad Helviam Matrem de Consolatione* (1994). The bibliography on Seneca is predictably large; for a start, note Miriam T. Griffin, *Seneca: A Philosopher in Politics* (Oxford, 1976). James Romm has a fine treatment of the Neronian phase of Seneca's life in his *Dying Every Day: Seneca at the Court of Nero* (New York: Alfred A. Knopf, 2014). The tragedies, we might note, have been the subject of especially lavish commentaries: Richard Tarrant has a Cambridge edition of the *Agamemnon* for the 'orange' series of classical texts and commentaries (1976); Anthony Boyle has produced major Oxford editions of several plays. Amanda Wilcox has treated the Senecan use of Caligula in her piece 'Nature's

Monster: Caligula as *exemplum* in Seneca's Dialogues', in *Kakos: Badness and Anti-Value in Classical Antiquity*, edited by Ineke Sluiter and Ralph M. Rosen (Brill, 2008).

2. He suffered an enforced suicide in AD 65, a victim of the so-called Piso conspiracy. The death is unforgettably related in Book 15 of Tacitus' *Annales*.
3. Costa argues for a date after 47, the year of the death of Valerius Asiaticus.
4. *De Constantia* 18.
5. The exact meaning of the Latin here is in dispute. The text is exceedingly difficult to construe (see Reynolds' Oxford Classical Text for the details). Costa accepts the conjecture *emendicaticiis*, which seems to describe false hairs that the sensitive Caligula tried to adopt. All that is certain is that Seneca is referring to the emperor's notorious baldness.
6. Dietrich Boschung has done an exhaustive study on Caligula's appearance through numismatic and portraiture evidence in his 1989 monograph *Die Bildnisse des Caligula*.
7. Again, this is part of how the dialogue may be dated; we know that Valerius died in 47.
8. The ithyphallic scarecrow god of Roman lore.
9. We know him only from Seneca's brief mention of him here.
10. A rare mention of the emperor's attitude toward his infancy nickname.
11. A twist, then, on the psychological attitude of the emperor. One might accept that Caligula was sick of a nickname that had been given to him when he was an infant; the idea that it ill accorded with his imperial dignity is reasonable enough to countenance. But in fact he was upset because of how he had taken to the habit of wearing buskins, and this was the source of his dislike of the old name.
12. *De Ira* 1.20.8 ff.
13. *Iliad* 23.724.
14. *De Ira* 2.33.3 ff.
15. Once again, we see that Caligula is presented as unable to sustain any rival or anyone else enjoying the attention of the public.
16. *De Ira* 3.18.3 ff.
17. The Latin is *animi causa* – in brief, Caligula did what he did because he felt like it.
18. The Latin is *soleatus*; Caligula was wearing dinner sandals; 'casual wear' of a sort.

19. *De Ira* 3.19.1 ff.
20. The Latin is *solet fieri*, literally, 'it is accustomed to happen'.
21. Again, the emphasis on the emperor's allegedly savage appearance, which Seneca commented on at length in the *De Constantia Sapientis*.
22. *De Ira* 3.19.2 *qui optabat, ut populus Romanus unam cervicem haberet.*
23. *De Ira* 3.19.4.
24. *De Ira* 3.21.5.
25. Gordon Williams' edition of the work for the Cambridge Greek and Latin Classics series examines the evidence (pp.1–2). Besides the material discussed in our text at length, we may note *De Brevitate Vitae* 20.3, where Caligula is mentioned briefly for having granted retirement to one Sextus Turannius after the man reached the age of 90 (no mean feat in his day).
26. *De Brevitate Vitae* 18.5 ff.
27. This was the man who expressed the wish that the people might have but one neck.
28. *De Tranquillitate Animi* 14.4 ff.
29. The game was the famous ancient board game *latrunculi*.
30. Fragment 211. The most convenient edition of the work is in the Loeb series; the fragments appear in Volume XV.
31. Rectus is completely unknown apart from this fragment of Plutarch.
32. *De Consolatione ad Polybium* 17.4 ff.
33. Again, the theme of inconstancy, of unpredictable behaviour and inconsistent action recurs.
34. And so the point for Seneca in context is that no Roman should take Caligula as a model for how to behave after the death of a loved one.
35. The charge was alleged adultery with Caligula's sister, Julia Livilla (cf. Dio 60.8; Tacitus, *Annales* 12.8.3).
36. *Ad Helviam Matrem de Consolatione* 10.4.
37. This is the longest of Seneca's *dialogi* at seven books, and is marked by a highly repetitious style. It occupies the third and final volume of the Loeb edition of Seneca's 'Moral Essays'.
38. *De Beneficiis* 2.21.5 ff.
39. *De Beneficiis* 4.31.2 ff.
40. The Latin is *quam si ore excepturus esset.*

41. *De Beneficiis* 7.11.

42. This is Demetrius the Cynic; on the episode as part of the evidence for Caligula's wastrel ways, see Barrett, pp.224-25.

43. Latin *dementia*.

44. The complete 'correspondence' may be found in three Loeb volumes, and there is a two-volume Oxford text. Summers' Macmillan edition provides a selection with notes for students of Latin.

45. *Epistulae* 4.7.

46. There is a convenient 1971-1972 Loeb edition in two volumes.

47. *Naturales Quaestiones* IVA, Pref. 15 *Non mihi in amicitia Gaetucili Gaius fidem eripuit.*

48. *Naturales Quaestiones* IVA, Pref. 17.

Chapter Nine: The Evidence of Pliny the Elder

1. The work is divided into thirty-seven books. The Loeb Classical Library edition is in ten volumes, with complete Latin text and English translation. There is a splendid Budé set in progress at the time of this writing, where each book of Pliny's work receives a separate volume for critical text, French translation and commentary (in some cases quite extensive); when completed, this will be the most extensive coverage available on the work, with the best available Latin text. The Clarendon Ancient History series has an edition of Book 7 (on the 'human animal') with detailed notes by Mary Beagon. Tyler Travillian has a useful student commentary on the same book (as well as the opening chapters of Book 8), with general introduction. There is a Penguin Classics volume of selected passages, including all of the major references to Caligula.

2. The dramatic story of the end of Pliny the Elder is told by his nephew in a famous letter to Tacitus (*Epistulae* 6.16).

3. Admittedly, almost all of the references (as is to be expected given the nature of the work) are of interest at best as passing instances of trivia; cf. *Historia Naturalis* 7.39, where Caligula's wife Caesonia is cited as an example of a pregnancy of unusual length (merely seven months). 'She was the daughter of Vistilia, a woman married six times and whose remarkable gestation periods earned her a place in Pliny's *Natural History*' (Barrett, p.95).

4. *Historia Naturalis* 4.10.

5. *Principio terrarum Mauretaniae appellantur, usque ad C. Caesarem Germanici filium regna, saevitia eius in duas divisae provincias.* On this matter note D. Fishwick, 'The Annexation of Mauretania', in *Historia* 20 (1971), pp.467–87.

6. *Historia Naturalis* 5.11.

7. Dio 60.9.5.

8. Barrett, p.119.

9. *Historia Naturalis* 7.45. For commentary on the passage, note Mary Beagon, *The Elder Pliny on the Human Animal: Natural History Book 7* (Oxford, 2005), *ad loc.* At 7.57, Pliny cites nine children for Germanicus' wife Agrippina. The context is a passage in which Pliny mentions that some couples are physically incompatible; children are produced when they take different partners – witness Augustus and Livia. Others have only boys or girls; most have alternating sexes – witness Germanicus' wife. The passage has occasioned some question as to its relevance to the question of the order of the children of Germanicus. Beagon notes in her commentary that it is possible that Pliny does not mean that the alternation was to be taken strictly, but rather simply that some people have both boys and girls.

10. *Historia Naturalis* 9.117.

11. On this episode see especially Barrett, p.89.

12. *Historia Naturalis* 11.143.

13. The Latin is *Gaio principi rigentes.* Pliny says that Nero's eyes were weak unless he squinted.

14. Cf. Barrett, p.73, with a discussion of the suspicion of hyperthyroidism (of which Pliny's passage is not evidence).

15. *Historia Naturalis* 12.10.

16. Apparently a reference to height and/or obesity.

17. *Historia Naturalis* 13.22.

18. *Historia Naturalis* 14.64. Again, a small detail into the emperor's habits and preferences – and, in this case, to his wit. There is also a reference to wine pricing that cites the reign of Caligula at 14.56, though with no explicit comment one way or another on the emperor, unless we are to assume that Caligula is being indicted for decadence because the passage refers to a lavish banquet given by the *vates*, or bard, Pomponius Secundus.

19. *Historia Naturalis* 16.201. The obelisk is a famous archaeological landmark in St Peter's Square in the Vatican City State; the present location of the obelisk,

however, dates only to 1586. Cf. Barrett, pp.200-01. Barrett draws attention to the fact that the sixteenth-century transfer of the obelisk was considered a major engineering feat, thus making the original transport of the monument all the more outstanding for its difficulty; he also discusses the fate of the Caligulan ship (which was eventually sunk in the harbour at Ostia as part of the construction work for the erection of a lighthouse under Claudius), including the relevant archaeological discoveries made when Rome's airport was being built in the late 1950s. The obelisk is also referenced by Polydore Vergil in his *De inventoribus rerum* (3.11.4-5; cf. 3.13).

20. *Historia Naturalis* 32.2. Pliny may have thought that it was appropriate for the same fish to be responsible for attacking the vessels of both Antony and his notorious descendant. As for the veracity of the event, John Healy notes in his Penguin edition of Pliny, 'The powers with which it [i.e. the goby] is credited by Pliny are, of course, completely fictitious.' But cf. the remarks cited by E.W. Gudger in his article, 'Some Old Times Figures of the Shipholder, Echeneis or Remora', in *Isis* 13.2 (1930), pp.340-52.

21. *Historia Naturalis* 33.33.

22. *Historia Naturalis* 33.53.

23. *Historia Naturalis* 33.79.

24. Orpiment is a yellow sulfide of arsenic. It is found in hot springs, and has a deep orange-yellow hue. See further the detailed treatment of John F. Healy, *Pliny the Elder on Science and Technology* (Oxford, 1999), pp.235-36.

25. *Historia Naturalis* 35.18.

26. Tiberius is said to have had a pornographic image of Atalanta with Meleager; one wonders if there is any connection between the two stories. Caligula's coveted Atalanta painting was of a nude virgin, and the emperor may have had salacious interest in the image (cf. Suetonius, *Tiberius* 44.2). Tiberius is said to have commissioned the work from Parrhasius on the condition that if he was displeased, he was to have a million sesterces instead. Far from being unhappy, he had the scandalous painting set up in his bedroom.

27. *Historia Naturalis* 36.122-23.

28. *Historia Naturalis* 37.6.

29. Though Pliny was certainly willing to denounce the tyranny of Nero in vivid terms (he had experienced it, though obviously to a far less serious degree than did Seneca); see further Beagon on Pliny, *Historia Naturalis* 7.45.

Chapter Ten: The Evidence of the Fragmentary Roman Historians and Additional Sources

1. Essential now for the study of these figures is the magisterial edition of *The Fragments of the Roman Historians* edited by T.J. Cornell (Oxford, 2013). The three-volume set contains texts and translations (with detailed, dense commentary) on a vast range of authors.

2. Caligula's father Germanicus does not seem to have tried his hand at historical compositions.

3. Claudius is cited by Pliny the Elder as a source for his *Historia Naturalis*. Livy is said to have encouraged his early historical pursuits. Suetonius (*Claudius* 41.1-3) also notes that Claudius commenced his history from after the death of Julius Caesar, but then decided to pursue the more politic course of avoiding the whole period of the civil wars. Like Agrippina, he is also said to have written his own memoirs, in eight books.

4. Claudius also made revisions to the Latin alphabet and to Latin punctuation. His three letters did not survive his reign.

5. In Tacitus' *testimonium*, Agrippina is said to have written of her own life, and of the fates of her family (Latin *casus suorum*); in Pliny's *Historia Naturalis*, we find a note that the detail about Nero being a breech birth was cited in Agrippina's own memoirs.

6. Balsdon, p.224 (cf. Josephus, *Antiquitates* 19.284).

7. Balsdon observes (p.225) that 'surviving references to Gaius in the *Natural Histories* do not allow us to infer anything concerning the tone of Pliny's history. He refers to his cruelty ("saevitia") and to his insane extravagance – which he compares with that of Nero – but that is all. An encyclopedia is the place for facts, not for judgements.' Different readers will have differing levels of assent with Balsdon's Plinian assessment.

8. The family was of some distinction, it would seem, at least from the later Republic. The historian may well be the same Cluvius Rufus who was governor in Spain under Galba in AD 69.

9. *Antiquitates* 19.19.91-92.

10. T.P. Wiseman has an appendix on Cluvius in his edition of Josephus (pp.109-16).

11. Cornell's edition concludes, 'In general, cautious minimalism is in place. We do not know when Cluvius was consul, and it is uncertain whether or not he is the source of Jos. *AJ* 19.91-92' (Volume I, p.559).

12. Cf. Cornell, Volume I, p.559. For the Cluvii as a family from one of the areas of Italy that was most influenced by Greek culture (i.e. Campania), see Wiseman, p.109. For the theory of the influence of Cluvius on Suetonius from the number of Greek quotations, see the foundational article of Gavin B. Townend, 'The Sources of the Greek in Suetonius', in *Hermes* 92 (1964), pp.467-81. Townend's thesis that Cluvius was a sensational author, much given to polemic and editorializing commentary of a salacious nature, is critiqued by Wiseman. Cf. also David Wardle's 'Cluvius Rufus and Suetonius', in *Hermes* 120.4 (1992), pp.466-82; G.B. Townend, 'Traces in Dio Cassius of Cluvius, Aufidius, and Pliny', in *Hermes* 89 (1961), pp.227-48.

13. Plutarch, *Quaestiones Romanae* 107; *Otho* 2.102; Tacitus, *Annales* 13.20.2; 14.2.1-2. The anecdote appears in a letter of Pliny the Younger about Verginius Rufus (*Epistulae* 9.19.5).

14. 'The evidence is all circumstantial, and so the conclusion can never be final. But I think it is as certain as we could ever expect it to be' (p.113).

15. Wiseman, p.114. Wiseman does not, however, subscribe to the view that Cluvius alone was the source for Josephus' account of the assassination (cf. pp.xxiv ff.). Balsdon notes: 'Finally there was the history of Cluvius Rufus, a consular who survived the year of the four emperors. Tacitus quotes from this in his account of Nero's principate and – more important for our purposes – it is highly probable that Mommsen ('Cornelius Tacitus and Cluvius Rufus', *Gesammelte Schriften*, 7, pp.224-52) was right in thinking this the source of Josephus' detailed account of the conspiracy against Gaius, his murder, and the events which followed his death' (pp.223-24).

16. Wiseman, p.43. Wiseman takes issue with the thesis of Arther Ferrill that Caligula was simply mad, noting that 'Ferrill's own position largely depends on the tacit premise that cruelty, extravagance and irresponsibility necessarily connote madness.' This is of course the major scholarly division in Caligula studies: on the one hand you have a Balsdon and on the other a Ferrill; Barrett is somewhere betwixt the two, though leaning more to the Balsdon side of the debate.

17. *Agricola* 10.3 ... *Livius veterum, Fabius Rusticus recentium eloquentissimi auctores.* We have no way to evaluate the reasonableness of Tacitus' judgment.

18. Tacitus, *Annales* 13.20.2.

19. Tacitus, *Annales* 15.60.2-61.6, where Rusticus is cited as a source of evidence for details in the account of the death.

20. Balsdon writes: 'Agrippina in her memoirs and Seneca at Fabius Rusticus' elbow doubtless made common cause in avenging with their pen the insults which Gaius had offered them in his lifetime. That Fabius was over-partial to the credit of Seneca we know from Tacitus' (pp.224-25). Once again, the speculation is eminently reasonable, though of necessity it remains speculation.

21. Smallwood's aforementioned edition of *Documents Illustrating the Principates of Gaius* ..., etc., contains the texts discussed here. For the coinage of the Caligulan reign, note Barrett's 'Appendix II: Coins, Inscriptions, and Sculpture' (pp.244-54).

22. A valuable volume is Ruskin R. Rosborough's 1920 Pennsylvania doctoral thesis entitled *An Epigraphic Commentary on Suetonius' Life of Gaius Caligula*, which contains much useful material to explicate various Suetonian passages, including the *Acta* and such inscriptions as the so-called *Fasti Ostienses*, a fragmentary calendar from the Roman seaport of Ostia that provides some evidence of the keeping of records, some of them relevant to the study of Caligula's reign. The Ostian calendar provided relatively recent discoveries of at least two important Caligulan era facts: that of the death of Antonia, and the names of the consuls who succeed Caligula and Claudius in 37. A fire in the Aemilian granaries from AD 38 is recorded in the calendar; Rosborough comments (p.46) that we might have expected Suetonius to have mentioned the disaster (though he notes that fires were both all too common and all too destructive in Rome).

23. Smallwood, No. 88, p.42.

24. We should note that Caligula's sister Livilla has a similarly plain funerary inscription (Smallwood, No. 87, p.42).

25. Smallwood, No. 86, p.41.

26. Smallwood, No. 85, p.41.

27. Cf. Smallwood, pp.28-30.

28. Smallwood, No. 34, p.29.

29. Smallwood, No. 124, p.48.
30. Smallwood, No. 125, p.48. Like the Caligula-Tiberius coin, the Pietas piece dates to 37-38; we may remember the emphasis on *pietas* from Caligula's early reign.
31. Smallwood, No. 222, p.65.
32. Smallwood, No. 276, p.77; the date is 37-38, the military reference quite uncertain (it may simply refer to Caligula accepting an oath of allegiance from the army).
33. Smallwood, No. 361, p.92.
34. Barrett, p.248. Barrett thinks that the soldiers represent the Praetorian Guard receiving their donative, but there are other theories, all unprovable.
35. Cf. Barrett, p.12.
36. Cf. Barrett, pp.249-50.
37. Barrett (p.252) admits, 'Inscriptions are of enormous potential value as a historical tool. In practice their use for the reign of Caligula is somewhat limited.'
38. The most convenient edition of Orosius' work is the three-volume Budé set with complete critical Latin text, French translation and some annotations (edited by Marie-Pierre Arnaud-Lindet). The relevant material for the study of Caligula appears in Volume III, which contains the seventh and final book. Van Nuffelen's *Orosius and the Rhetoric of History* (Oxford, 2012) in the Oxford Early Christian Studies series is a valuable introduction.
39. *Historiae* 7.5.1.
40. *Historiae* 7.5.2.
41. Virgil, *Aeneid* 1.294-96.
42. *Historiae* 7.5.5. Cf. Suetonius, *Caligula* 44.
43. See further Barrett, p.137, for analysis of the significance of the evidence of this passage: 'A tradition linking the two [sc., events – namely the defection of the British prince and the episode at the English Channel] seems to survive in the fifth century writer Orosius, who says that Caligula set out with a large force, scouring Germany and Gaul, and stopped at the edge of Ocean in view of Britain, and that when he had received the surrender of the son of Cunobelinus he returned to Rome because of a deficiency of war material.'

44. The reference is somewhat obscure; it seems to mean that there was a lack of materiel, as in supplies and provisions. The noun often refers to wood and lumber.
45. *Historiae* 7.5.6.
46. Like Philo and Josephus, Orosius is most interested in the connection of Caligula to Judaeo-Christian affairs.
47. *Historiae* 7.5.8.
48. 2.7.1.
49. See further on this Cerulli, E., 'Tiberius and Pontius Pilate in Ethiopian Tradition and Poetry', in *Proceedings of the British Academy* LIX (1973), pp.141-58; cf. the same author's 1968 Florence work *La letteratura etiopica: L'Oriente cristiano nell'unità delle sue tradizioni*. Note also the forthcoming work of Paul Burke, 'Saint Pilate and the Conversion of Tiberius', appearing in the edited volume of Mary C. English and Lee M. Fratantuono, *Pushing the Boundaries of Historia* (Routledge). Note also Paul L. Maier, 'The Fate of Pontius Pilate', in *Hermes* 99.3 (1971), pp.362-71; Helen K. Bond's *Pontius Pilate in History and Intrepretation* (Cambridge, 1998).
50. *Historiae* 7.5.9.
51. *Historiae* 7.5.10.
52. Orosius also notes that the reign of Caligula engendered significant interest in the restoration of the Roman Republic and the overturning of the house of the Caesars, which of course failed to materialize (cf. *Historiae* 7.6.3).
53. 2.4.1.
54. There is a three-volume Loeb edition entitled *Scriptores Historiae Augustae*, with complete Latin text and English translation. The Penguin volume (*Lives of the Later Caesars*) by Anthony Birley offers selected lives (i.e. the first part of the collection). The Budé editions of the set (in progress at the time of this writing) have especially extensive commentaries, and offer the best editions available for the lives that are covered in the series.
55. *Marcus Aurelius* 28.10. Tiberius had apparently succeeded in his wish to appear better by being succeeded by one such as Caligula – he managed not to be mentioned here (but cf. *Elagabalus* 33.1).
56. Like Caligula, we might note, he was a partisan of the Green faction in the chariot races.
57. *Avidius Cassus* 8.4.

58. *Commodus Antoninus* 10.2.
59. *Elagabalus* 1.1.
60. *Elagabalus* 33.1. Interestingly, Elagabalus is said to have surpassed even the *spintriae* of old – that is, precisely the perverts Caligula had ordered banished from Rome in the wake of Tiberius' death.
61. *Elagabalus* 34.1. Of course Caligula remained in power for almost four years, and Nero had a respectably long reign.
62. *Aurelian* 42.6.
63. The best edition is the Budé text with French translation, *Aurélius Victor: Livre des Césars*, edited by Pierre Dufraigne (Paris: Les Belles Lettres, 2003). There is an English translation with introduction and commentary by H.W. Bird for Liverpool University Press (1994) in the 'Translated Texts for Historians' series.
64. The Latin is *cum senatus atque optimi cuiusque multiplici clade terrarum orbis foedaretur.*
65. There is again a Budé edition, *Pseudo-Aurelius Victor: Abrégé des Césars*, edited by Michel Festy (1999).

Chapter Eleven: Towards a Reconstruction of the Caligulan Reign

1. For Winterling, the opening of Caligula's reign represented an attempt to return to Augustan policies that maintained an autocracy with a republican veneer (in alleged contrast to Tiberian practice). Relations between Caligula and the Senate became considerably strained in the wake of the conspiracy of 39.
2. The film has had its defenders (predictably enough); most of the praise it has been accorded focuses on its alleged political insights. The author has not seen the film, and with no regret; if there is anything surprising about the film, it is the number of leading actors who somehow managed to find themselves appearing in it.
3. It was commenced in 1938, and published only in 1944.
4. And here, too, there was controversy; the scene in which Hurt's Caligula removed the foetus from his eviscerated sister Drusilla in some horrific parody of pseudo-Jovian emulation was aired but twice in 1976 before it was removed (and is now considered lost); the episode closes with Caligula's uncle Claudius looking on in horror, though the audience mercifully does not see what he sees.

5. Barrett (p.12) takes this occasion as further evidence for the tradition of Caligula's apparently outstanding rhetorical skills.

6. Cf. John Hurt's portrayal of the young Caligula as bringing Tiberius a rare pornographic book that he hopes to borrow some day, when Tiberius is not using it.

7. We can only speculate on the point, but one might reasonably wonder if Caligula were indeed a fairly talented intellect, with if anything a tendency not to follow through on his pursuits. Claudius may well have been possessed of greater perseverance, but there can be little doubt that Caligula devoted a good portion of his formative years to the study of Greek literature in particular.

8. Cf. Ferrill, p.100, for the question of whether or not the emperor was more or less already insane (or at least seriously mentally hampered) by genetic disorders, and/or whether the experience of his formative years exacerbated an already existing problem.

9. P.90.

10. It was either 28 or 29 March when Caligula was granted his powers; he entered the city on the 28th.

11. There is the question of the death of Antonia on 1 May AD 37; again the ancient sources are keen to blame Caligula, though we can do little but choose either to accept or reject the claims. Some suspicions were no doubt fomented in light of later Caligulan atrocities.

12. Suetonius, *Claudius* 7. According to Suetonius, Claudius was hailed with popular favour when he appeared in public as the uncle of the emperor and the brother of Germanicus, though he was mocked in private by the imperial family, notably by having olives and dates thrown at him when he dozed off at meals, or by having his slippers removed as he slept and put onto his hands (*Claudius* 8).

13. Suetonius, *Claudius* 9.

14. Cf. Barbara Sidwell, 'Gaius Caligula's Mental Illness', in *The Classical World* 103.2 (2010), pp.183-206. Sidwell argues that there is no real evidence to reconstruct what was wrong (if anything) with Caligula, and that the tradition of his madness is part of a hostile senatorial tradition (cf. Winterling's thesis). Robert S. Katz's 'The Illness of Caligula' (*The Classical World* 65.7, 1972, pp.223-25) considers the possibility of glandular disorders, and notes that were

Caligula alive today, he would be seen by an endocrinologist or internist, not a psychiatrist. Katz defended his theory of hyperthyroidism in his 1977 article 'Caligula's Illness Again' (*The Classical World* 70.7, 1977, p.451), a response to M. Gwyn Morgan's 'Caligula's Illness Again' (*The Classical World* 66.6, 1973, pp.327-28). Morgan questions the Katz diagnosis, though he concludes that the mysterious illness of the autumn of 37 was purely physical and not some nervous breakdown. Morgan responded to Katz's response with his 'Once Again Caligula's Illness' (*The Classical World* 70.7, 1977, pp.452-53), again with criticism of the hyperthyroidism diagnosis, and the conclusion that whatever the malady, it was 'serious'. Note also D. Thomas Benediktson, 'Caligula's Madness: Madness or Interictal Temporal Lobe Epilepsy', in *The Classical World* 82.5 (1989), pp. 370-75, the title of which offers more than a clue as to his conclusion (cf. C. Dumont's 1964 Liège thesis, 'C. César: empereur épileptique. Quelques aspects d'une personalité'). Encephalitis is the diagnosis of A.T. Sandisson in 'The Madness of the Emperor Caligula', in *Medical History* 2 (1958), p.207; note also V. Massaro and I. Montgomery, 'Gaius – Mad, Bad, Ill, or All Three?', in *Latomus* 37 (1978), pp.894-908, and the same authors' 'Gaius (Caligula) doth murder sleep', in *Latomus* 38 (1979), pp.699-700 (Caligula as a schizoid); J. Lucas, 'Un empereur psychopathe: Contribution à la psychologie du Caligula de Suétone', in *Acta Classica* 36 (1967), pp.159-89. Note also G.C. Moss, 'The Mentality and Personality of the Julio-Claudian Emperors', in *Medical History* 7 (1963), pp.165-75.

15. In his *Sons of Caesar* (p.173), Philip Matyszak comments, 'it may be that, after spending a decade and a half under the sword of Damocles, Gaius Caligula understood that he was finally safe, and the realization precipitated a long-overdue nervous breakdown.'

16. For the Drusilla question, note Ferrill, p.111, who takes issue with the view of Barrett in particular. For Ferrill, there is no question that Caligula's act in deifying his sister was indeed evidence of madness; Barrett compares the case of Queen Victoria erecting lavish monuments in memory of Prince Albert. It is quite true, however, that neither Livia nor Antonia had been deified; Drusilla was the first Roman woman to ascend to the pantheon of the immortals. Her worship and cult, of course, did not survive her brother's reign. Ferrill correctly notes that no Roman emperor would have been much interested in restoring the cult of Drusilla. Drusilla may have been a

relatively 'safe' woman to promote to high honours – she had essentially no political significance, unlike Livia and Antonia, let alone Agrippina (who was also not deified – sister came before mother) – but the whole business was undoubtedly viewed as bizarre (and there is no compelling reason to believe that the story was made up by hostile biographers and historians). Certainly the episode is evidence of Caligula's no doubt genuine, extraordinary grief. As Ferrill does well to note, 'For one only in his mid-twenties, Caligula had already experienced a lifetime of tragedy and triumph' (p.112). It may all have been overwhelming for him – a banal but quite plausible explanation. Ferrill argues (p.158) that Caligula was crafty, though not intelligent; had he not been emperor, he might have been merely eccentric or peculiar – but imperial power corrupted him utterly. Ferrill is surprised that he lasted for as many years as he did – though noting that Nero and Commodus survived for much longer. Winterling (p.83) argues that Caligula behaved entirely rationally in the aftermath of his sister's death, largely on the grounds that the succession was quite undetermined, and that the development of Drusilla's cult would aid in buttressing the claims of the imperial family on a dynasty. He notes that Livia was deified by Claudius – but did anyone seriously compare Drusilla with Livia? – and that Poppaea Sabina was deified by Nero. The Poppaea deification could easily be seen to be just as ludicrous, however, as the Drusillan.

17. On this question see especially Arthur Keaveney and John A. Madden, 'The *Crimen Maiestatis* under Caligula: The Evidence of Dio Cassius', in *The Classical Quarterly* 48.1 (1998), pp.316-20. Keaveney and Madden exhaustively consider the question of treason charges under Caligula, including such cases as that of Gemellus, who was accused of having prayed for the emperor's death. Certainly Caligula had forgiven a number of Tiberian treason defendants early in his reign, and later, he was to use the same charge himself against his enemies (real and perceived). Keaveney and Madden argue that at no time did Caligula abolish the charge of *maiestas*, noting that at some points in his reign it was simply less likely to be employed. The happy period of clemency ended in 39, possibly in response to reports and rumours of possible conspiracy. 'Now under threat, he could identify with Tiberius and saw what seemed to him the gains accrued from a ruthless pursuit of senators on the model of his predecessor' (p.320). More generally on the vast

problem of freedom in the early principate, see the classic treatment of Mason Hammond, '*Res olim dissociabiles*: *Principatus ac Libertas*: Liberty under the Early Roman Empire', in *Harvard Studies in Classical Philology* 67 (1963), pp.93-113.

18. Cf. Ferrill, p.115, for the question of how much of the reports of Caligula's sadistic nature can be trusted. For Ferrill, even if some of the reports are untrue, the resulting picture is of an emperor who 'was one of the cruellest rulers Rome ever had, and the competition for that title is great'.

19. The wedding was probably early in 39, though the exact date is uncertain; the infant was born one month later.

20. Winterling (p.111) notes that while Gaetulicus was killed, Caligula's sisters received the comparatively more lenient punishment of exile. He argues that no one in Rome would have faulted Caligula for having had them slain – and that had he killed Agrippina, the world would have been spared a Nero. Certainly true – but there are shades here of Balsdonian willingness to rationalize away everything the sources report about Caligula.

21. He had been a partisan of Sejanus, and a rare survivor of his fall; see further here Raphael Sealey, 'The Political Attachments of L. Aelius Sejanus', in *Phoenix* 15.2 (1961), pp.97-114; also Zeph Stewart, 'Sejanus, Gaetulicus, and Seneca', in *The American Journal of Philology* 74.1 (1953), pp.70-85.

22. For the theory that Gaetulicus had connections to Ptolemy of Mauretania that explain the death of the latter, see Duncan Fishwick and Brent D. Shaw, 'Ptolemy of Mauretania and the Conspiracy of Gaetulicus', in *Historia: Zeitschrift für alte Geschichte* 25.4 (1976), pp.491-94. For more on the matter, cf. S.J.V. Malloch, 'The Death of Ptolemy of Mauretania', in *Historia: Zeitschrift für alte Geschichte* 53.1 (2004), pp.38-45.

23. Tiberius reigned for almost a quarter of a century, and yet he never left Italy once in that whole time.

24. And we do well to note that Caligula was planning to visit Egypt at the time of his assassination. This visit may well have inspired concern in some in Rome that Caligula was following in the footsteps of his ancestor Mark Antony – though no doubt some people felt safer with Caligula out of Rome than in the capital (cf. Levick's *Claudius*, p.29).

25. *Breviarium* 7.12. Eutropius composed an abridgement of Roman history in ten books; it is perhaps best known for its traditional place early in the Latin

curriculum (the style is quite easy and fluid). The 'Breviary' of Eutropius is a simple, unadorned account of Roman history; it is usually reliable and sometimes provides useful evidence to supplement other more major surviving sources.

26. Cf. Balsdon, p.59, for how this attestation 'is probably the most sympathetic notice that the undertaking received in antiquity'.

27. Cf. Balsdon, pp.71–72.

28. Cf. pp.78 ff.

29. Balsdon, p.81.

30. Balsdon argues (p.83) that many senators were doubtless disappointed that the conspiracy had failed; he concludes that the plotters had allies ready to move in their interests in Rome once Caligula was dead.

31. Cf. Suetonius, *Claudius* 9.

32. Suetonius, *Vespasian* 2.

33. Cf. Balsdon, p.84, for the question of the Latin text of Suetonius, which may read that Vespasian was hateful of the Senate – in other words, that the future emperor had no more love for that body than Caligula. Lipsius emended the text so that Caligula is the one hateful of the Senate – perhaps an example of the blackening of the reputation of the *princeps*.

34. See Barrett, pp.126–127, for the place of Caligula's foreign policy in the wider context of the earlier Julio-Claudian principates. Barrett argues that after the conservative foreign policy of Tiberius (in part inherited from Augustus), Caligula's more expansionist vision may have had significant popular support.

35. There is some numismatic evidence that Adminius became something of a client king of Rome, but the extent of his domains – if they existed – is quite unknown. See further the treatment of Birgitta Hoffmann, *The Roman Invasion of Britain: Archaeology Versus History* (South Yorkshire: Pen & Sword Military, 2013). We do not know when Cunobelinus died; it may have been as early as AD 40. His death would trigger the crisis that would lead directly to Claudius' decision to finish what Caligula had in some sense 'started'.

36. Cf. p.89. The Germans were certainly masters of insurgency and guerrilla warfare, and they made excellent use of their natural defences.

37. Dio 62.4.1.

38. Balsdon, pp.90 ff.

39. Again, the whole matter of the seashells is so confused that theories range from the aforementioned plan of insult to the idea that the soldiers were being encouraged to find wealth from pearls; cf. J.G.F. Hind, 'Caligula and the Spoils of Ocean: A Rush for Riches in the Far North-West?', in *Britannia* 34 (2003), pp.272-74.

40. For a start, cf. E.J. Phillips, 'The Emperor Gaius' Abortive Invasion of Britain', in *Historia* 19 (1970), pp.369-74.

41. Balsdon (pp.93-94) notes that Claudius would finish what his nephew had started; it is in some sense a verdict on the essentially sound character of Caligula's idea that his successor – for all his eagerness to erase other aspects of memory of the Gaian principate – did decide to follow through on a major expedition to invade the island. In terms of the more ludicrous aspects of the story of Caligula's dealings in Britain, Balsdon (pp.94-95) is correct that Agrippina and Seneca were in a position to influence the recording of history, and that both of them had great animosity toward Caligula. For the speculative theory that the whole British venture was not intended as an invasion of the island, but rather as a movement against the Canninefates, see P. Bicknell, 'The Emperor Gaius' Military Activities in AD 40', in *Historia* 17 (1968), pp.496-505. The Canninefates gave their name to the modern Kennemerland in the Netherlands.

42. For a sober appraisal of the question, see Barrett, pp.117-18.

43. The locale had long been an interestingly anomalous region of Roman interest. Notwithstanding its status as a client kingdom, Augustus had sent colonies there (cf. Nicola K. Mackie, 'Augustan Colonies in Mauretania', in *Historia: Zeitschrift für alte Geschichte* 32.3, 1983, pp.332-58).

44. Cf. Ferrill, p.148, who notes that Caligula may have avoided immediately entering Rome (he headed instead first for Campania) because he was afraid of a senatorial conspiracy/probable assassination in the wake of the Gaetulicus episode. Wiedemann wonders if he simply wanted to avoid being in Rome at the height of the summer (*Cambridge Ancient History*, p.228).

45. Balsdon – ever quick to praise Caligula in the face of his hostile critics – notes that Caligula was 'not a coward' (p.98).

46. One almost gets the impression that Balsdon frowns on the impolite action of those who marred the closing day of the Palatine Games with violence.

47. Cf. Seneca, *De Tranquillitate Animi* 14.4 ff.

Chapter Twelve: Assessing the Foreign Policy of the *Princeps*

1. Barbara Levick notes, 'Caligula spent nearly four years exploring what it meant to be Princeps and the limits of what he could do as Princeps' (*Claudius*, New Haven-London: Yale University Press, 1990, p.29).

2. Levick (*Claudius*, p.29) notes that perhaps morale was restored on the German frontier as a result of Caligula's actions, but nothing more; she mentioned the surrender of the son of Cunobelinus in 39, and otherwise can find no foreign policy achievement in the north with which to credit Caligula.

3. For the theory that all that Caligula intended was a show of force, a spectacle, as it were, to intimidate more than anything, see R.W. Davies, 'The "Abortive Invasion" of Britain by Gaius', in *Historia* 15 (1966), pp.124-28.

4. For a summary of the rebellion, note Levick's *Claudius*, pp.149 ff.

5. Barrett, p.182.

6. 'The stage was already set for a final confrontation that would culminate less than thirty years later in the devastating sack of Jerusalem by Rome' (Barrett, p.191).

7. Levick's *Claudius*, p.29.

8. Philip Matyszak comments in his *Sons of Caesar* (p.167) on Caligula's fascination with Agrippa: 'Given the restrictive atmosphere in which he had lived until then, it is unsurprising that the young Gaius Caligula was fascinated by this free spirit, a relative of the infamous Salome who had received the head of John the Baptist on a platter.'

9. Even apart from the religious dimensions of their work, for Philo, we might note, Caligula was planning nothing less than the utter destruction of the Jewish people. For Philo, Caligula was little more than a genocidal monster. The historical record does not permit verification of Philo's judgement. Caligula may have had a quite inappropriate sense of humour and willingness to make despicable 'jokes' like wishing that the Roman people had but one neck, but there is no evidence that he planned to launch a major war to destroy the Jews.

10. Barrett (p.191) sees the destruction of the altar of Caligula at Jamnia as evidence of a 'religious zeal that must have been largely independent of Caligula'. But it was Caligula who initiated the whole problem of his alleged divinity.

11. Cf. Levick's *Claudius*, p.34.

12. Cf. p.89. For Winterling, senatorial jealousy cannot be excluded as a motivating force for hatred of the *princeps*.

13. It would take the work of four legions under the command of Aulus Plautius; cf. Dio 60.19-23. Caligula seems to have planned for using four legions to cross over into Britain, too: the Fifteenth and the Twenty-Second, called *Primigeniae* after the birth of his daughter Drusilla, and the Fourteenth and Twenty-First from Germany. See further here Wiedemann in the *Cambridge Ancient History*, p.228. On the question of whether the two new *Primigeniae* legions were raised by Caligula or Claudius, see Humphrey, pp.218 ff.

14. *The Romanization of Britain: An Essay in Archaeological Interpretation* (Cambridge, 1990), p.40.

15. An idea, we must note, that many scholars discount as anti-Caesarian/anti-Caligulan fantasy.

16. *Aspects of Roman History*, p.73.

17. The question of whether or not Caligula felt that the Augustan system was some sort of 'sham' republicanism is ultimately irrelevant to the matter of how Caligula acted in his dealings with the Senate. Insulting them and subjecting them to arbitrary threats was certainly not a productive avenue to achieving some sort of better system of government, and absolute monarchy was foreign to the traditions of the Republic since the sixth century. If Caligula had concluded that monarchy was a more efficient and better system than republicanism, he does not seem to have absorbed the lesson that benign monarchies tend to survive longer than despotic ones.

18. Matyszak notes in his *Sons of Caesar* (p.176): 'As Gaius Caligula rose from his sickbed, he had apparently decided that the issue had been fudged for long enough. It was time to make the distinction between emperor and subjects unambiguously clear.' Certainly Caligula represents, in part, the problem of exploring the exact nature of what Augustus had brilliantly left undefined – or at least lacking in precise definition. That decision had been brilliant *for Augustus* – it was more difficult to maintain for Tiberius, or for Caligula. Something of a restoration of the Augustan policy would return under Claudius – but the genie of autocracy would prove quite difficult to return to its bottle. Cf. Matyszak's further remark (p.193): 'The true crime of Gaius Caligula was not homicidal mania, but pushing the trend of the past

century to its logical conclusion to show the Caesars as the autocrats they had become. This was not so much mad as several centuries premature.' For Denise Reitzenstein (in her *Bryn Mawr* review of Barrett's second edition), Winterling is 'der Epigone Balsdons'.

19. P.240. For an attempt to offer a balanced assessment of Caligula that acknowledges a 'kernel' of veracity to the stories of ancient lore, though with rhetorical exaggeration, note M.P. Charlesworth, 'The Tradition About Caligula', in *The Cambridge Historical Journal* 4.2 (1933), pp.105-19. Charlesworth also notes the extreme energy of Caligula's reign, though the inability to bring much to fruition (we may compare the emphasis on inconstancy in the surviving sources). It may well be that much of the lack of finish was the result of attempting too much, too quickly, and in the face of too much opposition. For Charlesworth, ultimately Claudius represented something of a restoration of the Augustan attempt at balance between representative government and autocracy.

20. Ferrill (in his *Bryn Mawr Review* of the first edition of Barrett) notes that rather than Hitler or Stalin, Caligula should be compared to Idi Amin or the Emperor Bokassa – a reasonable enough point.

21. *The Sons of Caesar*, p.193.

22. And of course Germanicus' loss was no doubt deeply felt. Of Tiberius' mentorship the pages of Tacitus offer the best verdict.

23. For Arther Ferrill, essentially all that Caligula bequeathed to Rome was a more autocratic vision of the principate. The position is not entirely without justification, though I would be inclined to be more charitable in terms of the Caligulan vision for foreign policy.

Conclusions

1. Britannicus.

2. On this point, the work of Philip Hardie has shown the way; cf. his article 'Virgil's Ptolemaic Relations', in *The Journal of Roman Studies* 96 (2006), pp.25-41.

3. Claudius would be poisoned in October of 54 – at least if we can believe the consensus of the ancient evidence. Not surprisingly, modern historians have sometimes cast doubt on the tradition.

4. Of Caligula, Finley Hooper writes (p.372): 'Yet it was the horror of the times that this twisted person could become the first citizen of Rome. It was a wonder that the Augustan system could survive him, a blessing that his reign was so short.' Hooper acknowledges that some of Suetonius' stories in particular may be embellished or untrustworthy, and that certain of Caligula's deeds may have been 'commendable', but in the end he subscribes to the thesis that the emperor was more *monstrum* than *princeps*.

Bibliography and Further Reading

1. Catharine Edwards has a perceptive review of Ferrill in *The Classical Review* 42.1 (1992), pp.114–15, in which she notes that both Ferrill and Barrett 'share the underlying assumption that we can arrive at a true picture of what Caligula was like'.

Bibliography and Further Reading

T he list that follows is highly selective, even idiosyncratic. Those interested in a scholarly appraisal of Caligula will want to turn to Barrett first; either the first or the second edition is perfectly serviceable. Further reading beyond Barrett should probably proceed to Balsdon and Ferrill (a study in contrasts, to put it mildly), and also Winterling. A briefer treatment of the Caligulan principate will be found in Wiedemann's contribution to Volume X of the second edition of the *Cambridge Ancient History*. For those with German, Gelzer's *Real-Encyclopädie* article on 'Iulius Caligula' (10.381-423) offers the standard treatment. In French, the works of Auguet and Renucci are highly recommended. On the death of Caligula, Wiseman's historical commentary on Josephus' treatment from Book 19 of his *Jewish Antiquities* is invaluable.

The footnotes of the present volume offer a wide range of relevant journal articles on specialized Caligulan topics. It should be noted that the commentaries on Suetonius' *Caligula* by Hurley, Lindsay and Wardle offer a wide range of historical comments on the period, and have notes that are largely accessible to those without Latin. Much information on Caligula may also be gleaned from the commentaries on relevant portions of Dio Cassius and Tacitus in particular. Biographies of Tiberius and Claudius (here the works of Barbara Levick hold just sway) also contain much useful material (Levick's *Claudius* is especially helpful on the question of just how complicit Claudius may have been in the conspiracy to kill his nephew). Note also that Barrett has produced exemplary biographies of Livia and Agrippina the Younger, and Kokkinos a fine volume on Antonia the Elder. An interesting, lightly amusing summary of the diverse schools of thought on Caligula can be found in *The New York Times* of 1 April 1990, 'Week in Review, "Ideas & Trends"', where Eric Pace comments on the publication of Barrett's book under the headline, 'Scholarship Yields a New Caligula, Who is Merely Obnoxious'.[1]

Adams, G.W., *The Roman Emperor Gaius 'Caligula' and His Hellenistic Aspirations* (Florida: Brown Walker, 2007).

Alston, R., *Aspects of Roman History AD 14-117* (London-New York: Routledge, 1998).

Auguet, R., *Caligula, ou le pouvoir à vingt ans* (Le Regarde de l'histoire) (Paris: Payot, 1975).

Balsdon, J.P.V.D., *The Emperor Gaius (Caligula)* (Oxford, 1934).

Barrett, A., *Caligula: The Corruption of Power* (New Haven-London: Yale University Press, 1989).

Barrett, A., *Caligula: The Abuse of Power* (New York-London: Routledge, 2015, revised second edition of the 1989 original).

Barrett, A., *Agrippina: Sex, Power, and Politics in the Early Empire* (New Haven-London: Yale University Press, 1996, first published the same year in London by B.T. Batsford Ltd as *Agrippina: Mother of Nero*).

Barrett, A., *Livia: First Lady of Imperial Rome* (New Haven-London: Yale University Press, 2002).

Bastien, S., *Caligula et Camus: Interférences transhistoriques* (Amsterdam-New York: Rodopi, 2006).

Bissler, J., *Caligula Unmasked: An Investigation of the Historiography of Rome's Most Notorious Emperor* (Thesis Kent State, 2013).

Bond, H.K., *Pontius Pilate in History and Interpretation* (Society for New Testament Studies Monograph Series 100) (Cambridge, 1998).

Boschung, D., *Die Bildnisse des Caligula* (Berlin: Gebrüder Mann Verlag, 1989).

Bowman, A.K., et al. (eds), *The Cambridge Ancient History, Second Edition, Volume X: The Augustan Empire, 43 BC – AD 69* (Cambridge, 1996).

Breeze, D.J., *The Frontiers of Imperial Rome* (South Yorkshire: Pen & Sword Military, 2011).

Burnand, C., *Tacitus and the Principate: From Augustus to Domitian* (Cambridge, 2011).

Campbell, J.B., *The Emperor and the Roman Army* (Oxford, 1984).

Cornell, T.J. (ed.), *The Fragments of the Roman Historians* (3 vols) (Oxford, 2013).

Dabrowski, A.M., *Problems in the Tradition about the Principate of Gaius* (Dissertation Toronto, 1972).

Edmondson, J., *Dio: The Julio Claudians: Selections from the Roman History of Cassius Dio*. LACTOR 15 (London: London Association of Classical Teachers, 1992).

Edwards, C., *The Politics of Immorality in Ancient Rome* (Cambridge, 1993).

Ferrill, A., *Caligula: Emperor of Rome* (London: Thames and Hudson, 1991).

Goodman, M. *The Roman World 44 BC - AD 180* (Routledge History of the Ancient World) (London-New York: Routledge, 1997).

Goodyear, F.R.D. *The Annals of Tacitus, Volume I (Annals 1.1-54)* (Cambridge, 1970).

Goodyear, F.R.D., *The Annals of Tacitus, Volume II (Annals 1.55-81 and Annals 2)* (Cambridge, 1981).

Hammond, M., *The Augustan Principate* (Cambridge, Massachusetts: Harvard University Press, 1933).

Holland, T., *Dynasty: The Rise and Fall of the House of Caesar* (London: Little, Brown, 2015).

Hooper, F., *Roman Realities* (Detroit, Michigan: Wayne State University Press, 1979).

Humphrey, J.W., *An Historical Commentary on Cassius Dio's Roman History, Book 59 (Gaius Caligula)* (Dissertation British Columbia, 1976).

Hurley, D.W., *An Historical and Historiographical Commentary on Suetonius' Life of C. Caligula* (American Classical Studies 32) (Atlanta, Georgia: Scholars Press, 1993).

Kokkinos, N., *Antonia Augusta: Portrait of a Great Roman Lady* (London-New York: Routledge, 1992).

Koll, R.A., *The Ruler Cult under Caligula* (Dissertation Case Western Reserve, 1932).

Levick, B., *Tiberius the Politician* (London-New York: Routledge, 1999, revised edition of the 1976 original from the *Aspects of Greek and Roman Life* series).

Levick, B., *Claudius* (New Haven-London: Yale University Press, 1990).

Lindsay, H., *Suetonius: Caligula* (London: Bristol Classical Press, 1993).

Marsh, F.B., *The Reign of Tiberius* (Oxford, 1931).

Martin, R., and Woodman, A., *Tacitus: Annals IV* (Cambridge, 1989).

Matyszak, P., *The Sons of Caesar: Imperial Rome's First Dynasty* (London: Thames and Hudson, 2006).

Maurer, J.A., *A Commentary on C. Suetoni Tranquilli, Vita C. Caligulae Caesaris, Chapters I-XXI* (Dissertation Pennsylvania, 1949).

Miller, F., *The Emperor in the Roman World (31 BC – AD 337)* (Ithaca, New York: Cornell University Press, 1977, reprinted by London: Duckworth, 1992, with a 1991 afterword by the author).

Nony, D., *Caligula* (Paris: Fayard, 1986).

Pagán, V.E., *Conspiracy Narratives in Roman History* (Austin, Texas: The University of Texas Press, 2004).

Powell, L., *Eager for Glory: The Untold Story of Drusus the Elder, Conqueror of Germania* (South Yorkshire: Pen & Sword Military, 2013).

Powell, L., *Germanicus: The Magnificent Life and Mysterious Death of Rome's Most Popular General* (South Yorkshire: Pen & Sword Military, 2013).

Renucci, P., *Caligula* (Paris: Éditions Tempus Perrin, 2011).

Rosborough, R.R., *An Epigraphic Commentary on Suetonius' Life of Gaius Caligula* (Dissertation Pennsylvania, 1920).

Salway, P., *The Oxford Illustrated History of Roman Britain* (Oxford, 1993).

Smallwood, E.M., *Documents Illustrating the Principates of Gaius Claudius and Nero* (Cambridge, 1967).

Talbert, R.J.A., *The Senate of Imperial Rome* (Princeton, 1984).

Wardle, D., *Suetonius' Life of Caligula: A Commentary* (Bruxelles: Éditions Latomus, 1994).

Wells, C., *The Roman Empire* (Cambridge, Massachusetts: Harvard University Press, 1992, second edition of the 1984 original).

Wilkinson, S., *Caligula* (Lancaster Pamphlets in Ancient History) (New York: Routledge, 2005).

Willrich, H., 'Caligula', in *Klio* 3 (1903), pp.85-118, 288-317, 397-470.

Winterling, A., *Caligula: Eine Biogaphie* (München: C.H. Beck, 2003).

Winterling, A., *Caligula: A Biography* (Berkeley-Los Angeles-London: The University of California Press, 2011, English translation of the 2003 German original, with a new epilogue).

Winterling, A., *Politics and Society in Imperial Rome* (Malden, Massachusetts: Wiley-Blackwell, 2009, translation of the original German text; Chapter 6, 'Meaningful Madness', concerns Caligula).

Wirszubski, C., *Libertas as a Political Idea at Rome during the Late Republic and Early Principate* (Cambridge, 1950).

Wiseman, T.P., *The Death of Caligula (Josephus Ant. Iud. XIX 1-273, Translation and Commentary)* (Liverpool, 2013, second edition of the 1991 Exeter original, entitled *Flavius Josephus, Death of an Emperor*. The title change, we might note, was recommended by Arther Ferrill in his review of the original work for the *Bryn Mawr Classical Review*, with the memorable admonition, 'Professional ancient historians and classicists should stop pretending that the rest of the world is intimately familiar with their field.').

Woodman, A.J., *The Annals of Tacitus: Books 5 and 6* (Cambridge, 2017).

Index

Vespasian, 51, 143, 167
Vesuvius, 139
victims of Caligula, 178
Vipsania Agrippina, 4, 6
Virgil, 30, 33, 37, 150, 183, 203–204
Vitellius, 73, 146, 153
Volsinii, 191

Xerxes, 15, 134
Xiphilinus, 43, 52, 60–2

Zeus, 20, 50, 63, 82–3
Zonaras (John), 43